LABOUR MARKET INEQUALITIES

LABOUR MARKET INEQUALITIES

Problems and Policies of Low-Wage Employment in International Perspective

Edited by
Mary Gregory
Wiemer Salverda
Stephen Bazen

OXFORD
UNIVERSITY PRESS

*This book has been printed digitally and produced in a standard specification
in order to ensure its continuing availability*

OXFORD
UNIVERSITY PRESS

Great Clarendon Street, Oxford OX2 6DP

Oxford University Press is a department of the University of Oxford.
It furthers the University's objective of excellence in research, scholarship,
and education by publishing worldwide in

Oxford New York

Auckland Bangkok Buenos Aires Cape Town Chennai
Dar es Salaam Delhi Hong Kong Istanbul Karachi Kolkata
Kuala Lumpur Madrid Melbourne Mexico City Mumbai Nairobi
São Paulo Shanghai Singapore Taipei Tokyo Toronto

with an associated company in Berlin

Oxford is a registered trade mark of Oxford University Press
in the UK and in certain other countries

Published in the United States
by Oxford University Press Inc., New York

© Oxford University Press 2000

The moral rights of the author have been asserted
Database right Oxford University Press (maker)

Reprinted 2002

ISBN 0-19-924169-4

Acknowledgements

We are grateful to the following publishers for permission to reproduce previously published material.

Fig. 3.1 from M. Keese, A. Puymoyen, and P. Swaim (1998), 'The Incidence and Dynamics of Low-Paid Employment in OECD Countries', ch. 12 in Rita Asplund, Peter J. Sloane, and Ioannis Theodossiou (eds.), *Low Pay and Earnings Mobility in Europe*, Aldershot: Edward Elgar.

Figs. 4.1 and 4.2 from *Employment Outlook July 1996*, copyright OECD 1996.

Table 7.3 from L. Bonnal, D. Fougère, and A. Sérandon (1997), 'Evaluating the Impact of French Employment Policies on Individual Labor Market Histories', *Review of Economic Studies*, 64 (4), 683–713.

Table 9.1 and Figs. 9.1–9.4 from T. Desjonqueres, S. Machin, and J. Van Reenen (1999), 'Another Nail in the Coffin? Or Can the Trade Based Explanation of Changing Skill Structures be Resurrected?', *Scandinavian Journal of Economics*, 101 (4), 533–54. Copyright The Editors of the *Scandinavian Journal of Economics*.

Figs. 9.5 and 9.6 from Paul Gregg and Jonathan Wadsworth (1999), *The State of Working Britain*, Manchester: Manchester University Press.

Table 10.1 reprinted from J. Hartog (1985), 'Earnings Functions: Testing for the Demand Side', *Economics Letters*, 19, 281–5, copyright 1985, with permission from Elsevier Science.

The editors would also like to thank Mary Silles, who compiled the index for this volume.

The editors and contributors are grateful to the European Commission for financial support to the Low Wage Employment Network (LoWER), whose activities are the origin of this book.

European Low-Wage Employment Research Network

Contents

List of Figures

List of Tables

Abbreviations

ALMP	active labour market policies
BHPS	British Household Panel Survey
BLPU	British Low Pay Unit
BLS	Bureau of Labor Statistics
CDD	*contrat à durée determinée* (fixed-term contract)
CDI	*contrat à durée indeterminée* (permanent contract)
CEA	Council of Economic Advisers
CERC	Centre d'Études des Revenus et des Coûts
CLS	Centre for Labour Market and Social Research
CGAS	Comparable German–American Sectoral Database
DARES	Direction de l'Animation, de la Recherche, et des Études Statistiques du Ministère du Travail
DOT	Dictionary of Occupational Titles
EALE	European Association of Labour Economists
ECHP	European Community Household Panel
ECVT	*Encuesta de Condiciones de Vida y Trabago* (Survey of Living and Working Conditions)
EITC	Earned Income Tax Credit
ETLA	Elinkeinoelämän Tutkimuslaitos (Research Institute of the Finnish Economy)
EU	European Union
FCT	factor content of trade
ILO	International Labour Office
ISCED	International Standard Classification for Education
ISSAS	Institute of Social Studies Advisory Service
LIS	Luxembourg Income Study
LoWER	Low-Wage Employment Research Network
NAIRU	non-accelerating inflation rate of unemployment
NBER	National Bureau of Economic Research
NES	New Earnings Survey
OECD	Organization for Economic Cooperation and Development
RMI	*revenu minimum d'insertion*
ROA	Researchcentrum voor Onderwijs en Arbeidsmarkt (Research Centre for Education and the Labour Market)
SCEL	Social Change and Economic Life Initiative
SEO	Stichting voor Economisch Onderzoek (foundation for Economic Research)
SIVP	*stage d'insertion à la vie professionnelle* (preparation for work)
SOC	Standard Occupational Classification
TSER	Targeted Socio-Economic Research Programme
TUC	Trades Union Congress
TUC	*travaux d'utilité collective* (community jobs)

Notes on Contributors

Rita Asplund is research director at the Research Institute of the Finnish Economy, Elinkeinoelämän Tutkimuslaitos (ETLA), Helsinki. Her particular responsibility at ETLA is the research programme Technology, Competences, and Competitiveness. Her main research interests are in the effects of technological progress on the labour market success of individuals, in mobility and careers patterns, as well as in low pay, unemployment, and social exclusion. She has co-edited *Low Pay and Earnings Mobility in Europe* (with P. Sloane and I. Theodossiou).

Stephen Bazen (Ph.D., London School of Economics) is Maître de Conferences in Economics at the University of Bordeaux. He has previously held posts at the Universities of Kent and Aix-Marseille. He has written widely on the issues of low pay and minimum wages and is co-author of *Les Bas Salaires en Europe* and co-editor of *Low-Wage Employment in Europe* (with M. Gregory and W. Salverda). He has acted as a consultant to a number of national and international organizations in the field of the design and evaluation of minimum wage policies.

Lex Borghans is a principal researcher at the Researchcentrum voor Onderwijs en Arbeidsmarkt (Research Centre for Education and the Labour Market (ROA)), Maastricht University. From his Ph.D. thesis at Tilburg University he has published *Educational Choice and Labour Market Information*, a microeconomic study of the effects of public labour market forecasts on students' educational choices and the functioning of the labour market. He has been involved in several research projects on education and the labour market, especially on forecasting the employment structure by occupation and type of education, and adjustment processes involved in labour market flexibility. Since 1998 he has been coordinating a research programme on investment in human capital and the utilization of competences in the labour market. His research topics in this programme include the measurements of skills, the way in which the learning context influences the production of skills, and the economic role of human capital.

Richard Freeman holds the Herbert Ascherman Chair in Economics at Harvard University. He is Faculty Co-Chair of the Harvard University Trade Union Programme, Director of the Labor Studies Program at the National Bureau of Economic Research, Co-Director of the Centre for Economic Performance, and a Visiting Professor at the London School of Economics. He is a member of the American Academy of Arts and Sciences, and is serving on the National Needs for Biomedical and Behavioral Sciences Panel of the US National Academy of Science. He has written or edited 23 books, including *Labor Market Institutions and Economic Success, Youth Employment and Joblessness in Advanced Countries, What Workers Want*, and *Generating Jobs: How to Increase Demand for Less-Skilled Workers*. In addition he has published over 250 articles dealing with topics in youth labour market problems, crime, higher education, trade unionism, economic discrimination, labour standards and globalisation, income distribution, and equity in the marketplace.

Andrew Glyn teaches Economics at Oxford University, where he is Fellow and Tutor at Corpus Christi College. He is an editor of the *Oxford Bulletin of Economics and Statistics*. His research interests centre on unemployment, inequality and profitability. His publications include

Capitalism since 1945 (with Philip Armstrong and John Harrison) and *Paying for Inequality* (edited with David Miliband).

Mary Gregory lectures in Economics at Oxford University, where she is Fellow and Tutor at St Hilda's College. She has been a Member of the Council of the Royal Economic Society and Editor of *Oxford Economic Papers*. Her research interests are in macroeconomics and labour economics. She has co-edited *A Portrait of Pay* (with A. W. J. Thomson) and *Low-Wage Employment in Europe* (with S. Bazen and W. Salverda). She has published articles on a range of labour market issues, recently including women in the labour market; unemployment and earnings; technology, trade, and the demand for skills; and labour market flexibility. She has been consultant and rapporteur to the OECD and the European Commission.

Andries de Grip is Head of the Division of Labour Market and Training of the Researchcentrum voor Onderwijs en Arbeidsmarkt (Research Centre for Education and the Labour Market (ROA)) and Professor of Economics at the Faculty of Economics and Business Administration, Maastricht University. He wrote his Ph.D. on *Education and the Labour Market: Schooling Mismatches*, at the Free University of Amsterdam, where he also taught. He has been at the ROA since 1987, and has published many studies in the field of manpower forecasting, occupational classifications, labour market segmentation, training and mobility, skill shortages, atypical employment, skill obsolescence, and employability.

Francis Kramarz is Head of the Research Department at the French Statistical Institute and an Associate Professor of Economics at the École Polytechnique. His professional interests are in labour economics and microeconometrics. His recent work has been published in *Econometrica*, *Journal of Labor Economics*, and *Review of Economics and Statistics*. He has also contributed, in collaboration with John Abowd, to the *Handbook of Labor Economics*, with a chapter on the use of matched employer–employee data.

Claudio Lucifora is full Professor of Economics at the Università Cattolica (Piacenza). He has previously held positions at the Università di Palermo, Université de Paris II, London School of Economics, and Université du Maine. He is a member of the Executive Committee of the Italian Association of Labour Economists (AIEL) and of the European Association of Labour Economists (EALE). His research interests and publications are mainly related to issues in labour economics. Recent publications include *Policies for Low-Wage Employment* (co-edited with W. Salverda) and *Policy Measures for Low-Wage Employment in Europe* (co-edited with W. Salverda and B. Nolan).

Stephen Machin is currently Professor of Economics at University College London. He is also the Executive Director of the Industrial Relations Programme at the Centre for Economic Performance, a Research Associate at the Institute for Fiscal Studies, and Director of the new Centre on the Economics of Education. His current research interests include: low wage labour markets, changes in the skill structure of international labour markets and shifts in wage inequality, crime, and the labour market, childhood and family influences on adult labour market success or failure, and income and earnings inequality within and across generations. He has been an editor of the *Economic Journal* since 1998. Some of his recent work on minimum wages, skill-biased technological change, and trade unions and training has been published in *Journal of Labor Economics*, *Quarterly Journal of Economics*, and *Industrial and Labor Relations Review*.

Ive Marx is a researcher at the Centre for Social Policy, Universitaire Faculteiten St Ignatius (UFSIA) at the University of Antwerp, where he researches on poverty and income distribution. He has published on trends in poverty and income distribution in Belgium and other OECD countries, with a particular focus on the adequacy of social protection arrangements. His current research focuses on the consequences for poverty and social policy of labour market change in OECD countries, particularly the increase in long-term labour market exclusion and insecure, low-paid employment.

Brian Nolan (Ph.D., London School of Economics) is currently Research Professor at the Economic and Social Research Institute, Dublin. He has published widely on income inequality, poverty, public economics, social policy, health economics, and health inequalities. His publications include *Resources, Deprivation and Poverty*, co-authored with C. T. Whelan, and *Policy Measures for Low-Wage Employment in Europe* (co-edited with C. Lucifora and W. Salverda). He is currently working on a programme of research on poverty and related issues based on the European Community Household Panel Survey.

Inga Persson is Professor of Economics at Lund University, Sweden, where she holds a chair in the Economics of Gender. She has published widely on labour market policy issues, unemployment, the welfare state, and the economic position of women. Her publications include *Generating Equality in the Welfare State: The Swedish Experience*, and, jointly with C. Jonung, *Economics of the Family and Family Policies* and *Women's Work and Wages*.

Wiemer Salverda is Director of European Labour Market Studies at the Amsterdam Institute for Advanced Labour Studies AIAS, University of Amsterdam. He has been the Co-ordinator of the European Low-Wage Employment Research network (LoWER) since its foundation in 1996. His research centres on the low-wage labour market and government policies, wage inequality and employment growth, minimum wages, the youth labour market, skills and employment, consumer demand for low-skill services, and the performance of the 'Dutch model' and its dependence on wage moderation and social consensus. He is co-editor of *Low-Wage Employment in Europe* (with S. Bazen and M. Gregory), *Policies for Low-Wage Employment* (with C. Lucifora), and *Policy Measures for Low-Wage Employment in Europe* (with C. Lucifora and B. Nolan). He has been consultant and rapporteur to the OECD and the European Commission.

Ronald Schettkat is Full Professor of Economics at Utrecht University, Netherlands. He has been a Senior Research Fellow at the Wissenschaftszentrum Berlin, and he has held visiting positions at Stanford University, University of California at Berkeley, Tinbergen Institute in Amsterdam, The Netherlands Institute for Advanced Studies at Wassenaar, and the Universities of Bologna and Modena. His research interests include macroeconomics, labor economics, the economics of technological change, and institutional economics. His books include *The Labor Market Dynamics of Economic Restructuring: The United States and Germany in Transition*, and *Flow Analysis of Labor Markets*. He has been consultant to the OECD, the European Commission, and the Federal Government of Germany.

Peter Sloane is Jaffrey Professor of Political Economy, Dean of the Faculty of Social Sciences and Law, and Vice Principal, University of Aberdeen. He is a Fellow of the Royal Society of Edinburgh. He has published widely on a range of issues in labour economics and on the economics of professional team sports. He has recently co-edited *Low Pay and Earnings Mobility in Europe* (with R. Asplund and I. Theodossiou).

Ioannis Theodossiou is Professor of Economics, University of Aberdeen. He is a Fellow of the Royal Statistical Society. His research interests include labour market segmentation, low pay and earnings mobility, socioeconomic status and health, on which he has published widely. He has recently co-edited *Low Pay and Earnings Mobility in Europe* (with R. Asplund and P. Sloane).

Introduction

MARY GREGORY, WIEMER SALVERDA,
AND STEPHEN BAZEN

Combining economic efficiency with social equity is an ongoing challenge, with the terms of the debate and the trade-offs it presents continually reshaped by events. Low-wage employment is one of the key areas where this challenge is currently posed. The 1980s saw the emergence of high and persistent unemployment throughout much of the European Union, in many instances involving groups who had not previously been affected. As inflation receded over the decade, combating unemployment was restored to a central place on the policy agenda. The 1990s, however, saw growing recognition that unemployment is only one dimension in an increasingly complex set of unsatisfactory labour market outcomes. Many countries are now confronting a growing gap between those who benefit from the new career opportunities created by technological developments and rising prosperity, and those who do not. This gap manifests itself in a number of ways. Alongside the well-paid new jobs that are being generated, the fastest employment growth has been in 'atypical' work, part-time, limited term, or outside conventional employment contracts, often offering little in the way of security or continuity. While salaries and incomes have been rising, so has the extent of low-paid work. This has led to the sharp rise in earnings inequality already pronounced in the UK, and increasingly evident elsewhere. As sluggish employment growth has limited job opportunities, a new pattern of 'joblessness' has become established. Premature withdrawal from the labour force, which emerged initially as a trend towards earlier retirement, now involves substantial numbers of men in mid-career or even earlier. This movement out of economic activity can be a more important source of joblessness than unemployment. The distribution of work has become polarized in some countries, as two-earner and no-earner households have become common, replacing those with a single breadwinner. This range of developments has put issues of income distribution, inequality, and social justice back on the policy agenda.

The main losers from these developments are workers with low educational attainment and few employment-related skills. Being disadvantaged in the labour market is a familiar and long-standing situation for these groups. But the pattern now emerging across the advanced economies is for the clear accentuation of this. Many explanations are on offer for this deteriorating position of the low skilled: the acceleration of technological change, automating away physical effort and 'simple' jobs; the bias in technological change, enhancing the employment of skilled workers at the expense of the low skilled; the emergence of the newly industrializing countries as major exporters of manufactures; pressures of competitiveness stoked up through the global integration of financial markets; or the 'bumping-down' of the low skilled when the total supply of jobs is insufficient. Whatever the economic cause, the effects on disadvantaged workers and households have given new emphasis to low pay, poverty, and the risk of social marginalization, even social exclusion.

The high levels of joblessness among low-skilled workers in Europe are often presented as evidence of the rigidity of European labour markets, by contrast with the experience of the USA. Over the past quarter century the US economy has generated some twenty-five million new jobs, sufficient to absorb its growing population, the continuing movement of women into paid work, and the flow of immigrants, all with no rise on average in unemployment. In Europe, on the other hand, employment growth has been sluggish, and in some countries negligible, while unemployment has doubled or worse. On the other side of the record, however, the earnings of lower-paid workers in the USA have experienced a sustained decline, falling by perhaps as much as one-quarter in real terms over the two decades following 1973. Only in the last years of the 1990s did they show the beginnings of a recovery. It is argued that this decline in earnings for lower-paid workers in the USA has allowed the expansion of jobs, obviating a rise in unemployment. In Europe, on the other hand, real earnings of the low paid have generally been maintained, and have often increased. Wage flexibility comparable to the USA, it is argued, could not be achieved in Europe, owing to pervasive collective bargaining, minimum wage laws, and other forms of regulation. The consequence has been that employment growth has been restricted, and unemployment has risen substantially. The living standards of lower-paid workers in employment have been protected, while the hidden cost is borne by the jobless.

The immediate thrust of this argument is to call into question the 'European social model', with its emphasis on employment rights, wage regulation, collective bargaining, and extensive social welfare support. How far do the institutions and forms of intervention that characterize labour markets in the European economies contribute to favourable outcomes, particularly for those who would otherwise be disadvantaged in the labour market? Or do these same features bring rigidities that inhibit effective responses to global changes, damaging the interests of those they aim to protect?

This complex of issues centring on the position of low-paid and low-skill workers in European labour markets forms the theme of this volume. To reflect these common concerns across the member states of the EU the European Commission funded an academic network, the Low Wage Employment Network (LoWER) aimed at encouraging the interchange of analysis and research results among academics working in this field. The contributions in this book bring together results from the work of the Network. Its purpose is to give a comprehensive overview of various dimensions of low-wage employment within the EU and of the ways in which the institutional context and policy approaches impact on these.

The first group of chapters aims to establish the general profile of the position of low-wage workers in Europe, drawing on data for most of the advanced economies.

The topics covered are the role of labour market institutions in influencing wage inequality and the extent of low pay; the employment position of low-skilled workers; the position of women—the largest group among the low paid, and too often neglected; earnings mobility and progression for the low paid; and the relationship between low pay and household poverty. In the next group of chapters the focus moves to policy interventions and their impact on the low paid. The impact of minimum wages, and programmes to promote employment, represented by the extensive French experience are each assessed. The final set of chapters examines more specific issues: the role of the services sector, a major area of employment, particularly for the low skilled, and one that is too often neglected; the debate on trade versus technology in the changing demand for skills; and 'the debate on bumping-down': the upgrading of skill requirements versus overqualification as the source of changing skill patterns of employment.

Labour market institutions—unions, collective bargaining, minimum wage regulation, employment protection—are often blamed for the alleged poor performance of the European economies. In the opening chapter Claudio Lucifora examines the role of labour market institutions specifically in regard to their influence on wage inequalities and low pay. The institutions considered are unionization and collective bargaining, along with the role of wage regulation through minimum wages and the mandatory extension of the terms of collective agreements to non-bargaining firms. Lucifora finds that unionization, collective bargaining, and centralization in wage negotiations all contribute to a reduced incidence of low pay. The power of unions to create a wage floor and reduce wage dispersion at the bottom of the pay distribution appears to be the outcome of a combination of union power, wage regulation, particularly through the mandatory extension of collective agreements and statutory minimum wages, and the generosity of unemployment benefits. He estimates that the varying strength of these institutional features, taken together, explains about 60 per cent of the differences across the advanced economies in the extent of low pay.

Andrew Glyn and Wiemer Salverda examine the employment position of low-skilled workers, as measured by educational attainment, across the OECD economies. They find employment rates among the best-qualified quartile of workers to be between 80 and 90 per cent, while for the least qualified they are generally between 50 and 75 per cent. This margin gives striking evidence of the withdrawal from the labour force by low-skilled workers, which is making unemployment an increasingly inadequate measure of joblessness. Glyn and Salverda find that the major influence on the extent of joblessness among the low skilled is the national employment rate. When the overall employment position deteriorates, those at the bottom of the qualifications scale suffer disproportionate employment losses. Greater wage dispersion, on the other hand, does not appear to reduce the gap in employment rates between the most and the least educated. The central conclusion that they draw is that labour market flexibility, encouraged by low minimum wages and social benefits along with weak employment protection, and reflected in high wage dispersion, has not been a successful route to minimizing the employment disadvantage of the least qualified.

Deregulation in the labour market has had at most a marginal effect on employment opportunities for the low skilled, relative to the influence of the overall demand for labour.

A striking feature of the low-wage situation in almost all countries, and one that rarely receives sufficient emphasis, is the position of women. Women have been moving into paid work in increasing numbers, making up most, if not all, of the growth of the labour force in many countries over recent decades. They have also been catching up on, and even surpassing, men in educational attainment. Yet, labour market outcomes for women remain inferior to those for men. Rita Asplund and Inga Persson show this comprehensively in regard to low pay. The incidence of low pay among women is greater than among men in all countries, and among the low paid women typically make up the majority. The gendered division of labour between market and non-market work allocates many women to part-time jobs, where pay is low, and training and prospects limited. Job segregation within market work crowds women into lower-paid occupations and the lower levels within occupations. Crucially, the gendered pattern of low pay remains marked even after allowance for differences in education, job tenure, and work experience; women are more likely to be low paid simply for being female, irrespective of their other personal or job characteristics. Poor labour market outcomes for women, and in particular the incidence of low pay among them, remain a serious failure across the advanced economies. Future policies towards low pay should pay particular regard to the disproportionate presence of women among the low paid.

To the extent that low pay is a transient phenomenon, involving individuals who are experiencing a temporary setback, or young workers acquiring skills and experience that will enhance their future earnings, the situation is self-limiting. But when workers are trapped in low-paid jobs and economic disadvantage becomes a persistent, even a lifetime, characteristic, serious issues of inequality and welfare arise. The question of how far low-paid jobs are stepping stones and how far they are dead ends is examined by Peter Sloane and Ioannis Theodossiou. Looking at the evidence for a number of advanced economies, they find substantial earnings mobility everywhere, particularly upwards among younger men and the better educated. However, this picture of mobility masks persistent low pay for a substantial number of workers, particularly women, older men, and the less qualified. The longer workers remain in low-paid jobs, the more difficult it becomes to escape from these. Moreover, a sustained spell in low pay is damaging not only to future earnings in work but also to future employment prospects. Workers from low-paid jobs tend to move from low-paid work into unemployment or inactivity, and possibly back into further low-paid work. For them low-paid jobs are more likely to be associated with a future of further low-paid jobs and joblessness—the low-pay/no-pay cycle. However, the extent of persistence in low pay varies widely across countries—a low-paid worker in the USA, for example, being four times more likely to experience continuing low pay than a low-paid Danish worker. This suggests that labour market institutions and policies may play a significant role in restricting lifetime disadvantage. Moreover, the evidence on persistence in low pay and the low-pay/no-pay cycle indicates that the pay-off to effective public policies in this area could be substantial.

An argument often advanced in support of wage regulation against low pay is that low wages bring poverty. Brian Nolan and Ive Marx examine the evidence on this for the advanced economies. Much the most extensive data linking earnings to household income relate to full-time workers. Nolan and Marx establish that for this group the overlap between low pay in employment and household poverty is more limited than is often assumed. On their definitions, across the advanced economies only around 10 per cent of low-paid full-time workers live in poor households (below half of median income). Even when the definition of poverty is extended to two-thirds of median income, the working poor provide only around 20 per cent. On the other hand, the vast majority of full-time workers who are low paid also live in poor households. How far low pay is a source of poverty depends crucially on the extent to which the household is dependent on the earnings of the low-paid worker. Poverty rates are higher for low-paid men than for low-paid women, and among prime-age than young workers, as most low-paid women and young workers—who comprise the majority of the low paid—live in households with more than one earner. It is among low-paid married men with dependent children who are household heads that poverty rates are generally highest. The role of low-paid secondary earners, often part-time or casual workers, in keeping households out of poverty is an important one. Nolan and Marx conclude that, if policies aimed at improving the situation of the working poor, such as minimum wages and earned income tax credits, are to be effective against household poverty, they will have to fit within a broad-based anti-poverty strategy.

The policy intervention that comes most naturally to mind against the worst of low pay is a minimum wage. This was prominent on the political agenda over the 1990s, particularly in the UK and the USA. A series of upratings of the level of the US minimum wage has provided important new evidence on its effects, leading to a remarkable change in the consensus view among economists on its impact. This debate and the evidence are reviewed by Stephen Bazen. Many benefits can be claimed for a minimum wage. It provides protection for the lowest-paid workers; it reduces wage and income inequality; it reduces pay discrimination; it reduces poverty among working families; it improves incentives for the unemployed to accept work; and it has potentially beneficial effects on consumption, investment, economic growth, and the public finances. The crucial offset to these is the threat of loss of employment. When the labour market is viewed as functioning competitively, job losses are inevitable, and the only issue is how many will occur, to be settled by estimates of demand elasticities. The 'new' economics of the minimum wage, by contrast, departs from the traditional competitive paradigm, emphasizing the role of market imperfections, particularly monopsony, leading to no clear a priori predictions on the effect on employment of an increase in the wage. The evidence marshalled by Bazen from the experience of the USA, France, and other countries indicates negligible job losses, except among young workers. Bazen's conclusion is that minimum wages do indeed have a marked effect on low-wage labour markets, but that effect is to reduce the dispersion of wages at the bottom end of the distribution, but without significant reductions in employment. Minimum wages enforced at prevailing levels appear to have at most very limited effects in destroying jobs, to set against their benefits in terms of maintaining earnings levels among the low paid.

Active employment programmes, to promote the employability and employment of the unemployed, feature in many countries. One of the most extensive sets of programmes is that used in France. Francis Kramarz describes the various programmes in operation there and analyses their effects. The programmes take two main forms, although with many subprogrammes within these: vocational training, to enhance employment prospects, and subsidies for job creation or preservation. As assessed by Kramarz, the programmes of vocational training are of mixed effectiveness. Participation in a work training programme in the private sector is found to help the low skilled out of unemployment. Participation in 'community jobs' in the public sector, on the other hand, does not improve employment outcomes for the low skilled; even worse, for the higher skilled who join the programmes participation appears to act as a negative signal, worsening their future employment outcomes. Kramarz notes that, in general, participation in training schemes has a tendency to become self-reinforcing, participation in a programme leading to further periods on these schemes rather than to stable employment. Tax exemptions for minimum wage workers, aimed at job creation for the low skilled, appear to have little effect in encouraging employment for those paid at minimum rates. This result is attributed by Kramarz to employers' uncertainty about the duration of the subsidy, when the costs of hiring and firing a new minimum wage worker are high.

How far is the expansion of jobs in low-wage services in the EU restricted by high wages? With services now the main sector of employment growth in the advanced economies and high levels of joblessness in Europe, this question becomes a crucial one. Richard Freeman and Ronald Schettkat examine it through a detailed comparison of the role of low-wage services in the USA and Germany. They establish that the same sectors feature as low paying in both countries, with Germany having a clear 'jobs deficit' relative to the USA in low-wage service sector employment. However, they find no support for the argument that this jobs deficit is due to excessively high German wages. In fact, they find that relative wages in low-wage sectors are extremely similar in the two countries, and even rather lower, relative to the national average, in Germany than in the USA. This is a striking finding, given that overall wage inequality is much lower in Germany, and the wage gap between the low-paid and the median German worker is substantially narrower than in the USA. Freeman and Schettkat find the main explanation for this outcome in differences in US–German wage and employment structures. The USA is characterized by a wide dispersion of wages within individual industries. As a consequence, low-wage employment is to be found throughout the economy. In Germany, on the other hand, the dispersion of wages within individual sectors is much narrower, translating into the concentration of low-paid workers in a narrow range of low-wage industries and occupations. Since low-wage services in Germany are not characterized by high relative wages, Freeman and Schettkat conclude that the sources of the jobs deficit in these sectors must be sought elsewhere than in excessively high German wages.

How far the loss of low-skilled jobs is due to developments in world trade over recent decades, with the emergence of many industrializing countries as significant exporters of manufactures, is an issue with potentially major policy implications as the World Trade Organization (WTO) strives for further liberalization of world trade. A leading alternative explanation focuses on the nature of technological change in contemporary conditions, particularly as associated with the microchip revolution. Computerization and information technology may be seen as complementary with skills, requiring them for their development and application, while simultaneously eliminating many routine jobs previously done by low-skilled workers. This is the debate that is evaluated by Mary Gregory and Stephen Machin. Drawing on a range of pieces of research to which they have both contributed, they come up with the clear conclusion that the role of trade in destroying low-skilled jobs has been a minor one, while the evidence on a connection between the declining demand for low-skilled workers and the pervasiveness of new forms of technology is strong. These findings have direct policy implications. If trade is not contributing importantly to the loss of low-skilled jobs, then policies of intervention are not well conceived. Rather, the important orientations for policy lie towards the development of education and the fostering of skills that will link into, and take advantage of, technological progress.

A significant development in labour markets in recent years has been the trend towards people with higher levels of education, notably college graduates, holding jobs previously held by people with lower levels of education, such as school-leavers. Lex Borghans and Andries de Grip examine the principal explanations of the processes giving rise to this. The 'overeducation' view sees it as evidence of the underutilization of skills, which is socially wasteful. The 'upgrading' view, on the other hand, emphasizes the higher skills now required within occupations; although the job is formally the same, it now involves greater complexity, possibly partly as a consequence of the higher educational attainment of its holders. Both views, however, have pessimistic implications for the position of low-skilled workers. On the overeducation view, the increased supply of more educated workers pushes the low skilled into the least favoured jobs, or even crowds them out altogether from the working population. The upgrading view sees low-skilled workers as increasingly marginalized as their skill levels no longer meet the minimum requirements of the labour market. Interpretation of these developments is crucial for public policies towards education and training: is more education or less education socially efficient?

The main message from the papers in this volume is that, while the 'European model' for the labour market cannot reverse the adverse trends that are impacting globally on the position of the low skilled, it does achieve significant success in tempering the winds of change to the disadvantaged and potentially low paid. Labour market institutions characteristic of the European economies, notably collective bargaining and wage regulation, have a favourable impact in reducing the incidence of low pay and its persistence, although to date they have not served women as well as they have served men. Minimum wages at prevailing levels provide significant wage protection for more vulnerable workers, without causing substantial job losses. The significant 'jobs deficit' of Germany relative to the USA in low-wage services is not the outcome of excessively high German wages. The level and structure of social security support are not major inhibitors of employment. Conversely, reliance on wage flexibility among low-paid workers to create jobs for the low skilled does not emerge as economically effective, and can no longer be regarded as the simple panacea for unemployment among the low skilled.

But, while employment creation and job development to improve the position of the low paid and the low skilled is an urgent need, the construction of effective policies is not a simple task. Expansion of education and training must be appropriately targeted if the low skilled are not again to be the losers and resources wasted. Training programmes must lead to better employment, and job subsidies must ensure job creation and not simply be used to support yet more 'precarious' jobs. Policies aimed at reducing the poverty associated with low pay must be set in the context of a broad-based anti-poverty strategy. These challenges remain, but the 'European model' has a valuable economic as well as social role, and provides a favourable context for these further policies.

Mary Gregory
Wiemer Salverda
Stephen Bazen

1 Wage Inequalities and Low Pay: The Role of Labour Market Institutions

CLAUDIO LUCIFORA

In recent decades a number of industrialized countries have experienced significant changes in the distribution of earnings. Various factors, economic and institutional, have contributed to reshaping the structure of wage differentials across different groups of workers. Major changes have also occurred in the distribution of employment and unemployment within the labour force, with declining employment rates and growing joblessness particularly in European countries.

In this context, some have argued that there is a trade-off between the extent of joblessness and overall wage dispersion, advocating greater labour market flexibility, especially in wage setting, to reduce unemployment. However, in the face of the increase in earnings inequality, concern has emerged for those individuals located at the bottom end of the earnings distribution who have been most strongly affected, in terms of social exclusion and poverty, by the changing economic conditions. In particular, the low paid, the low skilled, and less protected groups generally, such as women, young workers, and older men, appear to have borne most of the burden, in terms both of lower earnings and of the higher incidence of unemployment (OECD 1996*a*).

The degree of wage inequality and the employment rate (the proportion of the working age population who are in employment) are important indicators of the performance of an economy. On the one hand, inequality in the labour market typically translates into significant disparities in living standards and often also into increasing poverty among individuals. On the other hand, labour market inequality affects the structure of economic incentives that individuals face and influences social cohesion and worker solidarity. The overall pattern that has emerged over the 1990s shows

A preliminary version of this paper has been presented at the LoWER Conference 'Policies for Low-Wage Employment and Social Exclusion in Europe' (Groningen, Nov. 1998), at the annual conferences of the European Society of Population Economics (ESPE) and the European Association of Labour Economists (EALE) (Turin, June 1999, and Regensburg, Sept. 1999), at the conference on 'Unemployment, Poverty and Social Exclusion' held at the Athens University of Economics and Business (Athens, Sept. 1999) and in seminars at the Università degli Studi di Milano, Università di Napoli, and Libero Istituto Universitario C. Cattaneo (LIUC). I would like to thank L. Bardone, F. Kramarz, S. Machin, W. Salverda, P. Sestito, and participants at seminars for their useful comments. In particular, I am especially grateful to A. Glyn and M. Gregory for extensive discussion, suggestions, and help on earlier drafts. The European Commission under the TSER program (LoWER Network) has provided financial assistance. The usual disclaimer applies.

substantial differences across countries in the extent of earnings inequality and in labour market outcomes more generally. These underline the diversity of forces, incentives, and constraints operating in the global economy.

Among the leading explanations offered for these trends, emphasis has been placed on demographic changes, adverse shifts in supply and demand for products and skills, skill-biased technological change, increased globalization of trade, and new forms of work organization (OECD 1996a; Gottschalk and Smeeding 1997; Gottschalk *et al.* 1997). Alternative explanations have emphasized the institutional side, arguing that trade union activity, practices of collective bargaining, and labour market regulations may have played a more relevant role (Blau and Kahn 1996; Fortin and Lemieux 1997). Institutional pay setting may alter wage dispersion and the incidence of low pay in various ways. First, legislation on wages may reduce dispersion by gender and by skill. Second, pay standardization policies, by reducing management discretion, may compress pay differences within firms. Third, industry-wide bargaining and mandatory extension of the terms set in collective agreements may decrease wage differentials across establishments and reduce the mark-up of union over non-union wages. Fourth, when the structure of bargaining is more centralized and negotiations are better coordinated, wage differentials between industries may be reduced.

It has been widely noted that those countries that have experienced the largest increases in inequalities have also been those with the most deregulated and decentralized labour markets. This seems to suggest that centralized wage setting, institutional constraints and widespread welfare safety nets may have had a significant role in shaping the distribution of earnings across countries. Heavily regulated labour markets and highly centralized wage-setting mechanisms are characterized by more rigid wage structures and greater inertia of wages in the face of economic shocks and business cycle fluctuations. Moreover, in highly unionized labour markets, trade unions have traditionally pursued egalitarian wage policies to enhance worker solidarity and to protect those at the lower end of the earnings distribution. This has been particularly the case in those countries without a statutory minimum wage (Blanchflower and Freeman 1992; Bjorklund and Freeman 1996).

Considerable attention has been devoted in recent years to the 'evolution' of earnings inequality and to the analysis of the competing explanations for the observed phenomena. In addition, however, the existence and persistence of substantial structural differences across countries in the 'level' of wage inequality and the 'incidence' of low pay can shed light on further dimensions of the patterns of inequality. To the extent that differences in inequality across countries reflect differing rewards for labour market activity and the working of institutional constraints, their existence may imply different sets of economic incentives and social structures. This is particularly important for the lower part of the earnings distribution, where the availability of jobs and the associated wage rates are strongly relevant for labour market activity and social cohesion.

In this study, we investigate the role that various institutional features may play in shaping the distribution of wages across a number of OECD countries. In general there is some scepticism among economists about the actual role that institutions play in the functioning of labour markets, on the grounds that the institutional setting is merely a superstructure through which market forces continue to operate. Nevertheless, in the absence of full employment and perfect competition in both labour and product markets, the existence of economic rents and discretion in pay setting makes the impact of institutional arrangements relevant for labour market outcomes. In this study attention will focus on explicit and quantifiable measures of institutional forces and the analysis of their impact. Restricting the scope in this way will avoid excessive arbitrariness in defining the relevant 'institutions' for pay setting, or interpreting their impact simply as a residual for those features that cannot be otherwise explained. In particular, we shall focus on three specific features: the effects of trade unions, the structure of collective bargaining, and the existence of wage regulation. While by no means the only labour market institutions relevant for wage determination, these certainly play a central role in explaining differences in the structure and dynamics of wages across countries (Freeman 1996*b*). This way of proceeding obviously leaves aside the role of social norms and cultural factors, which, though more difficult to measure, are likely also to be important in explaining cross-country differences.

The chapter is organized as follows. First, in Section 1, we review some of the institutional features that characterize the functioning of the labour market and are considered relevant for wage inequality and the incidence of low-wage employment. These fall into two main categories: unionism and collective bargaining practices, and legal regulation of wages. Next, we provide an overview of the stylized facts on low-wage labour markets across a number of OECD countries (Section 2). In Section 3 we investigate the effects that labour market institutions may have on both the incidence of low-wage employment and the distribution of earnings. The last section contains some concluding remarks and discusses some policy implications.

1.   Labour Market Institutions and Wage Regulation: An Overview of International Differences

Institutional wage setting may involve direct government legislation on a number of pay issues, such as a minimum wage, legislation against discrimination, or the mandatory extension of collective agreements. Or it may operate via the 'voluntarist' route, through the activities of trade unions and collective bargaining. While it is largely undisputed that the presence of wage regulation and collective bargaining affects wage formation, the magnitude and direction of the impact that institutions have on the functioning of labour markets and the distribution of wages depend on how far the constraints that they impose are binding. Many institutional arrangements are directed towards a specific portion of the wage distribution or to selected groups of individuals, making it likely that the effects will be concentrated on those (although spillover effects onto non-covered workers should also be taken into account). To the

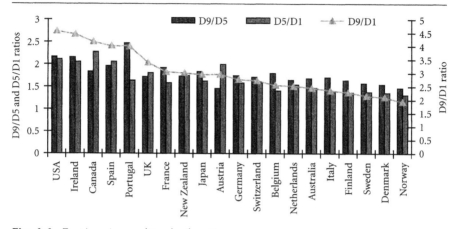

Fig. 1.1. Earnings inequality, decile ratios
Source: author's computations based on data supplied by OECD.

extent that the institutional constraint is binding, the wage outcome will differ from that resulting from the operation of market forces. It may be argued that as a general tendency institutionalized wage setting, by being targeted at the 'average' worker or firm, has the effect of reducing differences across groups. Market forces, on the other hand, by operating at the margin (i.e. through the 'marginal' worker or firm) tend to give rise to a wider dispersion in wage levels.[1] Moreover, we might expect market forces and institutional arrangements to interact in different ways in different parts of the earnings distribution, with a greater impact on the top or the bottom of the earnings hierarchy, depending on the types of institution at work.

Fig. 1.1 reports a range of indicators of earnings inequality across OECD countries, based on full-time, full-year workers.[2] We have ranked countries according to overall inequality as measured by the ratio of earnings at the ninth decile to the bottom decile (the D9/D1 ratio, right-hand scale). We also report the relative inequality in the top and bottom halves of the distribution (i.e. the D9/D5 and D5/D1 ratios, left-hand scale). First, significant differences in earnings inequality emerge across countries; in the USA, with the most unequal distribution, the D9/D1 ratio is close to 4.5, while in Norway it is less than 2. Second, in countries where overall inequality is relatively low (those located in the right-hand end in Fig. 1.1) it appears that earnings dispersion is particularly compressed at the bottom end of the distribution, more so than at the top. Conversely, those countries where earnings inequality is relatively high tend to have a wider dispersion at both ends of the distribution, often particularly at the top end.

[1] Since 'institutions' arise to represent and insure selected groups of individuals or firms, their focus is on the 'average' (median) and they may resist changes that affect the welfare of the 'average' worker, even if these might be perfectly consistent with optimizing behaviour based on the 'marginal' worker, such as that arising from the operation of the market mechanism (Freeman 1996*b*).

[2] These data have been kindly supplied by the OECD. Details are given in OECD (1996*a*: ch. 3 and annexes 3A and 3B). See also Bardone, Gittleman, and Keese (1998: esp. table 2 and annex 1).

The differences in earnings inequality observed across countries are reflected in the existence of similar disparities in the incidence of low pay; those countries characterized by wider dispersion in the bottom part of the earnings distribution also have a larger share of low-paid individuals. The remainder of the chapter is devoted to the analysis of the factors that might influence the pattern of inequality across countries and, in particular, their effects on the lower part of the earnings distribution and the incidence of low-wage employment. Following a widely used criterion, the definition of low-wage employment will be those workers whose earnings fall below two-thirds of median earnings.[3]

1.1. *Collective Bargaining and Unionization*

The extent of unionization and the practice of collective bargaining are important institutional features in wage determination. As shown in Table 1.1, columns (1) to (3), different patterns of union presence and activity characterize OECD economies. Moreover, during the 1980s and 1990s, a number of changes occurred in wage-setting institutions in several industrialized countries, notably declining unionization and progressive decentralization of bargaining. The interaction of wage regulation and union power may, therefore, have different implications for institutional wage setting across countries.

It has been argued that in decentralized systems with weak unions, such as the USA, the UK, and New Zealand, a decline in union density produces widespread effects on institutional wage setting, inequality, and the incidence of low pay. By contrast, in more regulated systems with industry-wide bargaining and high union coverage, such as the majority of European countries, the effect of declining unionization barely has an impact. The main explanation for these different outcomes resides in the institutional channels through which unions can influence wage formation—essentially mandatory extension provisions and centralization of bargaining (Freeman 1993; DiNardo, Fortin, and Lemieux 1996; Card 1998).

Much of the empirical evidence concerning the impact of unions on relative wages suggests that trade unionism can significantly alter the distribution of wages. One route is by raising the pay levels of those workers covered by collective agreements relative to non-covered workers (Lewis 1986). The impact on wage inequality then depends on the position of the workers affected by the union mark-up within the

---

[3] Various definitions may be used for the earnings cut-off determining low pay. First, this depends on whether an absolute or a relative measure is chosen. 'Absolute' measures are defined with reference to a given level of income in real terms—e.g. the official poverty line. Conversely, 'relative' measures are taken as the earnings level defined as a fraction of mean or median wages, or with respect to some specified quantile of the distribution. For the purposes of the present study, a 'relative' measure, closer to the idea of social distance, was chosen. Despite its apparent arbitrariness, this measure is in line with the Council of Europe's suggested 'decency threshold' (defined as 68% of full-time average weekly earnings), as well as with the level of the legal minimum wage enforced in several European countries. Different pay thresholds have been proposed by, among others, the Trades Union Congress (TUC) and British Low Pay Unit (BLPU). See OECD (1996a) for a thorough discussion of the properties and limitations of the different measures for the low-pay cut-offs. Keese, Puymoyen, and Swaim (1998) also deal with the issue.

Table 1.1. Union presence and wage regulation in OECD countries

Country	Unionization indicators			Wage regulations					Replacement ratio
	Union density	Coverage	Corporatism	Extension of collective agreements[a]		Minimum wage systems (MW)			
	(%)	(%)	Index	Description	Index	Description		Kaitz index	Index
	(1)	(2)	(3)	(4)	(5)	(6)		(7)	(8)
Austria	46.2	98	19	Almost all agreements	16	Nationally negotiated MW[a]		0.62	50
Belgium	51.2	90	14	Almost all agreements	15	Negotiated monthly MW		0.60	60
Denmark	71.4	69	12	By centralization	17	nationally negotiated MW[a]		0.64	90
Finland	72	95	16	Frequent (ministerial extension)	12	Nationally negotiated MW[a]		0.52	63
France	9.8	95	7	Very frequent	14	Statutory hourly MW		0.50	57
Germany	32.9	92	17	Frequent (small firms)	12	Negotiated MW by industry		0.55	63
Ireland	49.7	60	7	Limited to minimum wages	7	Statutory MW (selected industries only)		0.55	37
Italy	38.8	85	15	Almost all agreements (by industry)	16	Negotiated monthly MW by industry		0.71	20

Netherlands	25.5	81	7	Frequent (ministerial extension)	10	Statutory weekly MW	0.55	70
Norway	56	74	18	By centralization	17	Nationally negotiated MW[a]	0.64	65
Portugal	31.8	71	7	Frequent (ministerial extension)	16	Statutory monthly MW	0.45	65
Spain	11	78	7	Frequent by industry	15	Statutory monthly MW	0.32	70
Sweden	82.5	89	7	By centralization	17	Nationally negotiated MW[a]	0.52	80
Switzerland	26.6	50	12	Frequent (ministerial extension)	11	—	0.50	70
UK	39.1	47	4	No automatic extension	3	Statutory MW (before 1993, selected industries)	0.40	38
Japan	25.4	21	6	Rare (company agreements)	4	Statutory daily MW	0.53	59
Australia	40.4	80	5	Limited to min-wages	8	Negotiated MW	0.45	50
New Zealand	44.8	31	1	Limited cases (ministerial extension)	10	Statutory weekly MW	0.46	60
Canada	35.8	36	1	Limited cases	5	Statutory hourly MW	0.35	36
USA	15.6	18	1	No automatic extension	1	Statutory hourly MW	0.39	30

[a] Collective agreements covering most of the labour force.

Source: Nickell and Layard (1997: tables 3–6; 1999: tables 7–10). See also Bardone, Gittleman, and Keese (1998: table 2 and annex 1).

overall wage distribution. Inequality will be reduced if union workers have below-average pay levels, and conversely increased if union workers have above-average pay levels. A second is through 'standard rate' policies aimed at reducing inequality among individual workers. In particular, collective agreements seek to fix both the number of job categories in which workers are placed and the rate of pay for each job, thus limiting the ability of the firm to remunerate workers differently according to more individualized criteria.[4]

Some basic factors can be put forward to explain union preferences for a less dispersed wage structure among similar plants and within the organized sector, although their ability to achieve this will necessarily vary with market conditions and the institutional setting. First, worker solidarity requires a relatively uniform wage distribution, as the perception of marked differences in pay may reduce consensus among workers and therefore the strength of the union's 'collective voice' (Freeman 1980a,b). Hence unions tend to resist any decline in low pay relative to the average. Second, given the potential arbitrariness in measuring individual productivity, subject to supervisor evaluation, workers, being risk averse, will generally prefer narrower wage distributions. Finally, the union can be regarded as a political organization whose consensus depends on median preference. This implies that when the median wage is less then the mean wage a majority of workers will support a wage policy favouring the lower paid, thus further reducing dispersion and the incidence of low pay (Freeman and Medoff 1984; Hirsch and Addison 1986). In this respect, the effects that union presence is likely to produce on the distribution of wages, although indeterminate a priori, in practice tends to result in a marked compression of wage differentials and a lower incidence of low-paid employment (Blau and Kahn 1996).[5] This general proposition will be analysed in greater detail in Section 2.

1.2. Wage Regulation

The labour market regulations most relevant for influencing the distribution of wages are probably statutory minimum wages, antidiscrimination legislation, and the mandatory extension of collective agreements (see Table 1.1). These are not necessarily mutually exclusive, since in some countries wage minima are set by statute after consultation with the unions, while in other cases various aspects of industrial relations interact with legislation in a rather complex way.

Minimum wage legislation, by setting an explicit threshold for the lowest wage rate paid (hourly, daily, or monthly), impacts on the bottom end of the earnings distribution and tends to reduce wage dispersion (see column (6)). The actual effect

---

[4] In general unions have been very successful in removing performance evaluations as a factor in determining individual workers' wages. Also, seniority-based pay progression, requiring similar pay conditions to be applied to workers of comparable seniority, tends to reduce wage dispersion (Freeman 1980b).

[5] Care should be taken in interpreting the impact of institutional wage setting (i.e. statutory minimum wages or bargained wages) on earnings dispersion, since it could also be ascribed to a truncation of the earnings distribution resulting from negative employment effects on low-paid work. In general, however, the latter appear to be relatively small (Bazen, this volume; Bardone, Gittleman, and Keese 1998).

on the distribution depends on both the level of the minimum relative to the median (average) wage and on the number of workers covered. These may differ significantly across countries. Some systems do not have any statutory intervention in setting a minimum wage. Where it is present, the minimum may lose its 'bite' over time, if it is allowed to decrease both relative to average wages and in terms of coverage of the low paid (see columns (7) and (8)). A number of studies have found the abolition or reduction of statutory minimum wages to be the main determinant of widening earnings inequality, particularly in the lower part of the distribution, as well as being responsible for the increase in low-wage employment (DiNardo, Fortin, and Lemieux 1996; Fortin and Lemieux 1997; Bardone, Gittleman, and Keese 1998; Teulings 1998). Obvious examples are the decline (in real terms) of the Federal minimum wage in the USA over the 1980s and the abolition of Wages Councils in the UK (Machin and Manning 1994). Conversely, in France, where the minimum wage has remained relatively constant, no big changes in low-wage employment have been observed.

Antidiscrimination legislation and fair employment practices, by setting common standards of pay across otherwise different groups of workers, have the effect of reducing overall pay dispersion.[6] The actual impact on low pay, however, will depend on the groups affected; if those involved are located in the bottom part of the wage distribution, the legislation will move these workers upwards. With specific reference to female employment, it can be noted that, despite the fact that women are usually over-represented in low-wage jobs and show a higher propensity to experience long spells of low-wage employment, in most OECD economies women's pay rose relative to that of men over the 1980s and 1990s. Moreover, the effects of antidiscrimination legislation have to be evaluated against the contemporaneous massive increase in the participation of women in the labour market. Without institutional constraint, this increase could have pushed wage levels downwards in the bottom sections of the earnings distribution, further concentrating low pay among women (Freeman 1996b; Joshi 1998).

Finally, the mandatory extension of collective agreement provisions can have pervasive effects in reducing wage differentials among covered workers, irrespective of their union affiliation. In countries where such provisions exist, the effect of negotiated (minimum) wages are automatically (or *de facto*) extended to all workers, granting a high coverage to union bargaining activity (see columns (4) and (5) in Table 1.1). The USA and the UK, on the other hand, provide an interesting example of the absence of any form of mandatory extension. This appears to have been associated with wider wage differentials across groups of workers and firms, as well as with larger differences in the incidence of low pay. Conversely, in continental Europe, the various forms of extension provisions in conjunction with higher union coverage (see below) have had strong equalizing effects, compressing the earnings distribution at the bottom and maintaining a low incidence of low-paid jobs (Dell'Aringa and Lucifora 1994; OECD 1997a).

---

[6] Since institutions can affect men and women very differently, particular care should be used in interpreting their overall effects. In particular, while unionization and collective bargaining mostly affect the male wage distribution, female wages are more sensitive to minimum wage legislation.

2.   Low-Paid Employment and the Institutional Setting: Some Stylized Facts

Labour market institutions, such as those previously discussed, may influence the incidence of low-wage employment in a number of ways. Both the 'level' and the 'change' in labour market institutions may influence wage formation and the structure of earnings by altering the impact of market forces. Different institutional settings across countries provide different constraints and incentives for workers and firms involved in wage formation and can limit the impact of changing economic forces on the wage distribution. Changes in the institutional framework, loosening constraints and increasing incentives, may provide additional freedom to economic agents and favour changes in the structure of earnings. Whilst both the level and the change in institutions are certainly relevant, we concentrate our analysis on the structural differences in labour market institutions across countries rather than changes within countries in considering the effects of the institutional setting on low-wage employment and earnings inequality.

The well-being of individuals at the bottom of the earnings distribution is affected by the general level of real wages, the level and trend in overall inequality, and the degree of earnings mobility that characterizes the wage distribution. Whilst labour market institutions can influence each of these aspects, their implications for the low paid can be very different and should be distinguished.

Mean wage. Differences in the level of the mean wage across countries are relevant when low pay is measured with respect to some absolute benchmark. In countries characterized by a higher mean wage and living standards, what is classified as low-wage employment may be significantly different from that in substantially poorer countries. In general, a higher mean wage will be associated with a lower proportion of people falling below a fixed threshold. This seems to imply that economic growth can benefit everyone. However, if the variance as well as the mean of the distribution increases, there is no guarantee that everyone will be better off; some could become worse off in absolute as well as relative terms. International comparisons of low pay face a number of further difficulties arising from differences in productivity levels, definitions of subsistence levels, and purchasing power of each country's national currency. To avoid these, comparisons are most often made in relative terms. As an example of differing low-wage levels across countries, Fig. 1.2 reports for a number of OECD countries the real hourly earnings of workers located at the first decile of the earnings distribution, and the ratio of this to the mean wage. As shown in the figure, low wages on this definition tend to be notably low in the USA as compared with Europe and in particular with Germany. This suggests that, in addition to the differences in overall inequality (see also the D1/D5 ratio), the lowest part of the distribution varies significantly across countries (Freeman 1994; Gottschalk and Smeeding 1997; Keese 1998).[7]

---

[7] Considering the changes that have occurred over time in various countries can be useful for assessing the relationship between the evolution of mean wages and low pay. In particular, when measured in

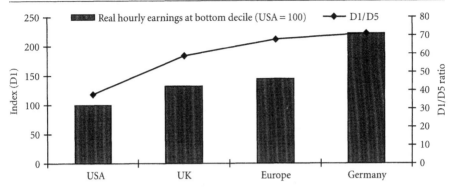

Fig. 1.2. Real hourly earnings index (D1) and D1/D5 ratio (men)

Source: author's computations based on data supplied by OECD.

Turning to the relationship that might exist between a country's institutional setting and its economic performance, although there is no general agreement among economists on the role that labour market institutions may have on economic growth, a number of hypotheses have been subject to extensive scrutiny (Calmfors and Driffill 1988; Brunetta and Dell'Aringa 1990). High levels of unionization and centralized bargaining appear to play an encompassing role, allowing economic policies that are growth oriented rather than centred on redistributive strategies. By limiting the negative externalities from the wage behaviour of self-interested groups, these features lead to a more favourable trade-off between real wages and employment growth from which low-wage employment may benefit. Conversely, when unionization is fragmented and different groups pursue their own interests, the lack of cooperative objectives may prove harmful to the country's performance. Redistributive strategies that favour more powerful groups at the expense of weaker ones may support rent-seeking behaviour. Low-wage workers, lacking power as a group, face a worsened trade-off between the real wage and employment. Finally, under decentralized bargaining and weak union power, the functioning of a quasi-market mechanism may adversely affect the relative position of low-wage workers even in the context of sustained real wage and employment growth. In this context, institutional constraints have a negligible effect, and the operation of supply and demand forces can severely affect the earnings of marginal (low-paid) workers (Pekkarinen, Pohjola, and Rowthorn 1992; Caroli and Aghion 1998).

Wage inequality. Differences in wage inequality across countries are a further dimension of the low-wage employment problem. Countries with wider wage differentials

absolute terms, the increase in real wages in Japan and the UK has brought a relative fall in the incidence of low pay. In contrast, in the USA the fall in real wages at the bottom of the earnings distribution has brought a rise in the proportion of workers with low real earnings.

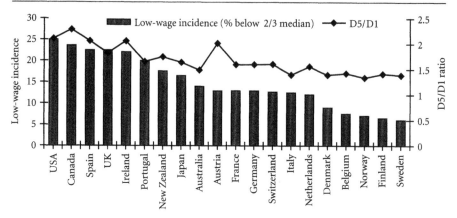

Fig. 1.3. Incidence of low-wage employment and D5/D1 ratio

Source: author's computations based on data supplied by OECD.

are often characterized by a larger proportion of low-paid individuals. In Fig. 1.3, we report for several OECD countries the proportion of low-paid workers—that is, those whose earnings fall below two-thirds of the median wage—as well as the ratio of the median to the first decile wage. The pattern that emerges, as documented in several studies, shows that countries characterized by a higher dispersion in the lower part of the earnings distribution also have the largest share of low-paid individuals (Blau and Kahn 1996; OECD 1997*a*).

International differences in earnings inequality can reflect a wide variety of factors, importantly including differences in measured and unmeasured characteristics (educational attainment, skills, age distribution, and so on) and the differing wage returns for those skills. Blau and Kahn (1996) find that differences across countries in the skill distribution, measured by years of schooling and other relevant worker characteristics, account for only a small part of the differences in the overall dispersion of male wages. Hence institutional factors could be relevant in explaining the residual (unexplained) variation. In the present context institutional differences in wage formation underline a different set of incentives and constraints that individuals take into account in making their choices.

A good starting point in comparing wage inequality and the incidence of low pay across countries is to decompose overall inequality into 'between-group' and 'within-group' components.[8] Since labour market institutions can have a pervasive effect both

---

[8] Inequality differs not only among these different groups but also within groups of workers with the same average characteristics. In terms of the methodology often used, the 'within-group' component can be approximated by the dispersion of the residual of the regression, with a wider dispersion showing greater inequality within groups.

on the distribution of observed characteristics and on the structure of returns to these characteristics, it is important to assess their role in shaping the cross-country pattern of inequality. In other words, differences in overall inequality and in the incidence of low pay may reflect not only the fact that there are differences across countries in unionization rates, and in the composition of the workforce by skill, gender, and other observable traits, but also that the mode of determination of economic returns may differ. Institutional pay setting, such as union pay policies, the structure of bargaining, the existence of mandatory extension of collective agreements, and legislation on wages more generally, may significantly influence wage dispersion and the incidence of low pay.

An alternative hypothesis, often neglected, is that different types of institutions may induce greater (in)stability in the earnings of people with similar characteristics and belonging to the same group. At any moment in time people may experience different earnings (and employment) patterns with short-term transitory increases or decreases in their earnings. If these fluctuations are larger in one country with respect to another, then both inequality and low-wage employment measured at a given point in time will differ (Gottschalk and Moffitt 1994; Gottschalk 1998).

Wage mobility. A further dimension of the functioning of the low-wage labour market and its interactions with the institutional setting relates to the mobility patterns that characterize the earnings distribution. Whilst measures of inequality and low-wage incidence can provide a measure of the diffusion of low pay at a given point in time, they do not offer any perspective on the transitions that occur between the pool of low-wage workers and the rest of the earnings distribution. In particular, when analysing low-wage employment, it is important to stress that it is not always the same people who are low paid: a person in the lowest percentiles in a given year will not necessarily be in the same percentile a few years later. Differences in mobility patterns both across countries and over time may reflect differences in the covariance structure of earnings for any given distribution. In general more dispersed distributions are expected to be characterized by higher (short-term) fluctuations in earnings and hence by larger transition flows across the different parts of the distribution. In terms of low-wage employment the greater dispersion may imply more frequent spells in low pay, while the duration of each spell may be shorter as individuals are also more likely to exit from low pay due to the larger transition flows. To get a rough picture of the relationship that links the extent of low pay to the mobility patterns of individuals located in the lowest deciles of the distribution, in Fig. 1.4 we compare across countries an indicator of low-wage incidence with a measure of transitions out of low pay— that is, the proportion of people moving from a low-wage job to a high-wage job.

The evidence does not seem to support the hypothesis that countries characterized by a larger pool of people earning a low wage are also more likely to have larger flows out of low pay. In particular, contrary to these expectations, in countries where the proportion of low-paid workers is higher, only a small proportion seem to transit to better-paid jobs. At the aggregate level, a significant degree of persistence in low pay

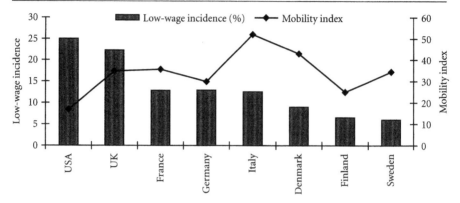

Fig. 1.4. Mobility patterns and low-wage incidence

Source: author's computations based on data supplied by OECD.

emerges: it is the same individuals who are still found in low pay several years later (OECD 1997*a*). Conversely, exiting low pay appears more likely in those countries where its incidence is smaller.[9]

In general, the empirical literature shows that earnings mobility is rather modest and not sufficient to override the effects of steady state inequality (Burkhauser, Holtz-Eakin, and Rhody 1995; OECD 1996*a*; Bigard, Guillotin, and Lucifora 1998). In terms of labour market institutions, the fact that the USA has a less regulated labour market and a more decentralized system of collective bargaining as compared to European countries does not translate into greater earnings mobility nor into a higher probability of leaving low pay. Likewise the more centralized wage-setting institutions in Germany and the Nordic countries do not imply a significantly lower mobility among the low paid. This evidence, even if only sketched, seems to imply that institutions produce their main effects on the permanent components of pay dynamics, whilst differences in the transitory components appear to have only marginal effects (Dickens 1997*a*; Cappellari 1998; Gottschalk 1998).

[9] Care in interpreting these results is necessary for three main reasons. First, given the definition of low pay (relative to the median wage) when earnings are more dispersed—particularly at the extremes of the distribution—the wage gain required to exit low pay might be larger, thus mechanically reducing transition flows. Second, persistence in the aggregate might be due to some specific characteristics of the low-wage pool that are correlated with earnings levels quite independently of pure state dependence (e.g. skill as well as unobserved heterogeneity). Third, year-to-year mobility into and out of low pay might also be affected by significant selection effects. Flows of workers out of low pay are often accounted for not only by a move into a higher-paid job but also by moves into non-employment (unemployment or out of the labour force). Similarly, flows into low pay may be associated with an earlier spell of unemployment (Bardone, Gittleman, and Keese 1998).

3.   Measuring the Effects of Institutions on Low-Wage Employment

The fact that over the 1990s several OECD countries experienced a general tendency towards increasing inequality, and are still showing considerable differences in the extent of inequality and low-wage employment, may be interpreted as evidence that institutional structures under common shocks can produce substantially different outcomes. In this section we shall investigate the extent to which selected institutional features can influence the distribution of wages and the incidence of low-wage employment across a number of OECD countries. In particular, since the impact of institutional features is typically concentrated in specific parts of the distribution, we shall centre our attention on those institutions that are most likely to impact on the bottom part of the wage distribution—namely, trade unions, the structure of collective bargaining, and wage regulation. Their main effects, as well as those of selected control variables, are reported in Table 1.2 and discussed thereafter.

Table 1.2. Institutions and the incidence of low wages (cross-country correlations, 20 countries)

Labour market institutions	Bivariate correlations	Simple univariate regression dependent variable: log(LWI)		
	$\rho(LW, x)$	Constant	x	R^2(adj)
Union density	−0.68**	3.23	−0.015**	0.44
Union coverage	−0.60**	3.33	−0.010**	0.33
Centralization	−0.72**	3.20	−0.069**	0.50
Kaitz index	−0.64**	4.07	−0.028*	0.38
Benefit replacement ratio	−0.53*	3.37	−0.021*	0.41
Other controls				
Women employed part-time	−0.30		—	
Proportion of self-employed	−0.36		—	
Test-score ratio	0.58[a]		—	
Enrolment/population rate (high-school age)	−0.23		—	
GDP (per capita)	−0.17		—	
Services share (employment in services /total employment)	−0.22		—	
Share of home-ownership	0.05		—	
Product and labour market regulation	−0.17		—	

* 5% significance level; ** 1% significance level;
[a] based on only 11 countries.

Note: Data refer to full-time, full-year workers in private sector employment.

Source: author's calculations based on data supplied by OECD and from Nickell and Layard (1997, 1999).

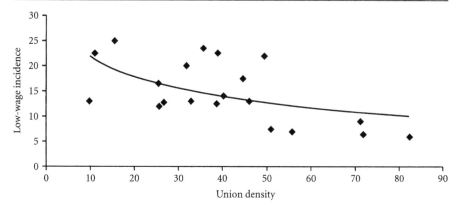

Fig. 1.5. Union density and low-wage incidence

Sources: Low-wage incidence: data supplied by OECD; union density: Nickell and Layard (1999: table 7).

3.1. Unions and Collective Bargaining

There are several routes through which trade unions can alter the overall distribution of wages and in particular the incidence of low pay. Although union pay policies tend to reduce wage dispersion by raising wage floors in almost all countries, the extent to which unions are able to reduce the gap between low pay and average pay levels appears to be correlated with the degree of unionization (or union density) observed in each country. In Fig. 1.5, we plot the incidence of low pay against union density. The empirical evidence, summarized in simple bivariate correlations (rank correlation in the case of the index of centralization) shows that where unionization is generally low a larger pool of low-wage workers is observed. In the USA, where only 14 per cent of workers are members of a trade union, the proportion of low-paid workers is over 25 per cent, whilst in Sweden, where union density is over 80 per cent, less than 6 per cent of workers fall below the low-pay threshold (see Table 1.1). Similarly in Italy, Germany, and Belgium, where nearly one worker out of two is a member of a union (i.e. Italy 40 per cent; Germany 33 per cent; Belgium 51 per cent), the proportion of low-paid workers lies between 8 and 13 per cent. Hence, at a purely descriptive level, the extent of unionization appears to be negatively correlated (rho = −0.68) with the extent of low-wage employment (see Table 1.2).

However, unionization has been traditionally low in some countries, such as France, which have also experienced a fairly low incidence in low-wage employment. In this context the existence of mandatory extension provisions for collective bargaining, as previously described, can make the degree of union coverage a more appropriate indicator of the effective 'strength' of unions in protecting low wages. When the extension of collective agreements is taken into account, as in Fig. 1.6, the evidence of a negative correlation between union power and low-wage employment is confirmed (rho = −0.60). In particular, looking at the estimated coefficients from simple univariate regressions, it emerges that an increase of 1 per cent in union

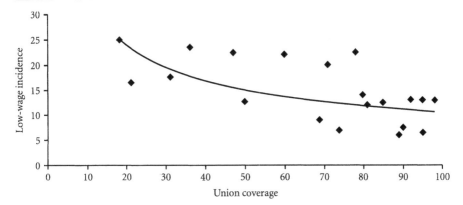

Fig. 1.6. Union coverage and low-wage incidence

Sources: Low-wage incidence: data supplied by OECD; union coverage: Nickell and Layard (1999: table 7).

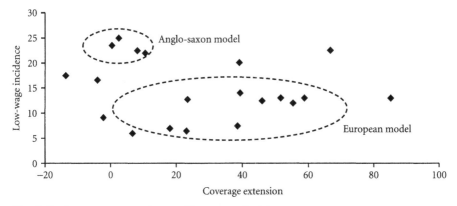

Fig. 1.7. Coverage extension and low-wage incidence

Sources: Low-wage incidence: data supplied by OECD; coverage extension: Nickell and Layard (1999: table 7).

density or coverage—considered independently—is associated with a reduction of 1 and 1.5 per cent, respectively, in the incidence of low pay. In other words, the power of the unions to create a wage floor and reduce wage dispersion at the bottom of the distribution seems to be the result of a combination of factors: on the one side, 'pure' union power given by actual membership and, on the other, some form of wage regulation that can extend the power over the outcomes from collective negotiations far above that provided by union presence.

In order to see this, in Fig. 1.7 we have computed an indicator of coverage extension, measured as the excess of bargaining power over and above union membership, and related it to the incidence of low pay. The pattern that emerges, with the exception of some outliers, shows two clusters of points: on the top left (i.e. high low-wage employment and low coverage extension), we find countries belonging to the

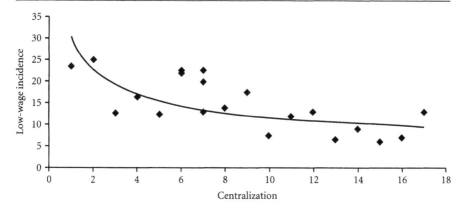

Fig. 1.8. Centralization and low-wage incidence

Source: Low-wage incidence: data supplied by OECD; centralization: Nickell and Layard (1999: table 7).

Anglo-Saxon model of industrial relations characterized by limited mandatory extension provisions; conversely, on the bottom right, it is the European model of industrial relations, with high coverage and frequent mandatory extensions (see Table 1.1), that predominates.[10]

Finally, the structure of collective bargaining might be related to the extent of low pay. In particular, centralization of collective bargaining through the encompassing role played by the unions is shown to reduce significantly wage dispersion in the bottom part of the wage distribution and limit the incidence of low pay. Both Table 1.2 and Fig. 1.8 show a negative and statistically significant correlation between an index of centralization and the proportion of low-wage workers (rho = −0.72). An upward move in the centralization ranking reduces the percentage of low-pay employment by almost 7 per cent.

3.2. Wage Regulation

As already discussed, both the existence of a statutory minimum wage and the generosity of unemployment benefits are further labour market institutions, which may have an impact on the bottom end of the wage distribution as well as on the propensity of individuals to take up low-paid jobs. In general, a high (low) minimum wage relative to the average wage (the Kaitz index) tends to be associated with lower (higher) levels of low-wage employment. This is confirmed in the strong negative correlation that emerges from Fig. 1.9 between the Kaitz index and the proportion of low-wage workers across countries (rho = −0.64).

---

[10] Note that most of the outliers are represented by Scandinavian countries, for which unionization and coverage are both high. In some cases, coverage extension turns out to be negative—that is, union density is higher than coverage.

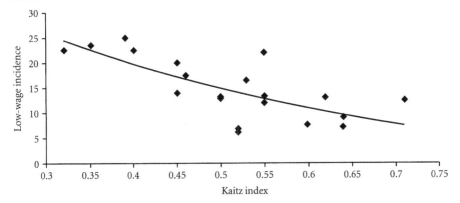

Fig. 1.9. Kaitz index and low-wage incidence

Sources: Low-wage incidence: data supplied by OECD; Kaitz index: Nickell and Layard (1999: table 9).

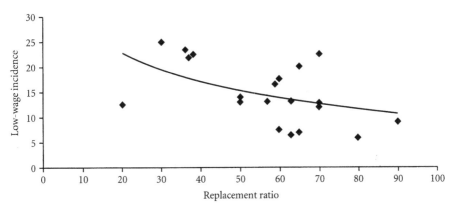

Fig. 1.10. Replacement ratio and low-wage incidence

Sources: Low-wage incidence: data supplied by OECD; replacement ratio: Nickell and Layard (1999: table 10).

The generosity of unemployment benefits, as measured by the replacement ratio in Fig. 1.10, also appears to be negatively related to the extent of low-wage employment (rho = −0.53).

In general, as it emerges from coefficient estimates, a unit increase in the ratio of the minimum to the average wage or in the replacement ratio shows a statistically significant negative impact on the proportion of workers in low pay. The evidence presented thus far seem to confirm the significant role played by labour market institutions in shaping the distribution of earnings and the incidence of low-wage employment. Different institutions concerned with wage-setting practices have, taken one by one, shown that various forms of wage floor, by reducing dispersion at the bottom end of the distribution or more directly by truncating the distribution from below, can

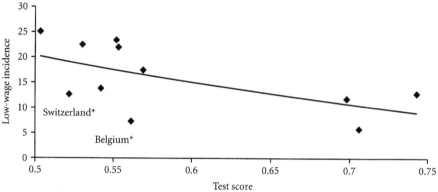

Fig. 1.11. Test scores and low-wage incidence
Source: data supplied by OECD.

play a relevant role in alleviating low pay. However, a number of caveats apply to the above evidence and further discussion is required before any policy implications can be drawn.

First, bivariate correlations across countries between different measures of labour market institutions and the incidence of low pay provide a description of the 'stylized facts' but do not involve any investigation of the causation that may generate the observed patterns. Furthermore, the exclusive focus on labour market institutions (since further aspects of low-wage employment are addressed in other chapters of this volume) neglects the role that market forces or other factors may play in determining a different incidence in low-wage employment across countries. Some of these (observed) factors are reported in Table 1.2 and have been further experimented with in the empirical analysis below. They include: the share of women employed part-time, proportion of self-employed, GDP per capita, the share of employment in services, and the extent of home-ownership. Each of these factors is often indicated as having some role in shaping the distribution of wages and the incidence of low pay. However, simple correlations show that there is no statistically significant relationship between any of the factors listed above and the share of low-wage employment.

Second, when using evidence from aggregate data, compositional effects—originating from a different distribution of observed as well as unobserved characteristics across countries—may distort the observed pattern in an unpredictable way. The obvious factor to be considered is the differing distribution of skill levels, either measured in years of schooling or, more appropriately, using average test scores. In Fig. 1.11 we plot literacy test score ratios against low-wage employment.[11] This shows a clear positive correlation between skill dispersion and the incidence of low pay: the more

---

[11] The index is based on the OECD's Literacy Skills Test Scores, and is the ratio of the fifth percentile divided by the mean (available for eleven countries only). I am particularly grateful to A. Glyn for making the data available to me.

Table 1.3. Estimates of the effects of labour market institutions on low-wage incidence (20 countries)

Labour market institutions	Low-wage incidence dependent variable: log(LWI)			
	(1)	(2)	(3)	(4)
Union density	−0.0101*	−0.009*	−0.008**	−0.008**
Union coverage	−0.006°	−0.005*	−0.007**	−0.007**
Centralization	−0.021	—	—	—
Kaitz index	—	−0.014**	−0.011*	−0.011*
Benefit replacement ratio	—	−0.007**	−0.008**	−0.008**
Other characteristics				
Test score ratio	—	—	0.003	—
'No score' dummy	—	—	0.001	—
Enrolment/population rate (high school age)	—	—	—	0.003
Constant	3.59**	4.45**	5.08**	5.07**
R^2	0.61	0.73	0.84	0.85
No. of observations	20	20	20	20

* 5% significance level; ** 1% significance level.

Source: author's calculations based on data supplied by OECD and from Nickell and Layard (1997, 1999).

heterogeneous are workers in the bottom part of the skill distribution in terms of skills, the higher are both earnings inequality and the proportion of people falling below the low-wage threshold.

The third and most fundamental criticism, which applies to all studies that investigate the role of institutions as a potential explanation for differing economic outcomes, relates to the fact that the variety of institutional features of labour markets may be the consequence rather than the cause of the differing incidence of low pay. For example, countries with low dispersion of wages for reasons other than those attributable to the institutional setting may set a relatively high minimum wage to protect workers from adverse shocks, knowing that very few would be affected. In the remainder of the section, we shall take up these points in order.

3.3. Institutions and Low Pay: Is the Evidence Robust?

As far as the first criticism is concerned, in Table 1.3 we report some evidence drawn from a simple multivariate analysis. The proportion of low-wage workers (in logs) is regressed against a set of institutional features that, as previously described, are expected to reduce earnings dispersion in the lower part of the distribution.[12] When

---

[12] Given the limited degrees of freedom, the results reported here should be interpreted with some care. A similar approach, though with fewer observations and fewer control variables, can be found in Freeman (1996b). The results obtained here are very close to those reported in that study.

we look at the joint effects of unionization, union coverage, and centralization in collective bargaining across countries, we find that they contribute to reducing the incidence of low-wage employment. Coefficient estimates are negatively signed and in general statistically significant (although centralization on its own is not). However, since institutional wage setting is also strongly influenced by the generosity of unemployment benefits and by a high minimum wage relative to the average wage, we include both of these as additional controls. In line with previous results, our findings also suggest that wage regulations have a significant impact on low-wage employment (DiNardo, Fortin, and Lemieux 1996; Fortin and Lemieux 1997; Teulings 1998). Finally, as a further test for the significance of the above results, we experimented with additional control variables, including the proportion of self-employed workers and the share of women employed part-time.[13] None of these, however, seemed to play any role in explaining the distribution of low-wage employment across countries. When considering the distribution of skill levels (as shown in Table 1.3, columns (3) and (4)) both the test score variable and enrolment ratios in higher education—while leaving the previous estimates largely unaltered—never achieved statistical significance.

Regression estimates can provide a basis for estimating the potential effects of differences in labour market institutions on the incidence of low wages. For example, if we consider the difference in the incidence of low-wage employment between the USA and Germany ($\Delta LW = 12\%$), the regression results suggest that 64 per cent of that difference ($\Delta LW_{(est)} = 7.7\%$) can be explained by differences in labour market institutions. Alternatively, repeating the exercise for the USA against Sweden ($\Delta LW = 19\%$) the proportion accounted for by differing institutional settings is close to 61 per cent ($\Delta LW_{(est)} = 11.7\%$).

Since many institutional arrangements are targeted towards a specific portion of the wage distribution, we may expect their effects, as previously discussed, to differ between the bottom and the top end of the distribution. In Table 1.4 we evaluate, for the same set of OECD countries, the effects of labour market institutions on various measures of wage inequality. In particular, do the institutional arrangements considered in the previous exercise have an impact on inequality at the top of the wage distribution that is different from their impact at the bottom?[14] In order to do this we regress various decile ratios (i.e. D9/D1; D9/D5; D5/D1) on different institutional features. Considering overall inequality (measured by the log of the ratio of the top to the bottom decile), higher union density appears to be associated with lower wage dispersion while no (statistically significant) effect is detected for the coverage or the

[13] Note that, since earnings data refer to full-time private sector employees, the inclusion of both part-time and self-employment controls is essentially trying to capture a potential under-reporting in low-pay employment (since low pay is known to be higher among female part-timers and the self-employed). Results for the other control variables have not been reported in the tables.

[14] It should be stressed that the estimation of the effects of labour market institutions on different portions of the wage distribution is particularly demanding with respect to the data used, which is a cross section of twenty OECD countries. While parameter estimates, both in terms of sign and magnitude, are fairly robust to changes in the specification, the statistical significance on the individual coefficients sometimes weakens when sufficient non-linear terms and interactions are introduced.

Table 1.4. Estimates of the effects of labour market institutions on the distribution of wages (decile ratios, 20 countries)

Labour market institutions	Decile ratio log(D9/D1) (1)	(2)	Decile ratio log(D9/D5) (3)	(4)	Decile ratio log(D5/D1) (5)	(6)	(7)
Union density	−0.004**	−0.003*	−0.0015	−0.0011	−0.0030°	−0.0011	−0.0010
Coverage	−0.006**	−0.0022°	0.0002	0.0002	−0.0022	−0.0008	−0.0009
Centralization	—	—	—	—	0.0013	—	—
Kaitz index −0.0080**	—	−0.011**	−0.0151**	−0.0165*	−0.0019	—	−0.0077**
Benefit replacement ratio −0.0031°	—	−0.003*		—	0.0010	—	−0.0030*
Other characteristics Test score ratio 0.0898	—	—	—	—	—	—	—
'No score' dummy[a] 0.058	—	—	—	—	—	—	—
Constant	1.57**	2.58**	1.08**	1.12**	0.98**	1.17**	1.14**
R²	0.55	0.74	0.60	0.63	0.28	0.49	0.41
No. of observations	20	20	20	20	20	20	20

° 10% significance level; * 5% significance level; ** 1% significance level.

[a] Dummy variable that takes value 1 when the test-score variable is missing (i.e. set equal to zero in 9 cases).

Source: author's calculations based on data supplied by OECD and from Nickell and Layard (1997, 1999).

centralization of collective bargaining. Also, both a higher minimum wage, relative to the average wage, and a more generous benefit replacement ratio result in a lower dispersion. The effect of the minimum wage on the distribution seems particularly strong.

When the same set of institutional variables are tested on the top and the bottom of the distribution respectively, some interesting differences result. First, as one might expect, union density has a negative impact on wage dispersion at the bottom of the distribution, whilst it shows no effect at the top. The reverse is true when centralization of collective bargaining is taken into account. In other words, it seems that countries with more centralized bargaining systems promote corporatist objectives and worker solidarity mostly by reducing earnings dispersion at the top of the distribution. When it comes to the role of wage regulation factors, the minimum wage shows a (statistically significant) negative impact on wage dispersion both on the whole distribution and, particularly, on the bottom part. No effect is detected at the top. The generosity of the benefit system also shows a negative impact on the overall distribution and on the bottom end, while no statistically significant effect is detected at the top. Finally, the inclusion of a test score indicator as a proxy for low-skill heterogeneity and as a potential determinant of wage dispersion in the bottom part of the distribution fails to show up as statistically significant (see Table 1.4, column (7)).

The results suggest that the main factors that are effective in reducing dispersion at the bottom of the distribution are union power and the minimum wage. In particular, the latter appears very effective in protecting low-wage employment. Conversely, centralized bargaining systems are more effective in restraining wage differences at the top of the distribution. Finally, the evidence concerning welfare benefits shows that higher replacement ratios also provide a safety net for low wages, reducing dispersion at the bottom of the distribution.

Although it should be stressed that the above results have to be taken with care, since they are based on aggregate cross-sectional data and on a limited number of observations, nevertheless they appear to be consistent with the view that labour market institutions do play a relevant part in determining wage inequality and the extent of low-wage employment across countries.

Next we turn to the role of different characteristics within the labour force, addressed in a number of studies. Blau and Kahn (1996), after correcting for a wide range of worker characteristics, still find that institutional features represent one of the main factors that can account for the observed differences across countries in wage inequality and low-wage employment, although Leuven and Oosterbeek (1997) give alternative explanations. Freeman (1996b) and Bjorklund and Freeman (1996), using US and Swedish data, run a pseudo-experiment comparing earnings inequality between a 'treatment' and 'control' group. The first consists of a sample of men of Swedish descent living in the USA and the second of a sample of native Americans, along with samples of non-Nordic men and persons of Swedish ancestry living in Sweden. The results show insignificant differences in earnings inequality between the two groups in each experiment, suggesting that institutions more than observed and unobserved characteristics contribute to shaping the earnings distribution. In other words, Swedish institutional wage setting appears to be more committed to egalitarianism, showing less dispersion in earnings and a lower incidence in low-wage employment, while in the USA there is more inequality because the wage-setting system produces higher dispersion in earnings.

As a final point, we take up the issue of the nature of institutions *vis-à-vis* market forces. A number of features that have characterized the process of structural change across most industrialized countries appear hard to reconcile with the view that institutions are purely endogenous and therefore should not be considered as one of the key factors capable of explaining the observed differences. One feature that should be considered is that pervasive labour market institutions show strong persistence against economic forces. Moreover, common shocks affecting most countries produce very different responses in wages and employment depending on the underlying institutional settings. Countries characterized by similar institutional features share common patterns, as described above, irrespective of the magnitude of the economic changes occurring. If institutional settings were endogenous responses to more fundamental shocks resulting from globalization, technological developments and organizational change, the pattern of economic effects should have been stronger where institutions proved more sensitive to adjustment. The available evidence suggests that this is not the case. Differences in labour laws and collective bargaining practices, as opposed to demand and supply factors, appear to be the relevant features of the diverging patterns. Also, countries where institutional wage-setting practices are targeted to protect low-wage workers and reduce wage dispersion should exhibit larger employment losses among low-skilled workers as compared to countries where wages are set in a more market-oriented fashion. However, the relative employment rates of the low-wage/low-skilled workers evolved in a similar fashion in most countries, which appears in contrast with the view that institutions are endogenous responses to market shocks (Nickell and Bell 1995; Fortin and Lemieux 1997; Card, Kramarz, and Lemieux 1999).

4. Concluding Remarks

In this chapter, the issue of labour market institutions and low-wage employment has been investigated and tested empirically across a number of OECD countries. Since institutional arrangements are typically directed towards a specific portion of the wage distribution or towards given groups of individuals, we have focused the attention on selected institutions that are particularly relevant for low-wage employment. In particular the effects of trade unions, the structure of collective bargaining, and the existence of regulations on wages have been considered.

Labour market institutions, in general, influence wage formation and the structure of earnings by altering the effects of market forces and providing a different set of constraints and incentives for workers and firms involved in wage formation. Here, the focus has been restricted to the analysis of the structural differences that exist in labour market institutions across countries and the effects that these have on low-wage employment and earnings inequality. By looking at the different moments of the distribution of earnings, various dimensions of low pay have been analysed: the effects of the institutional setting on the mean, the dispersion and the (time) covariance of earnings. Consistent with previous work, our results suggest that institutions are a relevant factor in shaping the distribution of earnings and the incidence of low pay. We have shown that institutional settings differ substantially across countries and that institutional variety in the labour market is able to explain a great deal of the observed patterns in low pay across countries.

At a descriptive level, results from bivariate correlations indicate that union density, collective bargaining coverage, and the centralization of wage negotiations jointly contribute to reduce the incidence of low pay across countries. However, the power of unions to create a wage floor and reduce wage dispersion at the bottom of the distribution appears to be the outcome of a combination of union power and wage regulations, such as mandatory extension of contract, statutory minimum wages, and the generosity of unemployment benefits. When all the above factors are taken together to explain the pattern of low-wage incidence across countries, the results show that over 60 per cent of the cross-country differences in low pay can be accounted for by the different institutional settings. Looking at the effects of institutional arrangements on wage inequality, we show that high minimum wages lower dispersion at the bottom end of the distribution, while a more corporatist system is effective in containing wage differences at the top. The hypothesis that greater dispersion of skills could be the main determinant of differences in earnings inequality did not receive strong support in our findings. The test score variable and the ratio of enrolments into secondary education, introduced as a proxy for skill heterogeneity in the bottom part of the earning distribution, never showed any (statistically) significant impact on the incidence of low pay or on wage dispersion in the different countries.

Whilst the above evidence is far from providing any conclusive assessment of the complex interactions that exist between labour market institutions and the problem of low-wage employment, it provides additional evidence, consistent with other studies, that institutions do matter for the functioning of low-wage labour markets. From a more policy-oriented perspective, the above findings seem to suggest that governments can have a role in supporting or promoting those institutions that have proved effective in dealing with the problem of growing earnings inequalities and low-wage employment.

2 Employment Inequalities

ANDREW GLYN AND WIEMER SALVERDA

The deteriorating position of less-qualified workers has been a growing cause for concern in many OECD countries in the 1980s and 1990s. As well as contributing directly to rising inequality, it compounds the difficulties faced by workers already disadvantaged in the labour market for reasons of age, gender, or race. This chapter documents the employment record of the less qualified and examines the factors that help to explain the variety of experience among OECD countries.

The first section discusses some tricky but important problems about how to represent the impact of educational qualifications on employment. Cross-country patterns of differences in employment rates by education are then reported for the OECD countries. Section 2 discusses a range of factors that may bear on the extent of employment disadvantage suffered by the least qualified. These include the usual suspects, such as overall demand for labour, trade with the South, and aspects of labour market flexibility, but we have also examined the dispersion of educational achievement in the labour force. New light is thereby thrown on the widely held view that, in the face of global trends, the less qualified lost out everywhere, but that in the USA this took the form of falls in their relative pay whilst in Europe their chances of being in work declined.

1. Employment Differences in OECD Countries

1.1. *Measurement Issues*

Educational qualifications, although subject to problems of comparison between countries and over time, offer just about the only widely available measure of 'skill'. The major cross-country studies that propelled the international debate on the declining demand for unskilled labour all reported how educational qualifications affected employment outcomes across countries. The main measure used was the ratio of unemployment rates for low and high educational categories or variants thereof (Wood 1994: table A3; Nickell and Bell 1995: table 2a; OECD 1994: chart 7.1). Ratios exceeded one almost everywhere, reflecting higher unemployment rates for the less qualified, but the trend over time appeared much less clear. Nickell and Bell confirmed the OECD's finding that the ratio tended to rise between the 1970s and 1980s, but reported that this trend was partially (or in the case of the UK wholly) reversed in the early 1990s. These measures were supplemented, data permitting, with 'non-employment rates' (100 per cent minus the ratio of employment to population to working age), which could take into account differences in non-participation; by this measure (the ratio of non-employment rates for workers in low and high educational groups), the USA was also displaying *fewer* disadvantages for the less qualified in 1991 than in the early 1970s (Nickell and Bell 1995: table 6).

The problem with these measures is, first, that the *ratio* of unemployment (or non-employment) rates does not adequately reflect differences in the probability of having a job for workers with different levels of skill. Thus, whilst the UK unemployment ratio (low-ed to high-ed) fell from 2.9 in 1971–4 to 2.6 in 1992, the absolute difference in the unemployment rates nearly quadrupled from 2.6 to 10.3 per cent; the chances of having a job fell much more for the less qualified and thus the extent of disadvantage suffered by them rose. Similarly, while the ratio of male non-employment rates in the USA was 3.9 in both 1975–8 and 1991, the difference in non-employment rates rose from 19.1 to 24.1 per cent.[1] It is these absolute differences in un- (or non-)employment that measure the extent to which the less educated are less likely to have a job; comparisons of the ratio of unemployment rates do not convey differences in the probability of having work in situations where the unemployment rate for the most educated is not constant over time.[2] Nor is the ratio any better for measuring differences across countries. Sweden in 1991 and the UK in 1992 had the same ratio of unemployment rates; in the former case the difference in unemployment rates between the best and least educated was 2.4 percentage points, in the latter 10.3 percentage points. The degree to which the less educated were less likely to be in work was obviously far greater in the UK. Whilst the ratio of unemployment rates may be an appropriate indicator of the pattern of labour market slack in some models of wage pressure (Nickell and Bell 1995), it is a misleading measure of the comparative employment record of different groups. The use of absolute differences in unemployment (and employment) rates in the OECD's latest discussion of the issue is surely correct (OECD 1997a: ch. 4). The emphasis in what follows is on employment, rather than unemployment, rates—that is, on how different economies have generated work for the less qualified, rather than whether those without work are unemployed or inactive.

The second problem in interpreting educational differences in employment concerns differences between countries (or changes within a country) in the proportions of the labour force in the various educational categories. In 1994 the proportion of the

---

[1] UK male unemployment rates were 4.0% and 1.4% in 1971–4, and 16.9% and 6.6% in 1992. The US male non-employment rates were 25.8% and 6.7% in 1975–8, 32.4% and 8.3% in 1991 (Nickell and Bell 1995: tables 2a and 6).

[2] Suppose the chances of car accident on a particular journey went up from 10% to 50% whilst the chances of a train accident went up from 1% to 10%. The relative chances of having an accident (of being unemployed) have fallen from 10 to 1 for car versus train to 5 to 1. But the position of car travellers has surely deteriorated more, as reflected in the bigger differential in the chances of arriving safely by train (up from 9% to 40%) and in the decline in the relative chance of arriving safely by car (down from 91% to 56%).

Table 2.1. Measures of employment rate differences, men aged 25–64

Country	Educational level			Educational quartile		
	Lower secondary (1)	University (2)	Difference (3)	Q1 (4)	Q4 (5)	Difference (6)
Germany 1994	66.2	90.7	24.5	71.1	88.2	17.1
France 1994	62.1	86.0	23.9	60.5	85.0	24.5
France 1981	80.3	92.5	12.2	73.8	91.8	18.0

Source: See Data Appendix.

male labour force aged 25–64 with university education was 8.5 per cent in Italy and 26.7 per cent in the USA, whilst the proportion with lower secondary education was 15.3 per cent in the USA and 65.0 per cent in Italy (OECD 1997*a*: table 4.1a). So highly educated workers were almost twice as numerous in the USA as those with low education (on this definition), whilst in Italy the ratio was about 1 to 8. This makes it hard to compare employment patterns across educational groups in the USA and Italy. Changes over time are just as troublesome. For example, the proportion of workers in the lowest educational category halved in the UK between 1984 and 1994. Their deteriorating employment position may partly reflect a more refined process of 'sorting', whereby the shrinking membership of the bottom educational category is increasingly confined to those with other disadvantages in the labour market (in terms of intellectual capacity, attitude, and so forth). Plausibly, the distribution of talents among the population remained the same, but its mapping over the range of formalized educational categories changed.

The *Jobs Study* (OECD 1994) made a rough correction for differences in educational patterns by constructing unemployment by educational quartiles. By analogy with the distribution of wages, consistent definitions for the two ends of the employment distribution are applied by taking the top and bottom quarters of the population ranked by educational qualification. Table 2.1 shows that employment rate (employment over population) differences between educational quartiles can give a different picture from those between university graduates and those with only lower secondary education. Column (3) shows that in both France and Germany men with lower secondary education had employment rates about 24 percentage points lower than those with university qualifications. But the quartile comparison (column (6)) suggests a distinctly worse position in France, with employment rate differences nearly half as big again as those in Germany. The explanation is that less than half of those in the first quartile in Germany had only lower secondary qualifications, so that the employment rate of the first quartile is boosted by the higher employment rate of the next educational group; by contrast, in France most of the first quartile were in the lowest subsection of lower secondary, which pulls their employment rate (column (4)) below the average for lower secondary as a whole (column (1)).[3] The quartile calculations also suggest a much smaller deterioration in employment at the bottom end in France since 1981. This is because the proportion of the population in the very lowest educational category, with the lowest employment rate, was almost halved over the period.

These quartile measures capture both the experience of particular educational categories and the educational structure, and this is appropriate because inequalities in employment outcomes reflect both influences. Employment rate differences for quartile groups are analogous to the D9/D1 measures of overall wage dispersion rather than to measures of pay differentials between specific educational groups. The 'sorting' problem of using fixed educational categories over time is minimized, since the 'bottom' refers to a constant, rather than an ever-shrinking, share of the working population.

The third issue concerns age and gender. Including age groups with large numbers in full-time education (or national service) is confusing because their non-employment does not only reflect a lack of work. Educational participation by young people and consequently their labour market participation differs significantly over time and internationally. It seems best to treat youth separately and leave them out here (see OECD 1998a for a discussion of youth unemployment). Thus the OECD data used below, starting at age 25, probably provide the best single measure. There is a similar problem with older workers. Labour force withdrawal is very prevalent amongst those over 55, especially the least qualified. Given that these age groups contain a higher proportion of the least educated, they have an important weight in employment outcomes. There seems to be a case for concentrating on 'prime-age workers' between 25 and 54. On the other hand, early retirement has been a deliberate policy for dealing with lack of work for the least qualified in many countries and has had an important influence on labour force participation for those over 55. Leaving out these workers may paint an unrealistically rosy picture of the employment position of the least qualified. So the fact that the OECD data used cover only the whole age group 25–64 is not too serious a drawback. Finally, it is desirable to analyse men and women separately. Given the very strong historical and cultural influences affecting patterns of women's participation in the labour market, it may be that the data for men best display the influences of lack of work on employment outcomes; on the other hand, the labour market for men does not exist in isolation and the position of women obviously deserves analysis in its own right.

1.2. Employment differences

Table 2.2 presents data for employment rates (as a percentage of the population of working age) for nineteen OECD countries for 1994 calculated mainly from the background data used in OECD (1997a) (see Data Appendix for details). The data are

[3] In the International Standard Classification for Education (ISCED) ISCED 0/1 is the lowest educational category whilst ISCED 2 is also included in 'lower secondary'. Since employment differences are much less at the top of the educational spectrum, using quartiles, rather than educational groups such as university graduates, makes much less difference at the top end (as Table 2.1 shows).

Table 2.2. Employment outcomes by educational quartile, 1994
(employment/population, %)

Country	Women			Men			
	Q1	Q4	Q4–Q1	Q1	Q4	Q4–Q1	Q4–Q1 changes 1981–94
Australia	50.5	73.5	23.0	73.0	88.0	15.0	n.a.
Austria	47.0	70.5	23.5	70.2	86.6	16.4	n.a.
Belgium	23.2	76.9	53.7	52.8	88.0	35.2	n.a.
Canada	40.8	77.4	36.6	64.2	86.3	22.1	4.5
Denmark	55.5	85.6	30.2	65.7	87.6	21.9	8.2
Finland	50.9	77.1	26.2	54.6	80.3	25.7	10.7
France	40.5	72.4	31.9	60.5	85.0	24.5	6.4
Germany (1995)	37.4	70.9	32.5	71.1	88.2	17.1	9.5[a]
Ireland	18.2	67.7	49.5	58.6	89.1	30.6	n.a.
Italy	20.1	63.3	43.2	60.6	84.7	24.1	13.0[a]
Netherlands	30.1	70.9	40.8	66.6	86.9	20.3	1.5
New Zealand	46.3	75.7	29.4	67.5	90.3	22.8	15.2
Norway	56.2	86.1	29.8	72.9	90.9	17.9	6.7
Portugal	52.0	80.7	28.7	80.0	87.8	7.9	n.a.
Spain	22.9	57.3	34.4	63.6	80.8	17.1	8.6
Sweden (96)	63.6	87.0	23.4	73.1	87.2	14.1	−5.2[a]
Switzerland	58.7	69.8	11.1	90.6	93.3	2.7	n.a.
UK	52.0	79.0	27.0	65.1	88.3	23.2	13.2
USA	51.2	79.9	28.7	70.1	90.6	20.6	1.4
Japan	n.a.	n.a.	n.a.	89.6	97.6	8.0	2.2[a]
Europe (median)			30.2			20.3	

[a] Germany 1980–95, Italy 1980–94, Finland 1982–94, Japan 1979–92, Sweden 1981–94.

Note: n.a. = not available.

Source: See Data Appendix.

shown separately for men and for women. Employment rates for the least educated are generally in the range 50–75 per cent; the figure for Portugal is biased upwards by the fact that it actually refers to the nearly 70 per cent of the population in the lowest educational category, whilst the very high Swiss rate reflects the regulation of the numbers of less qualified through control of migration.[4]

With employment rates for the best-qualified quartile generally between 80 and 90 per cent, educational differences in employment outcomes (Q4–Q1) vary substantially between countries. Most fall in the range 15–25 per cent, with Ireland and Belgium outliers at over 30 per cent and Portugal, Japan, and Switzerland below 10 per cent. Differences in inactivity are very significant; thus Italy has one of the

---

[4] Migrants make up a high proportion of those with the lowest level of educational qualifications.

lowest unemployment rate differences between the best and least qualified, but its employment rate differences are greater than the average for Europe.

Perhaps most striking of all, the USA lies close to the average for the OECD countries as a whole, with the least-educated quartile of men 21 per cent less likely to have a job than the most-educated quartile. This was higher than in allegedly sclerotic Germany and little better than France. Even for women, whose overall employment rate in the USA is very high, Q4–Q1 is as large as the average for European countries. Thus wage flexibility clearly did not prevent the less qualified in the USA from suffering the high levels of joblessness.

Employment differences are greater for women than for men and more variable across countries, reflecting the fact that the longer-term rise in women's participation has generally had a bigger effect on better-educated women and an extremely uneven effect for the less qualified.

It is important to supplement the picture of the employment position of the less educated in the early 1990s with an analysis of how it changed over the 1980s. Here the data problems are even more severe, but some rough preliminary estimates can be made. The OECD data start for nine countries in 1981, far from ideal as many countries were deep in recession. With patching from national sources, estimates for another five can be included. The right-hand column of Table 2.2 shows the change in the male Q4–Q1 employment rates over the 1980s and early 1990s. There really is a very wide range of experience. The majority of countries experienced a rise of Q4–Q1 of between 6 and 15 per cent; of those with small increases (or even falls) only Sweden[5] and Japan were preserving what was still a low level of employment disadvantage for the less qualified.

The USA also suffered only a very small deterioration in the relative employment of the less qualified in the 1980s and early 1990s. To this extent the favourable comparison of US employment experience *during the 1980s* with many European countries is justified. But it must be emphasized that the position of the least-qualified men in the USA had become extremely bad by 1981, with (of the fourteen countries with data) only the Netherlands having a lower employment rate for the first quartile. Thus the less educated in the USA lost jobs in the 1970s and relative pay in the 1980s—simply comparing the small deterioration in their employment position in the 1980s with the larger deterioration in some European countries is only part of the picture.[6] The

[5] An improved method for ascertaining educational qualifications in the 1996 Swedish Labour Force Survey substantially reduced the measured employment rate for the least educated quartile and these are the employment rates shown in Table 2.2; however, the change in Q4–Q1 between 1981 and 1994 is based on the earlier series.

[6] The comparatively favourable employment trend for the less educated in the USA in the 1980s does not depend on the starting year being 1981 or on the calculations being made for educational quartiles. Between 1970 and 1979 the shortfall in the employment rate between those with less than four years of high school and those with more than four years of college increased from 9.3% to 19.1%; at the next peak in 1989 it had risen by only an extra 3.4%. Given the falling proportion of the least educated in the 1980s, the employment difference between the first and fourth quartiles actually declined between 1979 and 1989, having doubled between 1970 and 1979 (calculated from *The Handbook of Labor Statistics* and from *The Statistical Abstract of the USA*).

detailed findings of Card, Kramarz, and Lemieux (1999) that the less qualified in France did not suffer greater declines in their employment rates in the 1980s than comparable workers in the USA are broadly consistent with the aggregate data presented here. In France like the USA much of the radical deterioration in employment for the least qualified appears, surprisingly perhaps, to predate 1981. However in a number of other countries, including Finland, Denmark, Italy, New Zealand, Spain, and (the allegedly flexible) UK, there was indeed a major deterioration in the relative employment position of the least qualified in the 1980s.

2.   Why Employment Differences Differ

This section examines how far it is possible to account for the cross-country variation in the employment rate differences described in the previous section. A number of macroeconomic and structural factors are considered first, including overall labour demand, trade with the South, and the distribution of literacy skills. These are combined into a simple multiple regression before the impact of various dimensions of wage and labour market flexibility is examined.

2.1. Demand, Structural Change, and Educational Dispersion

It is conceivable that falling employment could affect all groups equally (in terms of the proportions of the working population losing jobs). However, overall lack of demand for labour may cause a disproportionate decline in the demand for the least qualified, as, by one means or another, they are 'bumped down' the employment ladder (Nickell and Bell 1995; De Grip and Borghans 2000). Fig. 2.1 suggests that, for men at least, lower employment generally does indeed have a disproportionate reflection at the bottom end of the labour market. The relationship is significant at the 0.0 per cent level and accounts for half of the cross-country variation in employment differences. Belgium and Ireland appear to have exceptionally high non-employment for the least qualified, even given their high levels of non-employment overall. Conversely, Spain and Portugal seem to have maintained comparatively small employment gaps between the more and less qualified relative to the overall demand for male workers, although this may simply reflect the very high proportions of the population in the least educated.

Nickell and Layard (1997) have shown that cross-country differences in the dispersion of earnings were related to the dispersion of academic achievement as measured by standardized literacy scores (see also Lucifora, this volume). Pryor and Schaffer (1999) report that literacy scores within the USA have a significant effect on the chances of being in work (even after education is controlled for). It seems plausible that the employment record of the less qualified was better in countries where their educational achievement was not so weak. The International Adult Literacy Survey

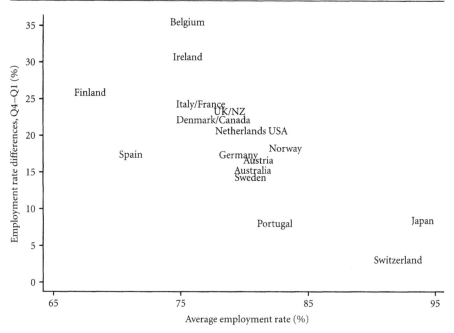

Fig. 2.1. Employment differences and average employment rates, men, 1994

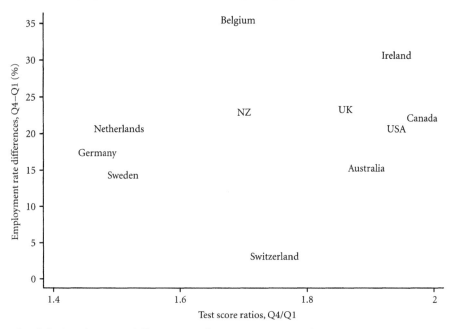

Fig. 2.2. Employment differences and test scores, men, 1994

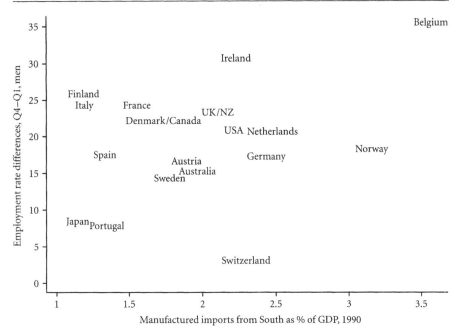

Fig. 2.3. Employment differences and Southern imports, men, 1994

(reported in OECD 1997*b*) provides data on test scores for samples of the working population, measured by three separate literacy tests in 1994–5 for eleven countries. From the underlying data from this study we constructed measures of the dispersion of literacy skills for men and women separately using the 'quantitative literacy' tests (see Data Appendix). Fig. 2.2 plots Q4–Q1 employment differences for men against the corresponding ratio of the scores of the top quartile of the men to the scores of the bottom quartile. The German, Swedish, and Dutch educational systems delivered notably less-dispersed literacy scores than the Anglo-Saxon countries and Belgium. The substantial dispersion in Switzerland appears to be related to the number of migrant workers with language difficulties; as pointed out earlier, the employment difference in Switzerland is actually held down by the safety valve of migration.

The less qualified may have suffered disproportionately from structural change— for example, when the least skill-intensive manufactures are displaced by imports from low-wage sources (Wood 1994). Fig. 2.3 suggests that there may be an effect, and to test for this the ratio of Southern imports to GDP was included in the regressions.

Table 2.3 shows the results of regressing Q4–Q1 employment rate differences in 1994 on the ratio of imports from non-OECD countries to GDP and on the dispersion of quantitative literacy, controlling for the important influence of the overall

Table 2.3. Regressions with employment rate differences, Q4–Q1 as dependent variable, 1994

Equation/ category	Constant	Average employment rate	Quantitative literacy		Manufacturing imports from south (% of GDP)	R^2 corr (N)
			(Q4–Q1)	No score		
(1a)	68.48	−0.977	10.98	18.99	4.871	0.643
Men	[0.002]	(0.228)	(3.46)	(6.07)	(1.70)	
		[0.001]	[0.006]	[0.007]	[0.012]	(20)
(1b)	46.25	−0.587	4.267	8.089	6.162	0.406
Women	[0.006]	(0.130)	(7.58)	[0.544]	(2.25)	
		[0.000]	(13.02)	[0.583]	[0.016]	(19)

Notes: The dependent variable is the difference in employment rates in percentage points between the fourth and first quartiles.
Huber standard errors ( ); p-values [ ].

employment rate. Since the literacy scores are only available for slightly over half the sample, a dummy variable is included for the countries with no score. The regressions are run for men and women separately. All variables are significant,[7] except that test score dispersion did not significantly affect the employment of less-qualified women.

A 1 per cent lower employment rate is associated with a 1 per cent point bigger gap between the employment rate of the first and the fourth quartiles for men. For women the effect is not quite so large but still highly significant. These results are certainly consistent with less demand for labour in general causing greater disadvantage (as when the least qualified get bumped down off the employment ladder). The Finnish recession in the early 1990s provides a spectacular example of a collapse in demand being reflected in disproportionate job loss for the least educated. The differential in employment rates between those with lower secondary education and those with tertiary education rose by nearly 10 percentage points between 1989 and 1994; such a sharp decline could hardly be attributed to long-term influences such as technical progress. Conversely, the more drawn-out 'employment miracle' in the Netherlands since the mid-1980s brought a substantial decline in Q4–Q1 for men (some 7 per cent between 1985 and 1997) as the employment rate of the first quartile rose steadily.

However, the causation may run in the reverse direction as well. Declining demand at the bottom, for longer-term reasons such as technology or trade, may generate the overall rise in non-employment (as in Wood's analysis, which sees the non-accelerating inflation rate of unemployment (NAIRU) increasing if less-qualified workers lose their jobs, since they have little impact on the general level of wage pressure). This

---

[7] The patterns of significance are similar in a regression for only those countries with scores.

would bring upward bias to the coefficient for the overall employment rate, which includes the employment rates of the first quartile, and would mean that the impact of the overall demand for labour on employment differences may be exaggerated in Table 2.3.[8]

Educational differences (ratio in the country of quantitative test scores for the fourth to the first quartile) lie in the range 1.4–1.9. According to equation 1a in Table 2.3 countries at the bottom of this range would tend to have a 6 per cent smaller gap between employment rates for the least- and most-educated men than those countries with most dispersed outcomes.[9] However, test scores are not at all significant in explaining employment differences for women; presumably their influence is swamped by the host of social factors that influence differences in women's participation across countries.

One per cent more imports from the South as a percentage of GDP (a range spanning most of the observations) is associated with a 5 per cent larger employment gap for men and probably a bigger one for women. This coefficient is still practically significant at the 5 per cent level if the outlier Belgium is omitted (see Fig. 2.3). A broader indicator of structural change would be the share of industrial employment in the total; once overall employment is controlled for, however, there is no significant tendency for lower industrial employment, or declining industrial employment as a share of population of working age, to be associated with fewer jobs for the least qualified.

Skill-biased technical progress is often regarded as the major influence on declining employment opportunities for the less qualified. A number of technological indicators, such as R & D intensity, have been found to be associated with the variation across industries in the decline in jobs for the less qualified (see e.g. Machin and Van Reenen 1998). It might be inferred that in countries where technology is developed more intensively the problems will be greatest for the least qualified. If measures, such as the ratio of R & D in manufacturing to value added or the ratio of total R & D to GDP, are added to the equations reported in Table 2.3, they are consistently positive, but never significant. This is hardly a decisive rebuttal for the importance of technology, since the national level of R & D may be a very weak indicator of the rate of implementation of technological advance.

---

[8] A simple way of reducing the bias is to replace the average employment rate by a measure that reflects the broader demand for labour but is not directly affected by the employment rate of the least qualified. The employment rate of the second and third quartiles is a suitable candidate. If equation 1a is re-estimated using this variable, its coefficient is a little smaller (−0.8) than when average employment rate is used; this is consistent with there being an element of bias in Table 2.3, but the coefficient on employment is still highly significant. When the predicted value of the male employment rate from Nickell's (1997) cross-country equation was used as an instrument the coefficient on the employment rate was actually much larger (and test scores no longer significant).

[9] The formal level of education at the bottom of the distribution is not significantly related to employment differences—if the proportion of the population with the lowest level of education (ISCED 0/1) is added to equation 1 it is quite insignificant.

2.2. *Wages and Labour Market Rigidity*

Many people believe that greater wage dispersion encourages employment at the bottom end of the labour market. This would imply a trade-off between two dimensions of labour market inequality. The less effective is wage flexibility, the more difficult it is to justify policies that reduce labour costs at the bottom end of the labour market as a means of generating jobs. The relationship between relative wage flexibility and the growth of employment became a major policy issue with the publication of *The OECD Jobs Study*. In the 'Facts' section of the summary report the OECD wrote that

All countries have experienced a shift in demand away from unskilled jobs towards more highly skilled jobs. In most countries where relative wages have been flexible (the United States, Canada, Australia) both the relative employment and unemployment rates of the unskilled changed little during the 1980s. In comparatively inflexible Europe, on the other hand, both relative employment and unemployment rates deteriorated.   (OECD 1994: 23)

The OECD's chart 15 showed data for just eight countries, including the significant counter-example of the UK (where both employment and pay of the less qualified deteriorated sharply) but omitting the (then) low unemployment of egalitarian Scandinavian countries.

A number of subsequent studies have examined the relationship of employment performance and earnings dispersion with less clear-cut results than implied in the *Jobs Study*. OECD (1996*a*) found no significant correlation between the relative employment rates of the low skilled and high skilled and the incidence of low pay. Nickell and Bell (1995: 46) examined the declining demand for less-educated workers over the 1970s and 1980s and from inspection of the data found no evidence that 'unemployment effects are any more severe in countries where wage effects [increases in wage dispersion] are small'. Blau and Kahn (1996), by contrast, found that the greater wage dispersion in the USA was associated with smaller differences in employment rates (especially between the low and middle skill categories) than in continental European countries; however, they used employment data for only six countries.

From these studies there is little consistent support for the idea that wage dispersion has been the main influence on employment for the less qualified (and a similar conclusion is reached in the much more detailed comparisons with US experience of employment rates in the 1980s in France by Card, Kramarz, and Lemieux (1999) and in Germany by Krueger and Pischke (1997)).

A fundamental problem in attempting to test for such effects in a cross section is that less pay dispersion could reflect less dispersion in the productivity of workers, and thus even be associated with relatively high employment of the least educated rather than the reverse. Moreover, there is a more general endogeneity problem, as anything that drives down employment of the least qualified will presumably tend to drive down their wages. So simply finding no correlation between employment differences and wage dispersion (as in Fig. 2.4) would not prove that wage dispersion had no influence. However, regressing employment rate differences on a measure of wage

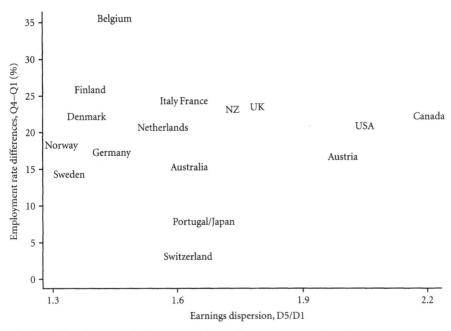

Fig. 2.4. Employment differences and pay dispersion, men, 1994

dispersion, including appropriate controls for the dispersion of productivity, can suggest whether differences in wage dispersion across countries have been the major influence on employment outcomes.

Two measures of earnings dispersion were added in turn to equation (1): the ratio of average earnings of the fourth to the first educational quartiles and then the usual OECD measure of the overall earnings dispersion (between the median and bottom decile). Table 2.4 reports the coefficients on the earnings dispersion variables and shows that the coefficients tend to be perverse (greater dispersion of wages being associated with larger differences in employment rates) and insignificant, despite the inclusion of the controls. Thus greater wage dispersion is not associated with higher employment at the bottom end of the labour market, given both the overall employment level, the educational level of the bottom end of the labour force, and imports from the South. It should be emphasized that this is not a test of whether wage dispersion has *any* influence on employment at the bottom end of the labour market. However, the results reported here do contradict the claim that wage flexibility is the *dominant* influence explaining why the less qualified are less employed in some countries than in others.

Minimum wages are sometimes thought to be an important influence limiting wage flexibility. Given the lack of significance of wage dispersion in accounting for

Table 2.4. Coefficients and significance levels *[p values]* when variables added (one by one) to equation 1 for employment rate differences, 1994

Additional variables	Men	Women
		(Test scores omitted from equation 1)
Ratio of earnings, Q4/Q1	1.072	4.607
(educational quartiles)	[0.773]	[0.269]
Overall wage dispersion	4.541	−1.446
D5/D1	[0.316]	[0.826]
Minimum wage (ratio to average)	12.39	8.202
	[0.297]	[0.542]
Replacement ratio (average	2.231	9.754
of years 2–5)	[0.535]	[0.144]
EPL (ranking of severity)	0.020	0.203
	[0.895]	[0.430]
ALMP (% of GDP	−5.857	10.68
normalized by unemployment)	[0.695]	[0.598]
Home-ownership (%)	0.053	0.183
	[0.647]	[0.223]
Trade union density (%)	−0.005	0.136
	[0.920]	[0.135]
Centralization of bargaining (rank 3–9)	−1.871[a]	−0.913
	[0.002]	[0.405]

[a] coefficient after dropping insignificant quantitative literacy.

Note: Only the first two variables are available for men and women separately.

employment rate differences it is hardly surprising that an index of the generosity of minimum wages is also insignificant when added to equation 1.

High and long-lasting benefits might decrease the labour supply (and thus reduce employment rates), an effect that could be particularly strong at the bottom of the labour market. Using the OECD replacement ratio database, a variety of summary replacement ratio measures were constructed, both for the first six months of benefit (either calculated at average earnings or at two-thirds of average earnings) and for years 2–5 of benefit (to capture the longer-term impact). When added individually, none of the coefficients was significant (the results for the longer-term benefits are shown in the table).[10]

Employment protection legislation is also criticized as inhibiting employment creation, and presumably the effect would be strongest at the bottom of the labour

---

[10] The measures of replacement ratios and benefit duration used by Nickell and Layard (1997) were insignificant, as was an indicator of the generosity of early retirement schemes (Blondal and Pearson 1995).

market. However if an index of the severity of employment protection is added to equation (1), it is quite insignificant. Conversely, active labour market policies (ALMPs) could help to prevent long spells out of work, and this might be particularly important for the less qualified. Expenditure on ALMP, normalized for unemployment to reduce endogeneity, is not significantly related to employment rate differences; this is disappointing perhaps, as ALMP should be of particular assistance to those with fewer qualifications. A high level of home-ownership has been suggested as an important influence on unemployment by inhibiting labour mobility (Oswald 1996); however, there is no extra impact on joblessness of the less qualified.

Finally, strong trade unions might be in a position to protect jobs at the bottom end of the labour market, or according to another view might inhibit job creation. Neither trade union density (shown in the table) nor the coverage of collective bargaining agreements is significant if added to equation 1.[11] However, a high degree of centralization of collective bargaining is significantly associated with a smaller employment difference for men (but not for women); when the centralization index is included, the literacy skills variable is no longer significant. This is probably because centralization of bargaining is associated with less dispersion of educational attainment (just as it tends to bring less dispersion of wages), but centralized bargaining may also foster better training and may have inhibited massive bursts of industrial redundancies, which tend to generate labour market withdrawal.

It is important not to claim too much for these results, especially given the very limited degrees of freedom and the difficulties of constructing a panel (the literacy data, for example, are available for only one year). Nickell (1997) found that a number of the variables considered here, in particular those concerned with the wage bargaining system, were influential in determining employment outcomes overall. It seems, however, that they did not have any *additional* effect on employment rate differences between educational quartiles over and above their influence, if any, through affecting the overall employment level.

The broad conclusion from this section is surprisingly strong. Neither greater wage dispersion nor other indicators of labour market flexibility were systematically associated with a better employment position for the least qualified given the overall employment level. The only significant effect was the opposite of that predicted by those advocating deregulation—bargaining centralization was associated with more jobs for the less-qualified men.

2.3. Unemployment Rate Differences

The focus of this chapter has been on differences in the employment rates of the best and least educated, on the grounds that labour market withdrawal (or non-entry in

---

[11] Including the coverage of collective bargaining makes the test scores variable insignificant. The two variables are strongly correlated; countries with egalitarian educational outcomes tend to have extensive collective bargaining. This underlines how a number of institutional and structural features may be clustered, making it very difficult to identify their individual effects.

Table 2.5. Regressions on unemployment rate differences, Q4–Q1, 1994

Equation/ category	Constant	Average unemployment rate (%)	Replacement ratio ratio years 2–5	Manufacturing imports from South (% GDP)	Quantitative literacy (Q4/Q1)	R^2 corr (N)
(2a) Men	−10.63 [0.077]	0.585 (0.134) [0.001]	9.593 (1.69) [0.000]	0.889 (0.465) [0.078]	5.387 (3.22) [0.118]	0.719 (19)
(2b) Women	−8.710 [0.489]	0.216 (0.158) [0.194]	13.19 (2.64) [0.000]	0.849 (0.978) [0.400]	5.267 (7.27) [0.466]	0.283 (19)

Note: Differences between fourth and first quartiles are given in absolute percentage points.

the case of women) has been a central part of employment inequalities. However, it is worth checking whether the factors that appear to influence employment rate differences also influence unemployment rate differences. Table 2.5 presents regressions similar to those in Table 2.3, but with unemployment rate differences as the dependent variable. The most striking result is that for women a higher overall unemployment rate is not associated with larger unemployment rate differences (equation 2b). Evidently, non-participation at the bottom of the labour market is subject to a host of social and historical differences between countries. The second difference from the employment results is that the long-term replacement ratio is very significant in accounting for the extent to which the less qualified exhibit higher unemployment and this holds for both men and women. An extended high replacement ratio appears to encourage a particularly high unemployment rate for the less educated; if it does not much affect employment (as the analysis reported earlier suggests), then the implication is that its main effect is on labour force inactivity—a result similar to that reported for the labour force as a whole by Blondal and Pearson (1995). Imports from the South are less significant in the unemployment regressions; the impact on employment noted earlier appears to have been reflected mainly in inactivity, which would be consistent with geographically concentrated redundancies leading to labour market withdrawal. Test score dispersion misses significance at the 10 per cent level in the regression for men and centralization of bargaining is not significant at all.

3.   Conclusions

This chapter has attempted to present systematically the differences in the employment rates of the best and least qualified in the OECD countries. These differences are large and vary considerably between countries, with the USA by no means displaying the superior performance that is often assumed.

The analysis has so far mainly been confined to a single cross section in the mid-1990s, with 'country effects' omitted.[12] Bearing in mind this limitation, the main conclusions are:

1. For both men and women a major influence on employment rate differences between the top and bottom educational quartiles is the overall employment rate; when the employment position deteriorates, those at the bottom of the qualifications scale suffer disproportionate employment losses.
2. The educational attainment of those at the bottom of the educational distribution significantly influences the employment differences for men. This effect does not show up for women, is very much weaker for unemployment rate differences, is significant only when the overall employment rate is controlled for, and is rendered insignificant when centralization of bargaining is included in the regression. Nevertheless, this constitutes some evidence that those countries that have less dispersed educational outcomes also display less extreme employment disadvantage for the least-qualified men.
3. Import penetration by manufactures from non-OECD countries reduces job prospects for the least qualified.
4. There is no significant association between employment differences across countries and the extent to which new technology is implemented, at least when measured by R & D intensities.
5. There is no observable tendency for countries where wage dispersion is greater to have smaller employment rate differences between the best and worst educated.
6. A high replacement rate from longer-term unemployment benefits is associated with larger unemployment differences between educational quartiles; there is no significant impact on employment differences, suggesting that benefits mainly affect the split between unemployment and inactivity.
7. Employment protection legislation, the generosity of minimum wages, and active manpower policies have no discernible impact on employment rate differences. However, centralized bargaining procedures are associated with smaller employment differences for men.

The central conclusion is that labour market flexibility, encouraged by low minimum wages and benefits and weak employment protection, and reflected in high wage dispersion, has *not* been the route by which some OECD countries have managed to minimize the employment disadvantage of the least qualified. Countries with centralized bargaining systems have fared better and any impact of deregulation appears to have been marginal as compared to the influence of the overall demand for labour.

[12] For men, employment differences between educational groups were rather small everywhere in 1973; thus the mid-1990s position will approximate to a 'long' first difference spanning back twenty years. For women, with very different patterns of participation twenty years ago, the 'country effects' left in a single cross section must be much bigger.

Data Appendix

Employment rates, unemployment rates, inactivity, employment rates by educational category: kindly supplied by OECD (background data for OECD 1997a: table 41.b); used to calculate quartiles. Data for 1981 supplemented by calculations from OECD (1994: tables 1.6 and 1.16) for Italy and Japan; data for Netherlands calculated from Labour Force Surveys; data for Germany from the Mikrocensus tables kindly calculated by Ronald Schettkat; data for Sweden calculated from Labour Force Survey Data supplied by Statistics Sweden (1996 is chosen as the first year of more satisfactory attribution of educational qualifications, which substantially increases differences between quartiles).

Test scores: ratio of average score of fourth quartile to average score of first quartile for five quantitative tests, calculated, for men and women separately, from CD of background data for OECD (1997b); data for Australia kindly supplied by Mark Chapman from ABS.

Imports from South 1990: manufactured imports from non-OECD as % GDP from Saeger (1995: table 2.6).

Research and Development: R & D spending in manufacturing as % of value added, business R & D as % of GDP from OECD (1992: tables 1, 4).

Minimum wage as % of average earnings: Dolado et al. (1996) refers to c.1993; Australia from Low Pay Commission (1998: table A6.2), plus Canada, New Zealand, and Japan from OECD (1998a: table 2.3).

Ratio of D5/D1 earnings, all workers c.1993: OECD (1996a); ratio of earnings of first to fourth educational quartiles constructed from OECD (1996c).

Replacement ratios: average of three different family situations, 40-year-old worker on two-thirds average wage and 2–5 years of benefit; OECD Unemployment Benefit database kindly supplied by OECD.

Union density, collective bargaining coverage, centralization of bargaining, coordination of bargaining: OECD (1997a: ch. 3) for average of values for 1980, 1990, 1994; for Ireland, centralization estimated.

Employment protection legislation ranking: OECD (1994: table 6.7).

ALMP: OECD (1997a) (normalized by unemployment)

Industrial employment 1994, share of total: OECD (1996d).

Home-ownership: Oswald (1996).

The authors would like to thank Esra Erdem and Peter Müchlan for invaluable assistance with analysing the data, and many colleagues for advice and suggestions.

3 Low Pay—A Special Affliction of Women

RITA ASPLUND AND INGA PERSSON

Over recent decades women throughout Europe have steadily increased their market work. Cohort by cohort, activity rates have gone up (Meulders, Plasman, and Vander Stricht 1993; Persson 1993). Particularly marked has been the increase in the labour market participation of mothers of small children. These developments have gone much further in certain countries, especially the Scandinavian ones, where the activity rates of women now resemble those of men, but the direction and pattern of this economic and social transformation are the same throughout Europe. In economic terms the transformation means that out of 100 persons in the EU labour force in the mid-1990s, forty-three were women (Eurostat 1998a). In social terms it means that in the overwhelming majority of households throughout Europe women are doing market work. Concomitant with the increase in women's participation in market work has been an increase in their educational investments so that in more recent cohorts young women tend to bring with them as much human capital to the labour market as young men. But, in spite of the increased similarities between European women and men in terms of labour market participation and educational investments, their positions and the economic outcomes for them in the labour market differ greatly. The types of jobs held and the economic rewards to work show a very clear gendered pattern in all the countries, even in those where the participation rates and the human capital investments of men and women are very similar.[1] Horizontal and vertical job segregation are extensive; women are paid less than men at given human capital characteristics; and female-dominated occupations are paid less than male-dominated ones (at given human capital and other job requirements).[2]

Women being, in general, less well rewarded than men in European labour markets, the existence of low pay could also be expected to be more frequent among women than among men. This expectation is, as we show below, borne out by empirical data

---

[1] See e.g. the studies undertaken for the European Commission within the framework of the European Network of Experts on the Situation of Women in the Labour Market, the studies published in Persson and Jonung (1997, 1998), the studies about Sweden undertaken within the framework of the Commission on the Distribution of Economic Power and Economic Resources between Women and Men (Ahrne and Persson 1997; Persson and Wadensjö 1997a,b, 1998), the studies for France undertaken within the framework of the Mage Network (published in different issues of *Les Cahiers du Mage*, 1995–8), the studies of the UK in Joshi and Paci (1998), and the studies of the USA surveyed in Blau (1998).

[2] See e.g. Le Grand (1997) and Meyerson and Petersen (1997a).

and holds both for low (annual) earnings and low (hourly) wages. Thus, low pay in Europe has a clear gendered pattern that needs to be dissected and addressed.

Other chapters in this book enumerate a number of factors, such as low educational qualifications and other skills, lack of job experience, job instability, or being in certain sectors of the economy, which seem to be crucial factors behind low pay. To account for women's low pay, the general analysis of the factors behind low pay should be extended in several ways. First, one should look at these 'crucial factors' from a gendered perspective and see whether, and if so why, these factors are more frequent and/or more pronounced for women than for men. Secondly, one should investigate whether these 'crucial factors' affect pay (and the probability of having low pay and remaining low paid) differently for women and men. Thirdly, being a woman (instead of a man) and being in a female-dominated occupation (instead of in a male-dominated one) may have an independent negative effect on pay not accounted for by other variables and their estimated coefficients. This analytical approach, obviously inspired by the decompositions utilized in econometric studies of the gender wage gap, will be used as a framework for this chapter.

In the next section we give an overview of the facts about women's low pay in Europe. We then take a closer look at the factors behind women's low pay, looking, for example, at the differences in women's and men's labour supply patterns and labour market positions. This is followed by a section where we survey the results of empirical studies of the determinants behind women's low pay in specific national labour markets, and by a section where we survey the results from studies of gender differences in low-wage mobility. In view of the reported findings, we also briefly discuss whether women's low pay matters. Some policy conclusions are drawn in a final section.

1.   Women's Low Pay

The number of workers who are classified as being low paid obviously depends on the definition adopted for low pay. In recent studies low pay is commonly defined as less than two-thirds of median full-time earnings.[3] Using this well-established definition, women face a clearly higher risk of being low paid, even when in full-time employment (Table 3.1). At the same time, the variation across countries in the share of women in low-wage employment is striking. In Finland and Sweden less than 9 per cent of all women in full-time employment are in low-paid jobs compared to close to one-third, or more, in Ireland, the UK, and North America.

The much higher risk for women of being in low-wage employment is equally pronounced when using an indicator of concentration that abstracts from cross-country differences in the overall incidence of low pay. In all countries the value of the indicator is greater than one for women, indicating that they are much more likely

[3] For detailed discussions of issues related to the measurement of low pay, see e.g. the various chapters in Asplund, Sloane, and Theodossiou (1998) and Bazen, Gregory, and Salverda (1998b). See also OECD (1996a, 1997a).

Table 3.1. Incidence, concentration, and distribution of low pay among men and women in full-time employment

Country	Incidence (risk)		Concentration		Distribution		D5/D1 ratio	
	Women	Men	Women	Men	Women	Men	Women	Men
Austria 1993	22.8	7.0	1.7	0.5	67.8	32.2	2.02	1.67
Belgium 1993	14.2	3.9	2.1	0.5	63.4	36.6	1.44	1.38
Finland 1994	8.7	3.3	1.5	0.6	71.8	28.2	1.30	1.46
France 1995	17.4	10.6	1.3	0.8	52.2	47.8	1.71	1.61
Germany 1994	25.4	7.6	1.9	0.6	61.1	38.9	1.42	1.37
Ireland 1994	35.6	16.7	1.5	0.7	56.7	43.3	n.a.	n.a.
Italy 1993	18.5	9.3	1.5	0.7	52.2	48.2	1.88	1.60
Netherlands 1994	26.8	8.1	n.a.	n.a.	46.1	53.8	n.a.	n.a.
Sweden 1993	8.4	3.0	1.6	0.6	65.6	34.4	1.30	1.36
Switzerland 1995	30.4	6.8	2.3	0.5	50.9	49.1	1.60	1.51
UK 1995	31.2	12.8	1.6	0.7	58.3	41.7	1.68	1.78
Czech Rep. 1995	24.7	7.0	n.a.	n.a.	71.9	28.1	n.a.	n.a.
Hungary 1996	26.5	15.6	n.a.	n.a.	50.0	50.0	n.a.	n.a.
Poland 1995	21.6	13.5	n.a.	n.a.	59.6	40.4	n.a.	n.a.
Australia 1995	17.7	11.8	1.3	0.9	44.3	55.7	1.58	1.68
Canada 1994	34.3	16.1	1.4	0.7	60.0	40.0	2.25	2.18
Japan 1995	36.4	6.1	2.4	0.4	73.1	26.9	1.41	1.60
Korea 1994	52.7	11.2	n.a.	n.a.	65.4	34.6	n.a.	n.a.
NZ 1994–5	20.7	14.4	1.2	0.9	47.5	52.5	1.67	1.77
USA 1994	32.5	19.6	1.3	0.8	54.6	45.4	1.98	2.13

Notes: Incidence measures the share of all women (men) who are low paid. The indicator of concentration (or, alternatively, relative incidence) is calculated by dividing the incidence of low pay for women (men) by the overall incidence of low pay (not shown in the table). Distribution reflects the share of women and men respectively among all the low paid. The D5/D1 ratio gives the ratio of median earnings to the earnings of the tenth percentile worker for the indicated (or the closest) year.

n.a. = not available.

Sources: OECD (1996*a*) and Keese, Puymoyen, and Swaim (1998). The figures for Ireland are from Nolan (1998*b*: table 5.5).

to be in low-paid jobs than their male colleagues. Indeed, in Belgium, Germany, Switzerland, and Japan women in full-time employment face a risk of low-paid employment that is at least twice as high as the average risk for all employees. Furthermore, in these relative terms, Finnish and Swedish women fare no better than women in other countries.

The incidence of low pay has been noted to be closely correlated with the earnings dispersion in the bottom half of the earnings distribution. The simple correlation between the incidence of low pay and the median (fifth decile) to bottom decile ratio (D5/D1) is reported to be over 90 per cent. Accordingly the conclusion drawn is that 'not surprisingly those countries with large earnings inequality are also the ones with a higher incidence of low-paid jobs' (OECD 1996*a*: 69; Keese, Puymoyen, and Swaim 1998: 228). Closer inspection reveals, however, that this conclusion holds only for men. The corresponding correlation for women is just below 50 per cent for the countries in Table 3.1; for the non-European countries it amounts to less than 32 per cent. Clearly, for women there must be other important factors in addition to the dispersion of earnings that affect the incidence of low pay and create variation in this incidence among countries.

Table 3.1 further shows that women are in the majority among the low paid, the only exceptions being the Netherlands, Australia, and New Zealand. Moreover, in most countries these low-paid women are typically in wholesale and retail trade, hotels and restaurants, and personal services, pointing to strong regularities across countries also in this respect (see OECD 1996*a*), an aspect that is explored in more detail in Section 3 below.

However, the above analysis can be criticized for understating the factual occurrence of low pay (and, especially, low pay among women) for two main reasons. First, by focusing on full-time employees only, it overlooks the influence on low-wage employment of the growing share of women particularly with part-time and other atypical job contracts. The few empirical studies on low pay that also include those employed on a part-time basis clearly show that part-timers are overrepresented not only among women but among the low paid as well (e.g. Sloane and Theodossiou 1998). Second, by restricting the analysis to employees in employment it disregards the fact that the flow into unemployment and non-employment is much larger from the bottom end of the earnings distribution than from higher earnings levels, an issue that we return to later. Experiments with British data indicate that this leads to the understatement of the risk of low pay by about 5 percentage points for women and some 3 percentage points for men when using the commonly adopted two-thirds of the median as the low-pay threshold (Stewart and Swaffield 1998).

Even though the incidence of low pay among women relative to men is still large, it has narrowed considerably over the past decades. As can be seen from Fig. 3.1, the decline in the relative risk of low pay among women has been particularly strong in the UK: from having been more than eight times as likely as men to be in low-paid jobs in the late 1970s British women were just over twice as likely in 1995.

The risk numbers for Finland and Sweden also point to a clear improvement in the position of women located at the bottom end of the wage distribution. For Finnish women the risk of being low paid, over three times greater than for Finnish men in the 1970s, had fallen to less than twice in the 1980s, with a further decline to 1.5 times by 1995.[4] In Sweden, in contrast, most of the improvement in the low-pay position of Swedish women took place in the 1970s.[5] In particular, at the end of the 1960s Swedish women were more than three times as likely as Swedish men to be in low-wage

---

[4] Calculations based on low-paid shares by gender kindly provided by Tor Eriksson. Low pay is defined as the lowest quintile comprising both part- and full-time workers.

[5] See Hultin and Szulkin (1997: table 12.2). In contrast to the risks illustrated in Fig. 3.1, the Swedish numbers comprise both full- and part-timers.

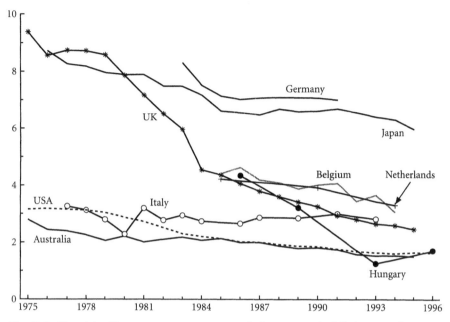

Fig. 3.1. The risk of low pay among women relative to men in full-time employment for selected countries, 1975–1995

Source: Keese, Puymoyen, and Swaim (1998: fig. 12.4). Reproduced with permission of the publishers.

employment; by 1981 this risk had declined to just over twice, remaining at this level in 1991. This trend is concomitant with the development of the overall gender wage gap in the Swedish labour market over the past decades.[6]

This improvement in the relative position of women located at the bottom end of the earnings distribution appears to be the combined outcome of increasing relative wages and 'stricter' institutional settings. Across all OECD countries, wage growth for the lowest decile of female workers has been greater than for the lowest decile of male workers (OECD 1996a: chart 3.3). And in some countries the lowest-paid women have succeeded in improving their earnings position even relative to male workers with median earnings. Simultaneously institutional settings that effectively limit the incidence of low pay have been maintained or even strengthened in many countries (e.g. OECD 1994, 1996a, 1997a).[7]

---

[6] See e.g. Persson and Wadensjö (1997a) and the references therein.

[7] In this context it may also be noted that simple correlations calculated by the OECD indicate that higher collective bargaining coverage and trade union density rates are associated with a lower incidence of low pay (OECD 1996a, 1997a; Keese, Puymoyen, and Swaim 1998). A strong negative association is also obtained between the incidence of low pay and the relative level of minimum wages, as well as between the incidence of low pay and benefit replacement rates. Moreover, these negative correlations are found to be stronger for women than for men. However, the OECD calculations represent only snapshots in time and obviously cannot be generalized to explaining long-term trends in the incidence of low pay nor the reduction in women's relative risk of low pay. See Lucifora, this volume.

More importantly, there is no strong empirical evidence in support of the hypothesis that these improvements in the relative earnings position of low-paid women
have impaired the labour market performance of women in terms of employment and
unemployment. Using the words of Keese, Puymoyen, and Swaim (1998: 243): 'The
absence of any strong association for women [and youths] between changes in wage
dispersion and changes in employment and unemployment is not being driven by
a few extreme or aberrant observations.' Women have been able to advance their
relative earnings position without jeopardizing their employment.

2.   Why are Women Low Paid?

Why do the working women of Europe have a higher risk than men of being low paid?
The answer must be sought in the gendered division of labour between market and
non-market work and in the gendered division of labour within market work. The
end result of the gendered division of labour in these two (interacting) spheres is
that women and men end up holding very different positions in the labour market,
positions that are differently rewarded, both in terms of current pay and in terms
of prospects for future economic advancement. In addition, it is also sometimes the
case that the difference in economic rewards is directly related to the fact that it is a
woman who holds the position (e.g. the case of direct wage discrimination) or to the
fact that the positions are predominantly held by women (e.g. female-dominated
occupations).

While the existence of a gendered division of labour seems to be a permanent
feature of all economies, its particular manifestation varies between countries and also
over time.[8] It can also be influenced by policies of different kinds, including policies
on the family, tax and social security, labour market regulation and wages, antidiscrimination and equal opportunities.

In this way the question about women's high incidence of, and overrepresentation
in, low pay is transformed into an investigation of the gendered division of labour
in the European economies of the late twentieth century, but where the types of
jobs generated by these economies are also a crucial factor. However, the types of jobs
generated are probably not independent of the existence of the gendered division of
labour.

2.1.   The Gendered Division of Labour between Work in the Home
         and Work in the Market

While women have increased their market work throughout Europe, there is still, in
all countries, a very marked division of labour, where women allocate much more

---

[8] See e.g. Rubery, Fagan, and Maier (1996), Blau, Simpson, and Anderson (1998), Jonung (1998a), and
the articles on 'The Extent of Occupational Segregation' reprinted in Ferber (1998).

Table 3.2. Inactivity rates for women aged 25–59 years by educational attainment level, 1997 (%)

Country	Educational attainment level		
	Tertiary level	Upper secondary level	Less than upper secondary level
EU15	14.2	26.0	47.6
Austria	13.8	28.8	41.8
Belgium	15.2	28.8	54.9
Denmark	9.5	20.1	34.0
Finland	10.1	17.3	29.0
France	14.1	21.0	36.2
Germany	14.8	26.0	45.1
Greece	18.4	43.9	55.3
Ireland	17.9	38.1	62.5
Italy	16.9	33.0	62.3
Luxembourg	22.2	40.0	55.7
Netherlands	14.8	27.9	51.0
Portugal	8.0	18.1	34.3
Spain	15.8	31.3	57.2
Sweden	9.3	12.9	26.2
UK	13.3	23.2	35.7

Source: calculated from Eurostat (1998*a*: table 029).

time than men to (unpaid) non-market work and men allocate more time than women to (paid) market work. This gendered division of market and non-market work serves to disadvantage women in the labour market and to impair women's labour market positions relative to those of men.

In the labour market this gendered division of labour is manifested in gender differences in labour force participation rates, part-time work, and career breaks. Today these gender differences in labour supply are most often connected with the birth and care of children, but because of anticipation effects on the part of women and via so-called statistical discrimination on the part of employers, they might still affect the labour market experiences of all women relative to men.[9]

The most extreme form of specialization, where women are outside the labour force and completely specialized in non-market work, is rapidly disappearing in Europe. But the picture varies very much with the level of educational attainment, and in several countries inactivity rates for women with low educational qualifications remain substantial (see Table 3.2).[10] Thus, in many countries one out of two women

---

[9] See the discussion in Fagan and Rubery (1996).

[10] One reason for illustrating the situation in Europe mainly with data covering only the member countries of the EU is the availability of comparable data for these countries via the EU Labour Force Survey.

aged 25 –59 years with less than upper secondary education is outside the labour force. But there are also countries where this group of women has relatively high participation rates (Denmark, Finland, France, Portugal, Sweden, and the UK), indicating that cross-country differences in economic structures and policies do influence the gender division of labour for women with low educational attainment as well. Indeed, it seems to be for these women that the variation across countries in inactivity rates is most pronounced, and thus for whom economic structures and policies might matter the most in the participation decision.

High inactivity rates are today likely to indicate not so much that women are permanently outside the labour force as that their labour force participation is characterized by more and longer career breaks—that is, it can be taken as an indicator of a less stable labour market attachment. This, in turn, means that groups of women with high inactivity rates are likely to spend more time in unemployed job search and temporary jobs in connection with re-entering the labour force, that they are more likely to lose accumulated firm-specific human capital, and that they are likely to acquire less job experience and on-the-job training. Hence, to their initial low level of education that already makes them more vulnerable to low pay will be added further disadvantages connected with their less stable labour force attachment. This can develop into a vicious circle where low rewards to market work serve to make the non-market alternative attractive, which makes for continued future low market rewards, and so on. Clearly here there are likely to be important roles not only for wage policy and wage distributions but also for the design of, for instance, childcare policies, parental leave policies, and tax and transfer systems (i.e. characteristics of the so-called gender regime (see Sainsbury 1996)).

In contemporary conditions, however, the gendered division of labour between non-market and market work often takes a less extreme form than complete specialization. Its most common manifestation in today's European labour markets is, rather, that of women's part-time work. The increase in women's employment in Europe has to a very large extent been in part-time jobs. While part-time work has increased also for men, that increase has been mostly among younger men (who often combine studies with working part-time) and older workers (where part-time work might be a form of partial retirement), and the total male rate of part-time employment remains well below 10 per cent in most of the EU countries (see Fig. 3.2).

For women, on the other hand, part-time work is very common also among those of prime age, and is related to their larger share in the total time input into household production. While women are heavily overrepresented in part-time work in all the EU countries, there is a wide variation between them in the extent of female part-time employment (see Fig. 3.2). Here too differences in economic structures and policies between countries (the so-called part-time regime (see Maier 1994)) seem to be important. From an overall EU perspective, part-time work is, nevertheless, clearly women's work. In 1997 women accounted for 80 per cent of all part-time workers in the union; among these women aged 25–49 years accounted for 53 per cent (Eurostat

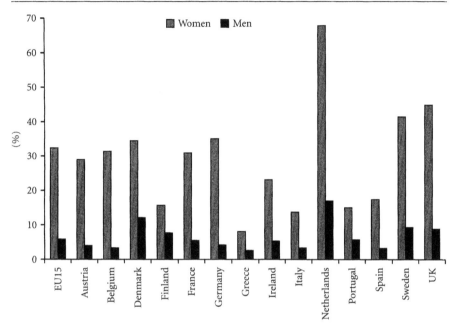

Fig. 3.2. The rate of part-time employment for all women and all men in employment, 1997

Source: Eurostat (1998*a*: table 051).

1998*a*: 118). About thirty out of 100 female workers were part-timers, to compare with only about five out of 100 male workers.

Part-time work is a mixed bag and also a mixed blessing for women. In Europe it is very heterogeneous (for some country examples, see Table 3.3). It ranges from 'long' part-time hours with, on the whole, the same social and legal protection and the same hourly wages as for full-time jobs, to 'short' part-time work in insecure jobs with low wages and social rights. Thus there is not necessarily a direct causal link from part-time work to a higher risk of low-wage employment; the relation between part-time work and low pay is more complicated and indirect, and also very much dependent on the country-specific character of labour market regulation, social security legislation, collective bargaining, and wage setting (see Maier 1994; Fagan, O'Reilly, and Rubery 1998).

Part-time work is also not evenly distributed over sectors, industries, and occupations in the economy, and also not evenly distributed over different categories of the (female) labour force. Women part-timers are, for example, more heavily concentrated into female-dominated (low-paid) service jobs than women full-timers, and women with higher educational qualifications are more likely to hold full-time jobs. The part-time outcome for women (in terms of both numbers and economic

Table 3.3. Employees in part-time employment, by range of hours usually worked per week (%)

Hours	EU15		Germany	Netherlands	Sweden	UK
	Women	Men	Women	Women	Women	Women
1–10	17.7	26.0	19.4	25.5	9.2	21.2
11–20	42.1	38.4	46.5	35.7	23.5	41.7
21–4	10.3	8.0	8.7	11.6	7.8	12.9
25–30	21.4	14.6	25.1	11.3	37.7	17.9
31+	8.4	13.0	0.4	15.9	21.8	6.2

Note: According to Eurostat instructions, individuals have been classified as part-time workers on the basis of their own spontaneous answers to questions about their working time, the motive being that working-time conditions vary considerably among member countries and sectors. This explains why some individuals working 31+ hours per week appear as part-timers.

Source: Eurostat (1998*a*: table 078).

rewards) represents an interaction between the supply side and the demand side of the economy, where both sides are heavily influenced by the specific character of supply-side policies (on the family, childcare, education, taxes, and transfers) and demand-side policies (labour market regulation, unionization and collective bargaining, structure of social insurance contributions).

Part-time work for women is a mixed blessing in that, on the one hand, it offers opportunities for women to combine market work and family life but, on the other hand, it could in the longer run endanger their human capital accumulation and future advancement.[11] A particular problem arises when part-time jobs are available only with certain categories of employers and within certain occupations, which might force women to change employer and type of job if they want to work part-time after having children.[12] This will lead to losses of firm-specific and occupation-specific human capital investments and consequent earnings losses.

Women's part-time work may also contribute to structuring work organizations and job ladders in ways that lead to (female) 'dead-end jobs' and 'mommy tracks'. Indeed, drawing on UK experience the distinction between the full-time and the part-time female workforce has been argued to be a crucial one and to form the basis for a growing dualization and polarization of the female workforce (Hakim 1996; Walby 1998). Joshi and Paci (1998) show that, while well-qualified female full-timers in the UK are making strong progress, and improving their pay position relative to their male peers, the situation for female part-timers relative to female full-timers has not

[11] See e.g. Meyerson and Petersen (1997*b*).
[12] See the discussion in Fagan and Rubery (1996), in Fagan, O'Reilly, and Rubery (1998), and in Joshi and Paci (1998).

improved, and even seems to be deteriorating. The increase in the pay differential between young female full-timers and young female part-timers in the UK is the result of two factors—a further increase in the differences between their respective human capital endowments and a slight increase in the (adjusted) wage premium for working full-time (Joshi and Paci 1998: 136). However, the UK experience might be an extreme one and part-time work in other countries might constitute less of a divide.

As discussed above, working part-time may be a voluntary choice by women (given the gendered restrictions facing them and their lower wages relative to those of their husbands) in order to reconcile market and household work. But in the Europe of the 1990s there is also a large number of women who work part-time because they have not been able to find a full-time job, so-called involuntary part-timers or 'part-time unemployed'. For these women, low earnings are the outcome of restricted opportunities for full-time jobs and not of (voluntary) labour supply choices. The share of male part-timers who work part-time because they have not been able to find a full-time job is higher than the share of female part-timers (27 per cent as compared to 18 per cent), but, since female part-timers, so far outnumber male part-timers, the overwhelming majority of the 'part-time unemployed' are women. Thus in 1997 3.6 million women as compared to 1.4 million men were 'part-time unemployed' in the EU (Eurostat 1998a: 138) and potentially suffered from negative effects on human capital accumulation and advancement associated with that status.

2.2. Job Segregation

Within the labour market the gendered division of labour is manifested in strong horizontal as well as vertical job segregation by sex. In the horizontal dimension, women and men are very differently distributed over sectors and occupations. This is the case in all the European economies. In 1997, for the EU as a whole, 16 per cent of women as compared to 39 per cent of men were employed in industry, 80 per cent of women as compared to 55 per cent of men were employed in services (Eurostat 1998a). Larger shares of the female than of the male workforce were found in wholesale and retail trade (16 versus 14 per cent), in hotels and restaurants (5 versus 3 per cent) and, particularly, in other services[13] (36 versus 12 per cent). The opposite was the case for transport and communications (with 3 per cent for females versus 8 per cent for males).

Studies of occupational segregation by sex reveal a high and only slowly changing level of segregation in industrial countries (Rubery, Fagan, and Maier 1996; Blau, Simpson, and Anderson 1998; Jonung 1998b). To measure the degree of occupational segregation, a 'dissimilarity index' is often used. This can be interpreted as the share of the female (male) labour force that would need to change occupation in order for the women (men) to have the same occupational distribution as men (women). Its minimum value is zero, when women are represented within each occupation with the

---

[13] Other services include educational, health, and social services as well as personal and cultural services.

same proportion as their share of the labour force. Its maximum value is 100, when women and men are completely segregated in different occupations. The index tends to be higher the more disaggregated the occupational classification used in calculating it. According to a study of the then twelve member countries of the EU, the occupational dissimilarity index in 1990, based on a two-digit occupational classification, ranged from 59 for Denmark and Luxembourg to 43 for Greece, and in most countries it had exhibited little change over the 1980s (see Rubery, Fagan, and Maier 1996). A similar study for Sweden showed an index of 60.5 for 1990, on a two-digit occupational classification, down from 60.8 in 1980, and an index of 64.5, down from 67.9 in 1980, based on a three-digit occupational classification (Jonung 1998b).[14] For the USA, Blau, Simpson, and Anderson (1998) calculate that the dissimilarity index on a three-digit occupational classification decreased from 59.3 in 1980 to 53.0 in 1990, suggesting a more marked decrease in US than in European occupational sex segregation during this decade.

The picture of marked occupational segregation by sex is reinforced when one looks behind the dissimilarity index to focus on the relatively low-skilled section of the labour force. The decrease in the dissimilarity index at the three-digit level that has been observed in, for example, Sweden and the USA over the 1980s mainly stems from women's increased share in initially male-dominated, white-collar, and service occupations, whereas little change seems to have taken place within blue-collar, craft, and technical occupations (Blau, Simpson, and Anderson 1998; Jonung 1998b). The sex segregation of the latter types of occupations and of traditionally female-dominated occupations at lower skill levels seems to be more entrenched, with sex-stereotyping remaining more pronounced, than among the high-skill, professional groups. This picture is confirmed by the study of the EU member countries mentioned above. There, too, the rather static picture of only small net changes in the level of segregation as measured by the dissimilarity index hides divergent processes and trends of desegregation and resegregation within different parts of the employment structure (Rubery, Fagan, and Maier 1996: 433–5). In particular, at lower levels of the occupational hierarchy the gendered division of labour has shown little sign of change. Most manual production and transport jobs are still done by men, and most low-skill service jobs are done by women. The part of the occupational structure where the low paid are likely to be found is thus characterized by particularly strong and entrenched occupational segregation. The same picture emerges when one looks at other measures of occupational segregation, such as the most common occupations among men and women respectively, and male-dominated versus female-dominated occupations.

It is furthermore the case that the vertical dimension of job segregation by sex is not revealed by occupational statistics. Even within occupations there is very often strong sex segregation, with men and women differently distributed over job categories that differ in their economic and other working conditions, as well as in the possibilities for training and advancement. The intra-occupational sex segregation is systematic in

---

[14] There were some changes in the Swedish occupational classification in 1985 so that the changes in the index between 1980 and 1990 must be interpreted with caution.

that women tend to be clustered at lower levels of hierarchies within occupations and in job categories with lower pay and less future potential. At higher skill levels the intra-occupational sex segregation is reflected in so-called glass ceilings and mommy tracks. At lower skill levels the correspondence seems to be special dead-end tracks for women, where they are trapped to a greater extent than men in low-paid job categories within occupations (see e.g. Granqvist and Persson 1997; Sundin 1998).

Job segregation matters, because it affects women's pay relative to men's. Indeed, it is one of the main channels through which pay differentials between men and women can be justified, maintained, and recreated. The results from empirical studies show that there is a marked wage penalty (for both men and women) for working in a female-dominated rather than a male-dominated occupation, at similar human capital and job requirements. For instance, for Sweden in the early 1990s Le Grand (1997) estimates the wage penalty for being in a strongly female-dominated occupation instead of in a strongly male-dominated one to be 9 per cent for women and 6 per cent for men. Studies of job mobility and advancement within occupations also show marked differences between men and women (see e.g. Meyerson and Petersen 1997b; Ohlsson and Öhman 1997). For the low-skilled part of the labour force we should then not be surprised to find that the very same processes of sex segregation and sex differences in pay and advancement possibilities turn out to create sex differences in the incidence and persistence of low pay.

2.3. Temporary Jobs, Job Instability, and Unemployment

Besides part-time employment, the other main category of so-called atypical work involves temporary jobs of various kinds. Their common characteristic is that the work contract is of limited duration, so that the individual runs a high risk of becoming unemployed upon its termination. In many labour markets temporary jobs have become more frequent over recent decades and they often serve as the main avenue for entering the labour market or for entering employment with a new employer.

In 1997 about 15 million people or 12 per cent of employees in the EU held a temporary job, but with considerable variation between countries, ranging from 6 per cent in Belgium to 34 per cent in Spain (see Table 3.4). The share of employees with a temporary job is somewhat, but not much, higher for women than for men. The gender difference in the incidence of this type of atypical work is thus much less marked than in the case of part-time jobs. Roughly the same share of men and women indicate that the reason for their having a temporary job is that they have not been able to find a permanent job (42 per cent for male temporary workers as compared to 39 per cent for female temporary workers). But here again there is large variation between countries, with the share of 'involuntary' temporary jobs ranging from just over 10 per cent in Denmark to 87 per cent in Spain (see Table 3.4).

The share of temporary workers within each occupational group is rather similar for men and women, with high shares found in production, service, and agricultural

Table 3.4. Share of employees with a temporary job and share of temporary jobs that are 'involuntary' (%)

Country	Temporary jobs			Involuntary	
	Women and men	Women	Men	Women	Men
EU15	12.1	13.0	11.5	39.0	42.2
Austria	7.8	8.4	7.3	18.1	8.7
Belgium	6.3	8.6	4.6	47.1	36.5
Denmark	11.1	11.6	10.6	44.7	31.9
Finland	17.1	18.9	15.2	79.4	72.4
France	13.0	14.2	12.1	n.a.	n.a.
Germany	11.6	11.9	11.4	12.3	10.0
Greece	10.9	11.9	10.2	76.9	78.9
Ireland	9.4	12.2	7.1	46.0	61.7
Italy	8.2	9.7	7.3	48.7	51.9
Netherlands	11.4	14.9	8.8	46.5	45.9
Portugal	12.0	12.6	11.4	82.8	82.8
Spain	33.6	35.7	32.4	87.0	87.3
Sweden	12.0	13.9	10.0	81.3	80.9
UK	7.3	8.3	6.4	34.4	45.2

Note: n.a. = not available.

Source: Eurostat (1998*a*: tables 032 and 064).

jobs. But in terms of numbers, female temporary workers tend to congregate in the same types of jobs as female permanent workers, and similarly male temporary workers shadow the employment profile for male permanent workers (*Bulletin on Women and Employment in the EU*, 1994). But there are certain differences. Female temporary workers are, for example, even more likely than women with permanent contracts to be found in female-dominated services and less likely to be found in clerical areas. Temporary employment is also more of a burden for women in southern Europe (Greece, Portugal, and Spain). Women in these countries are more likely to hold an insecure temporary contract than women in the north, and they are more likely to hold it outside the professional labour market, in a sector offering not only precarious but also low-paid work (*Bulletin on Women and Employment in the EU*, 1994).

The reason for focusing on temporary jobs is that they might be associated with lower pay than permanent jobs[15] and with job instability, risk of unemployment,

---

[15] For instance, evidence for Finland (Asplund 1998*a*) provides no support for the compensating wage differentials hypothesis of temporary jobs being, *ceteris paribus*, paid more than permanent jobs to compensate for the higher risk of job termination faced by people in temporary employment.

Table 3.5. Unemployment rates for men and women aged 25–59 years with less than upper secondary education and the ratio between their respective unemployment rates

Country	Unemployment rate (%)		Ratio of female to male unemployment rate
	Women	Men	
EU15	14.2	11.3	1.3
Austria	7.3	7.9	0.9
Belgium	17.6	10.0	1.8
Denmark	10.2	6.1	1.7
Finland	17.4	16.4	1.1
France	16.9	13.9	1.2
Germany	15.9	17.7	0.9
Greece	10.8	4.5	2.4
Ireland	16.0	14.6	1.1
Italy	15.3	8.5	1.8
Netherlands	10.1	5.3	1.9
Portugal	7.1	5.6	1.3
Spain	28.2	15.7	1.8
Sweden	12.1	11.9	1.0
UK	6.0	9.7	0.6

Source: Eurostat (1998*a*: table 025).

and meagre possibilities for human capital investments, which could contribute to a slower future wage growth. In terms of the risk of holding temporary jobs, we have found no marked gender differences, but it could still be that the character of the temporary jobs and their effects on job stability, wages, and wage growth differ between women and men. Even if the effects of temporary jobs turn out to be the same for men and women within particular occupations, the fact that male and female temporary workers are very differently distributed across occupations could play a role, and lead to differences between the outcome for women as a group and the outcome for men as a group.

Job instability and unemployment also tend to be concentrated among workers with lower educational attainment and skills. For the EU as a whole the ratio between the unemployment rate for persons aged 25–59 years without upper secondary education and the total rate of unemployment for this age group is 1.3. The ratio varies, though, from slightly over 1 for Spain, Italy, and Portugal, to 1.7 for Belgium, Denmark, and Germany. As a consequence, low-skilled workers are more likely than high-skilled workers to be exposed to losses of job experience and on-the-job training as well as to other scarring effects from frequent and/or long spells of unemployment.

But among low-skilled workers (those with less than upper secondary education) there are also clear gender differences in unemployment levels. For all EU countries except Austria, Germany, and the UK, the rate of unemployment is higher for low-skilled women than for low-skilled men (see Table 3.5). But again there is much variation among the rest of the countries as to how much worse low-skilled women fare relative to low-skilled men in terms of unemployment levels. Clearly, these gender differences in unemployment experience could be one factor that contributes to the observed gender differences in low pay.

2.4. Summary

In Section 2.1 above we have shown that there is still a very marked division of labour between work in the home and work in the market among European women and men. This division remains particularly strong for women with low educational qualifications and skills—that is, for women vulnerable to low pay—and is manifested in higher rates of inactivity (reflecting more and longer work interruptions) and higher rates of part-time work. This, in turn, might create a vicious circle, bringing this group of women further into being, and remaining, low paid. But there is also much variation between countries in these indicators of the extent of the gender division of labour, reflecting differences in family-related policies (gender regimes), working-time policies (part-time regimes), labour market regulation (inclusive of the existence or not of a minimum wage), and tax and social security policies. Thus it is also to be expected that there will be variation between countries in the impact of the gender division between market and non-market work on the incidence of women being low paid.

Within the labour market the gendered division of labour is manifested in very strong job segregation by sex. This segregation is generated from both the supply and demand sides of the labour market, as well as from the interaction between the two (see the discussion in Rubery, Fagan, and Meier 1996; Blau 1998; Jonung 1998a). Job segregation, in turn, can be expected to affect the relative earnings of women and men (see Johnson and Stafford 1998). As discussed in Section 2.2, job segregation takes several forms. First, there is a very strong occupational segregation between men and women. As measured by the dissimilarity index, this segregation has not decreased very much in Europe during the 1980s. This is particularly the case for the lower end of the job hierarchy, where occupational segregation seems more entrenched and sex-stereotyping more pronounced than for the high-skilled, professional part of the occupational structure. Secondly, even within occupations men and women are very differently distributed over job categories, and this intra-occupational sex segregation is systematic, in that women tend to be clustered at lower levels of hierarchies within occupations and in job categories with lower pay and less future advancement potential. In particular, at lower skill levels there seem to exist special dead-end tracks for women within occupations. It should come as no surprise then if the horizontal and vertical job segregation turns out to be an important factor behind gender differences in the incidence and permanence of being low paid.

3.   Women's Low Pay—a Matter of Characteristics?

It has been shown above that women are more likely than men to be in low-wage employment, a tendency that characterizes all industrialized economies for which data are available. But sex is not the only conspicuous difference between men and women in low-paid employment, as shown in the previous section. Comparing the individual and job-related characteristics of low-paid men and low-paid women reveals striking differences as well as interesting similarities, which again are largely repeated across countries. Let us look at some of these similarities and dissimilarities.

The higher probability of women being located at the lower end of the earnings distribution could be taken as an indication of low-paid women being, on average, younger than low-paid men. Put differently, women could to a larger extent be at the beginning of their working career and the low-paid job merely be a stepping stone into higher-paid jobs. Statistics for low-paid men and women do not support this hypothesis, however. On the contrary, low-paid women are generally older than their low-paid male counterparts. Figures for Ireland for 1994 reveal that two-thirds of low-paid men were under 25 years of age while over one-half of low-paid women were aged 25 or over (Nolan 1998b). Figures for the UK for 1993 show that one-half of all low-paid women were in the 35–50 age group compared to merely one-fifth of low-paid men (Sloane and Theodossiou 1998). Figures for Sweden for 1991 give an average age of 31.5 years for low-paid men compared to 35 years for low-paid women (Hultin and Szulkin 1997). A notable exception from this age pattern is Italy, where a large major-ity of low-paid men are found in the 30–55 age group, whereas low-paid women have persistently been more evenly distributed across age groups (Lucifora 1998). Moreover, the overall trend in Italy seems to have been—at least up to 1987—for a marked increase in the share of the oldest age group (over 55 year olds) among both men and women in low pay, with a corresponding decline in the relative shares of younger age groups (except for men under 25 years of age). This tendency has resulted in a considerable narrowing in the differences in the age distribution of low-paid men and women in Italy.[16]

The higher probability for women of being low paid than for men could be expected to be linked with marked differences in their accumulated human capital, with women

---

[16] From 1975 to 1987 the relative share of those aged 30–55 declined from 73 to 55% among low-paid men and from 53 to 45% for low-paid women. The relative share of those under 30 years of age dropped from 41 to 36% among low-paid women but remained roughly unchanged (about 25%) among low-paid men. Simultaneously the relative share of the oldest age group (over 55 years of age) increased to close to 19% in both gender groups from a modest level of 3% among low-paid men and close to 6% among low-paid women. See Lucifora (1998: table 10.1).

having accumulated less. Again, however, reality points in a totally different direction: the differences in human capital endowments between low-paid men and women are, on average, small or negligible. This holds for formal qualifications, for firm-specific human capital (as measured by tenure), as well as for training (Sloane and Theodossiou 1998). Evidence for Sweden indicates that low-paid women are, on average, more experienced in terms of total work experience and tenure than their low-paid male counterparts (Hultin and Szulkin 1997). This can be interpreted as further support for low-paid men being more often at the start of their working career than are low-paid women.

Drawing on the discussion in Section 2.2 above, the higher concentration of women among the low paid is the expected outcome from women being to a larger extent in service jobs, many of which are known to be low paid. This contention receives strong support when comparing the occupational and industrial distribution of low-paid men and women.[17] But the question may also be raised whether women are low paid because they are more likely to be in service jobs or if, instead, service jobs are often low paid because they are mainly occupied by women. The fact that, compared to the overall distribution of men across occupations, low-paid men tend to be overrepresented in female-dominated occupations[18] shows that the cause-consequence direction is not unambiguous.

Finally, larger establishments/firms are known to pay higher wages than small establishments/firms even for observationally similar workers.[19] Accordingly, the larger share of women among the low paid could be the result of women being employed in small establishments/firms more frequently than men. Statistics available for the UK indicate that this is certainly the case (Sloane and Theodossiou 1998). The evidence is not equally clear-cut when looking at the distribution of low-paid workers across differently sized workplaces in the southern parts of Europe dominated by small workplaces. Figures for Italy indicate that a large majority of the low paid are concentrated in small workplaces, but this tendency is stronger among low-paid men, although an increasing share also of low-paid women is found in small workplaces.[20]

Two major, highly interrelated hypotheses emerge from the above overview. First, being low paid seems to be largely dependent on individual as well as job-related characteristics. However, so far only a few attempts have been made to explore to what extent various characteristics actually contribute to explaining the incidence of low pay. Separating out characteristics with a major impact on the individual's risk of being low paid from characteristics with a minor impact is of crucial importance

---

[17] See e.g. Arai, Asplund, and Barth (1998) for the Nordic countries, Lucifora (1998) for Italy, and Sloane and Theodossiou (1998) for the UK.

[18] See evidence reported for e.g. Sweden by Hultin and Szulkin (1997).

[19] For more details on this wage premium induced by employer size, see Albæk et al. (1998) and the references therein.

[20] In 1975 some 70% of low-paid men and 50% of low-paid women were employed in workplaces with between one and twenty employees. By 1987 this share had increased to, respectively, 78% and 66% (Lucifora 1998).

for identifying potential low-pay traps with regard to employee as well as employer attributes. Of special interest also is whether the characteristics have the same impact for women and men. Second, low-paid men and women turn out to differ considerably when it comes to background characteristics. It could, therefore, be argued that the stronger concentration of women among the low paid is primarily a result of women having, on average, a more unfavourable set of background characteristics than men, and not a consequence of their sex. Again this hypothesis can be evaluated only empirically.

Existing empirical evidence provides support for the first hypothesis but not for the second. There are, indeed, certain individual and job-related characteristics that do contribute strongly to the risk of being low paid.[21] As pointed out by Stewart and Swaffield (1999), the results are much as would be expected from the earnings function literature. Thus, for both women and men, the probability of being low paid decreases with age and with increased human capital, as measured by educational attainment, work experience, tenure, and/or training. Among job-related characteristics, higher job requirements—as measured by the length of education required and the time it takes to learn the job—have been shown to decrease the probability of being low paid in Sweden. Holding a non-manual job and, especially, a managerial job significantly reduces the risk of low pay in Italy. Another important finding is that being in a female-dominated occupation increases the risk of being low paid very markedly for both women and men.

While the estimated effects of individual and job-related characteristics on the probability of being low paid most often turn out to go in the same direction for women and men, the few studies that have estimated whether the size of the effects differs across genders tend to find this to be the case.[22] For example, Hultin and Szulkin (1997) find for Sweden that the effects of experience and tenure in reducing risk are relatively smaller for women than for men, and that the risk-reducing effects of formal education are relatively larger for women than for men. Higher educational requirements for the job are found to reduce the risk of low pay somewhat more for women than for men, whereas a longer time required to learn the job reduces the risk of low pay more for men than for women. Furthermore, they find that the risk of being low paid increases with the share of women in the occupation, but more so for men than for women. Clearly, it would be of great interest to have similar studies of gender differences in impacts for other countries.

What about the second hypothesis? Does the gender difference in the incidence of low pay disappear when individual and job-related characteristics are taken into account? Available country-specific results overwhelmingly show that the gendered pattern of low pay is maintained also after controlling for differences in personal characteristics between women and men. For example, controlling for human capital

---

[21] See results reported in e.g. Hultin and Szulkin (1997) for Sweden, Stewart and Swaffield (1999) for the UK, Lucifora (1998) for Italy, Jepsen, Meulders, and Terraz (1998) for Belgium, and Nolan (1998b) for Ireland.   [22] See Hultin and Szulkin (1997) for Sweden and Lucifora (1998) for Italy.

(education, experience, tenure) and family characteristics (marital status, number of children) did reduce women's risk of being low paid relative to men's for Sweden in 1968. In 1991, however, this was no longer the case; instead, controlling for these characteristics increased women's relative risk of low pay.[23] Neither did the addition of controls for educational requirements of the job and time required to learn the job decrease women's relative risk of being low paid. On the other hand, controlling for the share of women in the occupation markedly reduced women's relative risk of low pay, indicating that occupational sex segregation is an important factor behind women's higher risk of being in a low-paid job in Sweden. But even after having controlled for occupational segregation, the risk of being low paid remained almost twice as high for women as for men.[24] In other words, the sex of the individual does exert an independent influence on the risk of being low paid; irrespective of the individual or job-related characteristics considered, women always face a higher risk than men of being in a low-paid job simply because they are women.

Studies focusing on the incidence of low pay in a single year can, however, be criticized for overlooking the dynamics of low pay—that is, the fact that a majority of people tend to move out of low pay. Some move more quickly, others more slowly. Some move permanently, others only temporarily. But they do move! The complex issue of mobility out of low pay is dealt with in the next section. It may, however, already be noted here that the characteristics that have been found to contribute most heavily to the observed incidence of low pay in cross-section analyses are largely the same as those that most strongly prevent the low paid from moving up the earnings ladder (cf. Section 4.3 below).

4.   Are Women Trapped in Low-Paid Jobs?

It is often argued that low-wage employment is less of a problem if people move higher up the earnings hierarchy within a few years. In labour markets characterized by a relatively high degree of earnings mobility, low-paid jobs thus have the character more of starting jobs than of dead-end jobs. The share of the low paid in a single year will, in that case, exaggerate the low-wage employment problem. It is, therefore, of great importance to separate the individuals who are low paid over a multi-year period from those who visit the bottom end of the earnings hierarchy only temporarily.

Our knowledge about the degree of earnings mobility has expanded rapidly in the past few years as panel data have become available for a growing number of industrialized countries. The comparability of results across countries is, however, still limited by major differences in the population and time span studied and the techniques and definitions used. Moreover, a major part of the existing empirical evidence relates to

---

[23] Hultin and Szulkin (1997). In 1968 the female odds ratio (as estimated by a logistic regression) decreased from 4.46 to 4.14 whereas in 1991 it increased from 3.11 to 3.63 when controlling for human capital and family characteristics.   [24] The female odds ratio decreased from 3.29 to 1.97.

all employees or male employees only. The limited evidence on the earnings mobility of women nevertheless displays interesting patterns pointing to striking similarities across countries.

4.1. *Mobility out of Low Pay into Higher Pay*

A well-established way of analysing the degree of earnings mobility between two points in time is to compare the relative earnings position of individuals in the starting year and the destination year using a transition matrix. For convenience, individuals are usually classified into deciles or quintiles.[25] In studies focusing primarily on the mobility of the low paid, various low-pay thresholds such as two-thirds of median earnings are commonly used. A major shortcoming of this latter type of threshold, however, is that it impairs the comparability of results across countries, as the share of low paid will vary with the overall dispersion in earnings.

Most analyses of mobility patterns are—mainly for data-related reasons—restricted to employees who are employed at both points in time, leaving out all those individuals who do not have positive earnings in either the starting year or the destination year. The consequent so-called sample attrition problem is known to affect the observed mobility patterns. Ignoring transitions into and out of employment has been shown to overstate the probability of moving up from low pay (Eriksson 1998; Stewart and Swaffield 1998). Another restriction common especially to cross-country comparisons is that the analyses comprise only individuals employed on a full-time basis.[26] This criterion again affects the outcome, although the impact varies across countries (see OECD 1996a: table 3.6).

Country-specific evidence clearly indicates that women have, on average, a much higher probability than men of remaining low paid over a sequence of years. This also explains their overrepresentation among the low paid. Results for Finnish non-manual workers point to a notably lower probability for women than for men of escaping low pay (defined as the lowest wage decile) within a spell of four years (Asplund 1998b). Moreover, this tendency strengthened markedly during the deep recession in the early 1990s compared to the early 1980s. In particular, both in the early 1980s and the early 1990s only one out of four low-paid women was higher up the earnings hierarchy four years later. Among low-paid men, in contrast, over half left the lowest wage decile within four years in the early 1990s, compared to one-third in the early 1980s.

Broadly similar results have been obtained for Swedish low-paid women (Hultin and Szulkin 1997). Of all women recorded as low paid in 1968, only one out of four had escaped low pay by 1974, the corresponding pattern being one out of two among

---

[25] Mobility is then measured as movements between one decile/quintile at time t to another decile/quintile at time $t + 1$.

[26] The mobility analyses performed by, for example, the OECD focus almost entirely on continuously full-time workers (e.g. OECD 1997a; Keese, Puymoyen, and Swaim 1998).

low-paid men.[27] The share of the low paid trapped in low-paid jobs declines slightly over the periods 1974–81 and 1981–91, but the gender gap remains: 68 per cent of the low-paid women in 1981 and 42 per cent of the low-paid men in 1981 were also low paid in 1991. It is further noted that women have a considerably lower probability than their male colleagues of moving quickly from a low-paid job to a high-paid job. Moreover, this tendency for low-paid women to have weaker chances than men of experiencing a 'high-pay career' has strengthened over time. A similar trend is discernible in Finland (Asplund and Bingley 1996; Asplund 1998*b*).

Results for the UK based on the 1991–3 waves of the British Household Panel Survey show that, of women, about one-third stayed low paid in all three years, with the corresponding share being just one out of ten among their male counterparts (Stewart and Swaffield 1998).[28] Only 24 per cent of the women who were low paid in the first year rise above the low-pay threshold in at least one of the next two years; only 11 per cent do so in both years. For men, the corresponding shares are 44 per cent and 17 per cent, respectively. The considerably higher state dependency of low-paid women is also reflected in the finding that the probability of remaining low paid conditional upon previous low-pay experience is notably higher among women than among men. The same database restricted to the 1991 and 1993 waves is used by Sloane and Theodossiou (1998). Not surprisingly, they also report the probability of moving from low-paid jobs—with the threshold defined as two-thirds of the median—to higher-paid jobs to be much higher among men than among women, pointing to a considerably higher probability of women to remain low paid.

The above analyses of mobility patterns out of low pay are based on rather short time periods (as are most studies of earnings mobility). Since the degree of earnings mobility tends to increase with the length of the time horizon studied, the probability of being trapped in low-wage employment could also be expected to diminish in the longer run.[29] However, few studies have followed the destiny of the low paid over longer time periods.

One notable exception is Eriksson (1998), who examines, using a Finnish longitudinal database, transitions out of the lowest quintile over the subsequent five-, ten-, fifteen-, and twenty-year periods. Eriksson finds that the gender difference in the share remaining in the bottom quintile changed markedly during the time period investigated, 1970–90. In particular, women were less mobile out of low pay in the 1970s. In the 1980s, in contrast, they were exiting low pay at approximately the same rate as their male counterparts and, moreover, had a higher probability than men of moving up the earnings ladder. A common trend for men and women when comparing the 1970s

---

[27] Low pay is here defined as the lowest one-third of the earnings distribution.

[28] Low-pay thresholds below two-thirds of median earnings produce smaller shares of continuously low paid, but retain the gender differences. This also holds when extending the analysis to a fourth wave (1994) of the panel (see Stewart and Swaffield 1998).

[29] Short-run mobility measures may, in fact, even be misleading in the sense that the short-run evidence turns out to be contradictory to observed long-run trends in earnings mobility (see e.g. Asplund, Bingley, and Westergård-Nielsen 1998).

and the 1980s, however, is an increasing share of people being trapped in low-wage employment in the 1980s,[30] a tendency that was slightly stronger among low-paid men. Finally, a large majority of the exits out of low pay are found to take place during the first five years; the exit rates after ten, fifteen, and twenty years are substantially smaller, with the overall trend being very similar for men and women.

Bigard, Guillotin, and Lucifora (1998) compare earnings mobility in France and Italy over a fifteen-year period (1974–88). Their findings reveal small gender differences in overall mobility patterns for France but, nevertheless, point to a slightly higher risk for women of remaining in low pay for a considerable part of their working career.[31] The mobility patterns observed for Italian women resemble those of French women. Compared to the French case, however, the highest degree of immobility is found among low-paid Italian men. More precisely, of those men who were classified into the two lowest earnings deciles in 1974, 70 per cent were still located at the bottom end of the earnings hierarchy in 1988. The reported share of immobile women amounted to 73 per cent but covered deciles 1 to 4 and not just the two bottom deciles (deciles 1 and 2), as in the case of their male counterparts.[32]

Another finding of crucial importance is the much higher probability for the low paid (compared to their higher-paid colleagues) of lagging behind in promotions and wage growth. A considerable portion of the low paid, having managed to move up the earnings ladder, have a tendency to slip back to their 'starting' point in the earnings distribution. In other words, the improvement in the relative earnings position of the low paid often turns out to be only temporary.[33]

Calculations of the average cumulated time spent in low pay during 1986–91 undertaken by the OECD indicate that women experience more time in low-paid employment than men (OECD 1997a; Keese, Puymoyen, and Swaim 1998). This is interpreted as low-paid women having greater difficulty than low-paid men of moving up the earnings ladder in a sustained way. However, evidence reported for the UK by Stewart and Swaffield (1998) indicates that women having been able to escape their low-pay status have a clearly higher probability of remaining higher paid, whereas their low-paid male colleagues have a higher tendency to fall back quickly into a low-paid job. Likewise, in both Denmark and Finland low-paid men have been found to be more downwardly mobile than low-paid women (Asplund, Bingley, and Westergård-Nielsen 1998). This most likely reflects the very different individual and job-related characteristics of low-paid men and women.

---

[30] This finding reflects the declining earnings mobility in the Finnish labour market in the 1980s among both male and female workers (see Asplund and Bingley 1996).

[31] Of the women who in 1974 were located in the bottom half of the earnings distribution (deciles 1 to 5), 81.9% were still placed there in 1988. The corresponding share for men was 75.1% (Bigard, Guillotin, and Lucifora 1998: table 7).

[32] The high probability among Italian workers of being trapped in low-paid jobs is also reported by Contini, Filippi, and Villosio (1998) and Lucifora (1998).

[33] See the evidence reported by OECD (1996a, 1997a) and Keese, Puymoyen, and Swaim (1998) for six OECD countries: Denmark, France, Germany, Italy, the UK, and the USA. Further support for the Italian outcome is provided by Lucifora (1998). For details on Denmark and Finland, see Asplund, Bingley, and Westergård-Nielsen (1998).

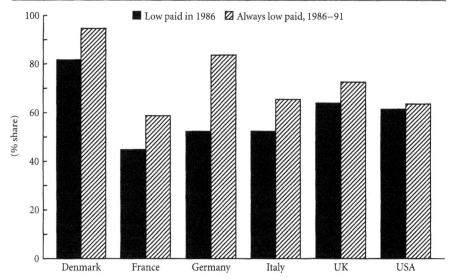

Fig. 3.3. Percentage share of women among all low paid in full-time employment

Notes: Low pay is defined as the bottom quintile of weekly/monthly earnings of all full-time workers; two-thirds of median earnings produces slightly different percentage shares but retains the overall pattern (see Keese, Puymoyen, and Swaim 1998). The data for France refer to 1984–9.

Source: authors' compilation, based on OECD (1997*a*: table 2.4) and Keese, Puymoyen, and Swaim (1998: fig. 12.12).

A totally different pattern emerges when analysing earnings mobility among the initially high(er) paid. In particular, there is strong evidence for a number of countries indicating that women have a considerably higher probability than men of dropping from high pay into low pay.[34]

In sum, existing evidence points to notable differences between men and women when it comes to experience of low pay. Low-pay traps stand out as more common among women (except in Italy). And, since women account for a considerably larger share of the persistently low paid than of the low paid in a single year, the gender distribution of the low paid reported in Table 3.1 understates the risk of women being low paid. As can be seen from Fig. 3.3, the compositional differences with respect to gender are particularly striking for Germany.

---

[34] See e.g. Contini, Filippi, and Villosio (1998) for Italy, and Stewart and Swaffield (1998) for the UK. Cross-country analyses undertaken by the OECD also point to a stronger tendency of downward earnings mobility into low-paid jobs among women (OECD 1996*a*, 1997*a*; Keese, Puymoyen, and Swaim 1998). Evidence for Finnish non-manual workers points to a clearly lower probability of women of retaining their relative wage position, especially when situated in the highest wage deciles (Asplund 1998*b*). Similar evidence has been reported for France (Bigard, Guillotin, and Lucifora 1998) and Sweden (Hultin and Szulkin 1997).

4.2. Mobility out of Low Pay into No Pay

Only a few mobility studies extend the analysis to movements into and out of employment, an aspect of crucial importance, especially when exploring the labour market performance of the low paid. Analyses focusing on five-year transition probabilities undertaken by the OECD reveal that, in all countries investigated, much of the movement out of low pay is out of full-time employment altogether, rather than into higher-paid jobs.[35] And, of those who left full-time employment, a large majority moved out of employment altogether rather than into part-time jobs or self-employment. Moreover, these exit rates are noted to be considerably higher for the low paid than for the higher paid. Another crucial similarity across countries is that most entries into low-paid jobs take the form of shifts from outside full-time employment. The pattern of strong concentration of both exits and entries at the bottom end of the earnings distribution is found to be particularly strong among women.

Country-specific results lend further support to these OECD findings. Evidence for the UK based on the three-year period 1991–3 points to a clearly higher probability of moving into non-employment among the low paid than among the higher paid —a tendency that is, moreover, much more pronounced for women (Stewart and Swaffield 1998). The low paid are also shown to be more likely to be low paid when moving back into employment, a pattern that, again, is clearly stronger for women (Stewart and Swaffield 1998). Furthermore, British women are over twice as likely as British men to be low paid when moving from an 'initial state' of non-employment to employment.

On the whole, the risk of cycling between low pay and no pay turns out to be much higher for women than for men. This also seems to have been the situation in Finland in the 1970s (Eriksson 1998). In the 1980s, on the other hand, Finnish men had a higher tendency to leave employment altogether. Simultaneously, the proportion of low-paid women exiting to housework fell considerably while their exits to non-employment states with a closer labour market attachment, such as self-employment and schooling, grew in importance.

4.3. Characteristics Affecting Mobility out of Low Pay

The country-specific results on the earnings mobility of the low paid reviewed in the previous sections point to considerable state dependence, especially among women. In particular, being low paid in one period has a relatively greater impact on women's probability of being low paid also in the next period. Likewise, periods out of employment tend to result in a higher risk of being re-employed in a low-paid rather than in a higher-paid job in the case of women than of men.

These aggregate transition probabilities of the low paid may, however, conceal substantial differences in individual transition probabilities, which may arise from

---

[35] See OECD (1996a, 1997a) and Keese, Puymoyen, and Swaim (1998).

differences across individuals not only in their sex but also in other crucial characteristics such as human capital endowments. More specifically, individuals with certain characteristics (for example, more education and skills) may have a clearly higher probability of moving out of low pay, while other characteristics (for example, low education and high age) may increase the individual's probability of being trapped in low-paid jobs. Remaining low paid may thus be the combined outcome of 'unfavourable' characteristics and the disadvantage to which previous low-pay experience tends to give rise.[36]

So far very few attempts have been made to identify the characteristics that most strongly influence the earnings mobility of the low paid.[37] This seems to be due not only to data restrictions but also to the sophisticated econometric methods that need to be applied.[38] Most econometric attempts to identify important determinants of the earnings mobility of the low paid focus on all employees, with the gender aspect being restricted to including a gender dummy in the estimated model specification. Being a woman is generally found to be one of the factors with the strongest influence on the probability of an upward move in the earnings distribution.[39] This is also to be expected in view of women's markedly higher probability of being low paid (see Section 3 above). The result is also in line with previous findings, pointing to a lower overall earnings mobility among women than among men.[40]

Using the gender-dummy approach means that it is implicitly assumed that all other characteristics affect the probability of men and women of escaping low pay in an equal way. This is certainly a strong assumption, as is evident from the following. A common finding obtained from gender-specific analyses of mobility out of low pay is that a higher educational attainment level is a precondition for women for leaving low-wage employment, whereas the influence of age is almost negligible. Among men, in contrast, the probability of moving out of low pay increases with age but not necessarily with education.[41] Moreover, these findings are well in line with those obtained when explaining the risk of being low paid; the characteristics reducing the probability of leaving low pay are, for the most part, the same as those found in cross-section analyses increasing the probability of being at the bottom end of the earnings hierarchy.

[36] Ignoring the latter aspect—that is, assuming the initial status to be exogenously given—has been shown to overstate the estimated effects on the conditional probability of remaining low paid (see Stewart and Swaffield 1999).

[37] A few studies focus on explaining overall earnings mobility: see e.g. Bingley, Bjørn, and Westergård-Nielsen (1995), Asplund and Bingley (1996) and Asplund, Bingley, and Westergård-Nielsen (1997).

[38] For different approaches, see e.g. Sloane and Theodossiou (1996, 1998), Asplund, Bingley, and Westergård-Nielsen (1998), and Stewart and Swaffield (1998).

[39] See e.g. Contini, Filippi, and Villosio (1998) for Italy, and Stewart and Swaffield (1998) for the UK. Sloane and Theodossiou (1998), in contrast, report a weak, if any, effect of gender on the estimated probability of staying low paid in the UK.

[40] See e.g. the review of earnings mobility in Atkinson, Bourguignon, and Morrisson (1992), Gregory and Elias (1994) for evidence for the UK, and Gittleman and Joyce (1995) for evidence for the USA. Opposite results have been reported for Sweden by Gustafsson (1994).

[41] See e.g. Stewart and Swaffield (1998). The crucial role of formal education for the chance of women of escaping low pay is also stressed in the analysis of Sweden by Hultin and Szulkin (1997).

5.   Does Women's Low Pay Matter?

Does all this then mean that the problem of female low pay is more severe than that of male low pay? The answer mediated by the empirical literature exploring the association between low pay and household poverty seems to be an overwhelming 'no'. The reasoning is simplistic: a majority of the low-paid women turn out to be married and mostly living in multi-earner households. In a recent comprehensive cross-country comparison of low-paid work and poverty among workers in full-time, full-year employment (Marx and Verbist 1998), it is found that low-paid spouses typically make up between 40 and 50 per cent of all low paid. It is also shown that poverty rates for low-paid women are, as a consequence, very low in a majority of the OECD countries studied, a conclusion that is repeated in a number of national studies.[42] Interventions in order to improve the relative wage level of the lowest paid—that is, mainly women—have therefore often been deemed as a poor weapon in combating household poverty.[43]

These conclusions can, however, be criticized on several grounds. As pointed out by Nickell (1996: 17), the low-pay problem 'is not just one of poverty but also of absence of work. At present, even if individuals have access to money but not to work, this is damaging to their self-esteem and socially corrosive'. Put differently, being a low-paid woman married to a high-income man does not change the fact that she is low paid with a rather weak labour market attachment.

Moreover, it seems reasonable to argue that the above conclusions would not hold with low-paid temporary and part-time workers, most of whom are women, included in the analysis. Results reported for Spain by Dolado, Felgueroso, and Jimeno (1998) lend strong support to this contention.[44] Analyses of the low-pay dynamics of women would definitely require a comprehensive account also of spells of part-time and temporary employment as well as of non-employment.

Equally importantly, the argument that women's earnings are only 'pin money' and 'supplementary earnings' to the earnings of male, primary breadwinners is rapidly losing ground.[45] First, demographics have changed, and higher age at first marriage, increases in divorce and separation rates, and differences in male and female life expectancy mean that women can expect to spend significant parts of their adult life cycle alone, dependent upon their own earnings. Quite a few women will also end up as lone parents during a certain period and consequently their earnings will also be crucial to the well-being of a significant number of children. Households are, in other

---

[42] A limited overlap between low pay and household poverty, particularly among low-paid women, is found in recent studies for Ireland (Nolan 1998b), Italy (Lucifora 1998), and the UK (Sloane and Theodossiou 1996). Similar findings are also reported in earlier studies for the UK (e.g. Bazen 1988) and the USA (Burkhauser and Finegan 1989).

[43] See e.g. Nolan (1998b) and Sloane and Theodossiou (1996).

[44] Dolado, Felgueroso, and Jimeno (1998) find that the typical minimum wage-earners in Spain are increasingly shifting from young, inexperienced workers to more adult people, mainly women, with temporary and/or part-time job contracts, living in households with scarce resources.

[45] See e.g. the evidence provided for the UK in Harkness, Machin, and Waldfogel (1997).

words, to an increasing extent becoming dependent on women's earnings as the main income source. Secondly, the share and role of women's earnings within married or cohabiting households have increased over time. The woman's market earnings are in many cases central to the household's well-being and escape from poverty and they can also provide an insurance and risk-spreading function against the risk of unemployment and job instability of her partner.[46] This is particularly so for low-wage and low-income households and has also become of greater importance in the more unstable labour markets of the 1980s and 1990s and with the deteriorating employment and wage position of low-skilled men. Thirdly, the change that is taking place in Europe towards individualization of tax and social security systems means that women's economic protection in case of illness, unemployment, and old age will increasingly be directly related to their own former market earnings.[47] And, finally, there is the aspect of power and freedom—having an income of her own affects a woman's bargaining power within the family and is a prerequisite of female economic independence and autonomy.[48]

6.   Policy Recommendations

There exists only sparse evidence on the incidence of and the mobility out of low pay. As revealed by our survey in this chapter, the available results are even more scattered and scarce when it comes to the gender aspect. Moreover, the use of different types of data, definitions, methods, and so on impairs the comparability of results across countries. This no doubt underscores the need to be cautious when drawing conclusions from the existing evidence on low pay among women, even though several crucial patterns do seem to be repeated across countries. Consequently also the possibilities of contributing empirically well-established recommendations on policy interventions and their expected implications for female low-wage employment are limited. The rather unsatisfactory state of the art within the field of women's low pay leads necessarily to the following suggestions.

We need broad-based, cross-country analyses of the labour market position and performance of low-paid women. Moreover, these analyses should not be restricted to women employed on a full-time basis but should also include part-timers and women having other types of atypical job contracts. The mobility aspect should cover mobility in and out of employment as well as mobility within the earnings distribution, and should focus both on the short run and the longer run. There are two main reasons for this need for comparative information displaying typical low-pay traps: women make

---

[46]   For empirical evidence, see OECD (1998a) and Harkness, Machin, and Waldfogel (1997).

[47]   See Jepsen et al. (1997) and Mage Network (1997b).

[48]   How having an income of her own is likely to affect female bargaining power in the family is analysed by so-called family bargaining models within the economics of the family; see e.g. Lundberg and Pollak (1996) and Persson and Jonung (1997). There are also empirical studies that confirm the existence of such effects: see e.g. Lundberg, Pollak, and Wales (1997).

up a major part of the low paid and women have a higher probability of being trapped in low-paid jobs. In addition, a growing number of industrialized countries are experiencing an increase in the share of the low paid owing to the overall increase in earnings dispersion.

But despite this need for new, comprehensive, and comparative information on women's low pay, existing evidence does reveal certain major factors behind women's higher incidence of and persistence in low pay. Overwhelmingly the most important single factor seems to be the job segregation (both vertical and horizontal) faced by women in employment. The measures undertaken so far to alleviate the problem of job segregation and to eliminate its consequences, not least in term of wages, have clearly not been enough.

The question of low pay, especially among women, should be given high priority in discussions of the need to increase flexibility in European labour markets and the different ways of achieving this. It is by now a stylized fact that collective bargaining and centralized wage setting have contributed substantially to improving the relative labour market position of women. A weakening of existing labour market institutions in combination with a growing use of atypical job contracts can be expected to have noteworthy consequences for the incidence and persistence of low pay among women.

The problem of low pay among women should not be played down by arguing that low-paid women do not generally live in poverty. The traditional European system of ensuring continuing employment among husbands has become old-fashioned. Low pay among women should be evaluated from the same premises as low pay among men. Analyses of the welfare consequences of low pay that are aimed to serve political decision-making should, as a consequence, be undertaken from a more 'objective' gendered perspective. On the whole, the question of women's low pay extends to a much broader range of policy areas than does the question of men's low pay. Of particular importance is the country's structure of family-related policies, working-time policies, education policies, as well as tax and social security policies. Women's low pay is thus a much more complex issue than is generally recognized. This is a challenge both for future research and for future policy initiatives on women's low pay.

4   Earnings Mobility of the Low Paid

PETER SLOANE AND IOANNIS THEODOSSIOU

Over a great part of the post-war period the earnings distribution has exhibited remarkable stability in many OECD countries. However, during the 1980s this long-term trend altered by varying degrees across countries and earnings inequality rose. This had the inevitable consequence of worsening the relative position of those at the lower tail of the distribution. Thus, the incidence of low-paid work has increased and become an important policy issue. In investigating this issue and for policy purposes it is important to consider issues concerning the ability of individual workers to increase their earnings capabilities through time. To the extent that low pay is merely a transient phenomenon in which young workers acquire the necessary skills to enhance their lifetime earnings, low pay is not a matter for particular policy concern. To the extent, however, that certain workers become trapped in low-paid jobs, a number of policy concerns are raised.[1]

In general, the main findings about earnings mobility have come from observations of the earnings histories of panel data sets. Economists have analysed these data to determine both the level and basic determinants of earnings mobility. This gives rise to a number of questions. First, how frequent are movements into and out of low-paid jobs and what form do they take? For example, is it necessary for workers to change employer or simply gain more experience in their present place of employment in order to improve their relative pay? How important are movements into and out of employment in determining the probability of low pay? Or more specifically does re-entry into employment imply a fall in wages compared with the previous job and if so by how much? Is such a decline in wages transient or permanent? How does mobility alter over the course of the life cycle? How do changes in the overall earnings distribution impact on earnings at the lower end of the distribution? These are only some of the questions that we need to answer if policy is to be properly informed.

The arguments put forward concerning the importance of wage mobility usually relate to the achievement of a particular objective—namely, equity. The implicit assumption is that a distribution of earnings with low inequality is more desirable than one with higher inequality.

The objective of moving towards higher equality can be justified by what is known as the 'Cardinalist' welfare criterion. If individuals have the same utility or welfare

---

[1] It should be noted that the concern of this chapter is with intra-generational mobility (or the advancement of individuals) rather than inter-generational mobility (the extent to which the advancement of children is constrained by the occupation or earnings of their parents).

function, and if this is an increasing and strictly concave function of earnings, then, for a given level of total earnings, total welfare is maximized if each person earns the arithmetic mean earnings. The implication is the desirability of a transfer of earnings from someone above the mean to someone below it, since this increases welfare. Thus, welfare economics can justify aiming at lower inequality, providing all the assumptions hold. However, the so-called Pareto criterion suggests that any policy that increases the welfare of some members of society, without changing the welfare of the remainder, is desirable. Thus, for example, if 1 per cent of the country's population is rich and the 99 per cent is below the low-pay threshold, then any policy that makes the 1 per cent even richer, without changing the welfare of the 99 per cent, is desirable. However, the merit of this conclusion is debatable. As Adam Smith (1776: 181) put it,

what improves the circumstances of the greater part (of the lower rank of the people) can never be regarded as an inconvenience to the whole. No society can be flourishing and happy of which the far greater part of the members are poor and miserable. It is but equity, besides, that they who feed, clothe, and lodge the whole body of the people, should have such a share of the produce of their own labour as to be themselves tolerably well fed, clothed and lodged.

Thus, in effect, one has to rely on value judgements in assessing the importance of the preoccupation with the low-pay issue.

However, the above focuses on a snapshot of the distribution of earnings, and, if there is mobility through the earnings, distribution is likely to exaggerate the degree of inequality. As Atkinson, Bourguignon, and Morrisson (1992) note, mobility may be desired intrinsically (for example, as a contribution to the attainment of equality of opportunity) or instrumentally (for example, as a contribution to the reduction of lifetime inequality). It may also be a means of improving the overall efficiency of the labour market in so far as wage or job mobility adjusts rapidly to changing demands or technologies.

In the remainder of this chapter we examine both the problems of analysing cohorts as they move through the earnings distribution and methods of estimating earnings mobility. We then consider the empirical evidence on earnings mobility in Europe, focusing on earnings mobility into higher-paid jobs and into joblessness, with an assessment of the impact of the latter on future earnings mobility potential. We then turn to the effects of institutions on low-pay mobility and the relationship between short-run and long-run inequality, concluding with some policy implications.

1.   Earnings Mobility: The Issue and the Problems of Analysis

The earnings distribution is merely a 'snapshot' of a complicated pattern of earnings dynamics, which is continuously changing through time. The study of such a distribution reveals the profiles of those in the different classes of the earnings distribution and consequently enables one to identify those who bear a high burden of low-paid employment. However, the picture is not complete if there is no information with respect to the movement of employees up (or down) the earnings distribution over time or over their life cycle. Thus, study of cross-section earnings distributions permits a static analysis of earnings, whereas an analysis of the earnings distribution over time permits the study of the underlying dynamics.

The structure of the earnings distribution for many countries has changed over the years. The OECD (1996a) has estimated that over the period 1979–95, although the trends in the overall dispersion of earnings, measured by the 90/10 percentile ratio, did not exhibit a generalized increase in earnings inequality across countries, over the first half of the 1990s the long-term trend towards stable or declining earnings inequality frequently altered dramatically. The UK and the USA exhibited the most pronounced increase in earnings inequality, but Australia, New Zealand, Italy, Sweden, and Finland also showed various degrees of increase in earnings inequality, especially after the end of 1980s (Fig. 4.1a,b).

However, comparing two or more such cross sections of the changing earnings distributions does not give much insight into earnings mobility and does not help the design of policy towards low-paid employment. To illustrate this point consider two earnings distributions with the same mean and dispersion but where one of them applies to an immobile labour force where workers are unable to move from one earnings class to another, and the other to a mobile labour force with workers moving up and down the distribution. Any design of policy to help the workers earning a wage below the low-paid threshold in the former case will benefit all those earning below this threshold. However, in the latter case policy efforts should be concentrated only on those who tend to stay below the low-pay threshold over a long period and not to those who quickly move up within the earnings distribution. Thus the dynamic analysis of earnings is of major importance and is mainly concerned with the earnings profile of the same workers over time.

The problem in studying the dynamics of earnings mobility using such a 'cohort' of workers has two strands. First, the investigation is able to evaluate earnings mobility only during the period of the panel data set, which is usually of short duration, and thus information about the life-cycle earnings and mobility of individuals in the earnings distribution are usually scarce. Secondly, any attempt to evaluate earnings mobility has to accommodate the issue of the employment propensity of the individual worker in terms of mobility into and out of joblessness or what has been referred to as the low-pay/no-pay cycle. It is normally the case that, over the life of the panel, information on the earnings of those who leave the cohort is not available, since they become unemployed or move out of the active labour market. Thus, if one wishes to estimate how long workers stay below the low-pay threshold but exclude those with no earnings from the sample for some period, then an important aspect of dynamics of earnings is excluded from the analysis.

Focusing only on the incidence of low-paid employment may also understate the extent of upward immobility, since workers' prospects of moving up the earnings ladder may worsen as the duration of a low-paid employment spell lengthens, which is sometimes referred to as the scarring effect of low pay. So the question arises: does

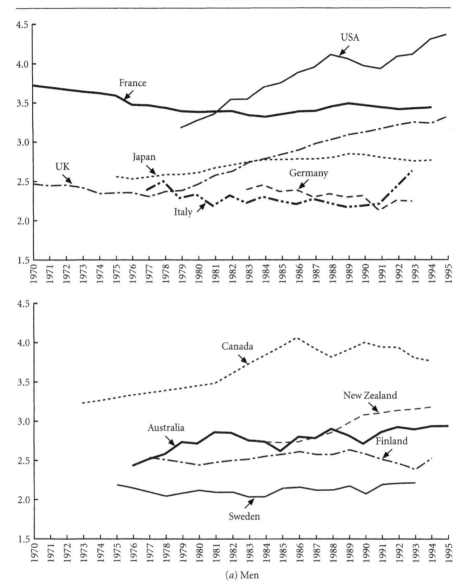

Fig. 4.1. Trends in earnings dispersion, D9/D1
Source: OECD (1996a: chart 3.1). Copyright OECD 1996.

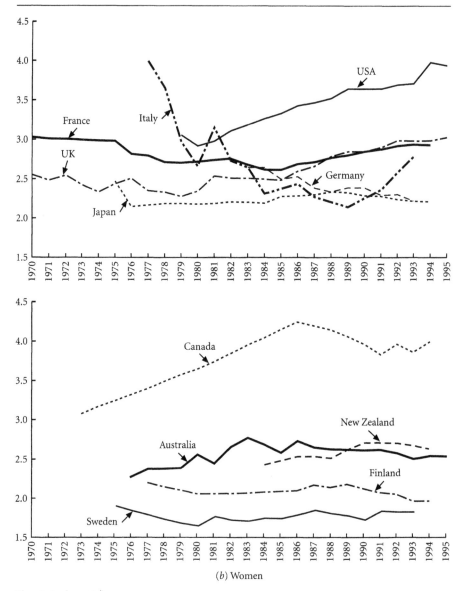

(b) Women

Fig. 4.1. (cont'd)

failure breed failure? Is the worker who has had a long cumulative spell of low-paid employment able to obtain a job above the low-paid threshold if he or she changes employer?

A further complication arises when one has to evaluate the low-pay/no-pay cycle effects, since prior unemployment spells and their duration may be expected to affect the risk of someone being in a low-paid occupation, which, in turn, may increase the risk of the job ending in unemployment. There are two interpretations of this phenomenon—heterogeneity, which is correlated with the initial conditions, and structural dependence, in which the earnings correlates are altered by the experience of low pay, perhaps because of scarring.

Finally, high earnings mobility may also entail high earnings instability. If mobility has only an upward direction, then it is highly desirable. However, if a worker has difficulties in retaining his or her position in the earnings distribution and the risk of joining the ranks of low-paid workers is high, then mobility may not be desirable.

2.   Estimating Earnings Mobility

A common approach to identifying earnings mobility over time is to classify earnings into discrete ranges and estimate the transitions between these ranges. Transition matrices are a useful way to summarize workers' movement over time. Each year workers are ordered from the lowest to highest earnings grouped into equal classes such as deciles or quantiles. The probability that an individual in class i in period t moves into class h in period $t + 1$ can be written as $P_i h$ and the matrix P with elements $P_i h$ such that $\Sigma h P_i h = 1$ is the transition matrix, (see Atkinson, Bourguignon, and Morrisson 1992). In focusing on such a transitions matrix, it is normal to count the proportion of immobile observations on or near the diagonal, while those above (below) the diagonal have experienced upward (downward) mobility. The more individuals' positions change over time, the stronger is the effect of mobility in reducing inequality below the inequality present at time t. Similarly, one may count the number of periods individuals stay below some defined low-pay threshold (Lillard and Willis 1978; Gottschalk 1982). This may be measured by the immobility ratio or the average jump. The properties of such measures have been identified by Shorrocks (1978a) and include normalization, monotonocity, immobility, and perfect mobility. The question is whether we can make valid mobility comparisons if the observation periods corresponding to the matrices are not identical. Unless some correction can be made for different time intervals, there will be a tendency for any mobility value defined over a longer time period to be too high.[2] An extension of the transition matrix

[2] A further problem arises from the fact that defining a low-pay threshold leads to the problem of 'wobble' around that threshold (see Gosling et al. 1997)—that is, relatively small movements in wages may move individuals across the threshold in either direction and this effect may be important when the threshold lies within a dense part of the earnings distribution such that a large proportion of observations is just above and below it.

analysis confronts the fact that many workers face a low-pay/no-pay cycle and these transitions between non-employment and positions in the earnings distribution should be examined too (OECD 1996a).

It is also important to distinguish between permanent and transitory components of earnings changes. At the extreme, one possibility is complete income stratification, in which knowledge of an individual's position in the earnings distribution in year t is a perfect predictor of his position in subsequent years. At the other is complete earnings mobility, in which an individual's probability of being in some discrete earnings class in a given period is independent of prior earnings status. Following this approach, Lillard and Willis (1978) utilize an earnings function of the following form.

$$E_{it} = X_{it}\beta + I_t + u_{it} \qquad i = 1, \ldots, N; t = 1, \ldots, T \tag{1}$$

where E_{it} is the log of real earnings of the i-th person in the t-th year, I_t are time dummies and $X\beta$ represents a vector of personal characteristics such as education, experience, race, etc. The error structure is assumed to be of the form

$$u_{it} = \delta_i + v_{it} \tag{2}$$

and

$$v_{it} = gv_{it} + \eta_{it} \tag{3}$$

where δ_i is a random individual component representing the effect of unmeasured variables, η_{it} is a pure random component, and γ is a serial correlation coefficient common to all individuals.

Lillard and Willis find that permanent income differences represent over 73 per cent of the total variation over a period of seven years in the USA. Of the remaining 27 per cent of transitory variation, over 22 per cent points result from purely stochastic variation and the remainder from serial correlation. Similar results were obtained by Gottschalk and Moffitt (1994) for the variance of earnings in the period from the 1970s to the 1980s. They utilized Friedman and Kuznets' (1954) approach which developed the following equation

$$E_{it} = P_{it} + U_{it} \tag{4}$$

where E_{it} is the i-th individual's earnings, P_{it} the permanent component of earnings, which does not vary with time, and U_{it} is the transitory earnings, which do vary over time. The total variation of E_{it} is the sum of the variance of permanent earnings and the variance of transitory earnings. Thus one can examine how much of the change in earnings can be attributed to a change of the variance in transitory earnings as opposed to a change in permanent earnings.

Buchinsky and Hunt (1996) allowed for the fact that using an average of several years earnings will cause inequality measured over a two-year period to fall, as it reflects the mobility of individuals through the earnings distribution. They estimate that inequality measured over a two-year period is between 7 and 18 per cent lower than the average inequality within the two years. For a five-year period the reduction in inequality is between 14 and 24 per cent.

It is clear that longitudinal data are vital for the estimation of earnings mobility. There may be either retrospective or panel data and each have problems of their own. While the use of event history data can overcome some of the problems encountered, they suffer from the problem of potential recall error. Indeed, Horvath (1982) has pointed out that recall error may even occur in retrospective surveys as short as one year. This may be a problem for earnings in particular, which, in addition, are likely to be distorted by inflation. A particular advantage of panel data is the ability to control for unobservables by the use of fixed effects models.

Suppose

$$W_{it} = X_i \alpha + Y_{it} \beta + u_{it} \tag{5}$$

where X is a vector of personal characteristics that cannot change over time, such as gender, race, and some types of education, Y is a vector of time varying characteristics, such as marital status or job and residential location, and u_{it} is the error term. Additionally, let us suppose that

$$u_{it} = Z_t + z_i(t) + v_{it} \tag{6}$$

where Z_t represents a set of variables common to all individuals in the panel at time t and that affect earnings (w_{it}), $z_i(t)$ represents the unobserved systematic earnings determinants, and v_{it} represents a pure transitory term. Such a model allows the researcher to control for any systematic individual characteristics or unobserved simultaneity biases that affect earnings. This is not possible with forms of data that do not contain a panel element.

While there can be no doubt that panel data offer considerable advantages for the estimation of earnings mobility over other kinds of data, they also raise a number of problems. First, it is necessary to collect data over a sufficient number of years to make examination of changes meaningful and this tends to reduce the number of individuals in the sample. Further, the size of the panel is likely to decline over time, giving rise to possible attrition bias. As Atkinson, Bourguignon, and Morrisson (1992) note, even a loss of say 5 per cent of the sample each year will eventually have a substantial cumulative impact on the proportion of the original cohort remaining in the panel. Attrition bias may lead us to understate the extent of earnings mobility by focusing only on those stable individuals who remain in the sample. Thus, for example, Keane, Moffitt, and Runkle (1988) found that a failure to account for this tended to bias real wages in a pro-cyclical fashion. This is a consequence of workers with low permanent wages as well as those with high transitory wages being more likely to lose their job in a recession.

Related to the above is the question of selectivity bias. This may arise from the fact that mobility is observed only for those who have a positive wage at both the beginning and the end of the period under analysis. Those with a weak attachment to the labour market may be ignored, thereby biasing the results by understating both upward and downward wage mobility (see e.g. Stewart 1998, 1999). A second aspect is that endogeneity bias may result from the fact that an individual's starting position in the wage distribution depends on his or her background characteristics. This is often referred to as the initial conditions problem—that is, conditioning on someone being in a given position in the earnings distribution and then modelling the probability of him or her moving to another position in the distribution in the next period will result in selection bias if being in the initial state is not exogenous. In much applied work two assumptions for the initial conditions are made—namely, that the initial conditions are exogenous and that the process is in equilibrium. A fully satisfactory solution to this problem requires a well-determined model of the process that influences an individual's probability of being observed in a particular position within the earnings distribution in question. A further complication arises from the fact that it appears for many workers there is a pay/no-pay cycle and for a substantial proportion of the population low-pay/no-pay mobility.

Earnings mobility will not be invariant to the prevailing underlying economic conditions. As Gottschalk (1997) points out changes in the absolute incomes of the low paid will be influenced by the rate of economic growth, changes in the earnings distribution itself, and change in mobility patterns. Increases in mean income will tend to reduce the proportion of the population falling below a fixed low-pay threshold as long as there are no other changes in the distribution. In other words, everyone should benefit from economic growth. However, if the mean and the variance of the earnings distribution both increase, we cannot be sure that everyone will be better off. Indeed, in the USA it appears that increasing inequality in the earnings distribution has fully offset the effects of increases in the mean of the distribution such that the earnings of the low paid have declined in both relative and absolute terms. The distribution itself may be influenced by a range of variables including changes in the supply of and demand for various categories of workers, changes in the distribution of workers' personal characteristics, changes in the degree of unionization, and changes in the real value of the minimum wage.

3.   Earnings Mobility and Low-Paid Employment in Europe

There is considerable mobility into and out of low pay and it is important to distinguish between those who are in continuous employment and those who are not. Stewart (1998, 1999), using the first five waves of the British Household Panel Survey (BHPS), has found, for example, that when one restricts the analysis to those who are employees at both the start and the end of the period analysed, the degree of persistence shown is quite strong for those who have been low paid for more than one period, and that the probability of becoming low paid declines the longer a person is higher paid. When one focuses on transitions into and out of employment, Stewart finds that the low paid are more likely to leave employment, so that restricting attention to those who remain in employment is likely to overstate the probability of the low paid escaping from low pay. Therefore, there is a low-pay/no-pay cycle, with one in six individuals below the threshold not in work one year later, and these are more likely to be low paid on re-entering employment. Furthermore, low-paid jobs seem not to be stepping stones to higher-paid jobs, since those previously in low-paid jobs have a lower probability of crossing the threshold into higher-paid employment than those whose previous state was unemployment.

3.1. Mobility in Continuous Employment

Low pay to higher pay mobility. In summarizing the situation in various OECD countries, Keese, Puymoyen, and Swaim (1998) find evidence of similar and substantial levels of mobility across countries. Thus, as a generalization, roughly half the workforce were in a different earnings quintile in 1991 compared to 1986 and somewhere between 11 and 17 per cent were at least two quintiles apart, suggestive of substantial changes in relative earnings. Table 4.1 reports evidence of mobility of low-paid workers between 1986 and 1991, restricting the analysis to those who remained in full-time employment. There is significant upward mobility by low-paid workers, especially when low pay is defined as less than 65 per cent of median earnings for all countries reported. Thus in Denmark only 8.1 per cent of those low paid according to this definition in 1986 remained so in 1991 and over a third of the low-paid group were earning more than 95 per cent of the median. Perhaps surprisingly, the lowest rate of mobility out of low pay occurred in the USA, where 55.8 per cent of the low paid in 1986 remained so in 1991. The authors note, however, that, in their sample of OECD countries over the period 1986 to 1991, owing to the substantial movement into low-paid jobs,[3] the share of continuously employed workers who were low paid at any time was between one and a half and two times as high as the share in a single year. Further, the share of full-time employed in the continuously low-paid sector is much lower than their share in a single year (3–5 per cent compared to 18–24 per cent). Despite this, such workers appear to accumulate a significant number of low-paid years—between two and four years on average. In summary, it appears that, though only a minority of low-paid workers continue to be low paid over a five-year period, this varies substantially across countries. For Britain, Gregory and Elias (1994) found that there is considerable mobility out of the bottom of the wage distribution, especially by younger men. Notwithstanding this degree of mobility, a substantial proportion of workers remain persistently in low-paid jobs, and it is on this group that economic and social policies need to be focused.

[3] It must be recognized that a substantial proportion of entry into low-paid jobs is accounted for by movements from outside full-time employment, including a large inflow of young people from nonemployment or some cases part-time work. For much of the two groups, duration of low-paid work will be short and one aspect of the school-to-work transition. There is, however, some movement from high-paid jobs into low-paid jobs. Thus, for Britain, Sloane and Theodossiou (1996) find that females as well as young persons are more likely than males to be in this position. In accordance with human capital theory, having recent job training makes it less likely that workers will move into low pay from a high-paid job. Other characteristics reducing the probability of downward movement are the possession of higher level educational qualifications, long tenure, full-time employment, and employment in larger enterprises.

Table 4.1. Five-year earnings mobility of low-paid workers who were employed full-time both in 1986 and in 1991

Country	Low paid defined as bottom quintile						Low paid defined as below 0.65 median earnings					
	1991 earnings status of 1986 low-paid workers			1986 earnings status of 1991 low-paid workers			1991 earnings status of 1986 low-paid workers			1986 earnings status of 1991 low-paid workers		
	Still in bottom quintile	Moved to second quintile	Moved to quintiles 3–5	In bottom quintile	In second quintile	In quintiles 3–5	Still below 0.65 median	0.65– 0.95 median	Above 0.95 median	Below 0.65 median	0.65– 0.95 median	Above 0.95 median
Denmark	43.8	27.9	28.3	54.0	24.7	21.3	8.1	58.1	33.9	22.0	53.2	24.8
Finland	39.1	27.3	33.6	43.0	23.9	33.0	36.9	34.6	28.5	37.0	32.4	29.7
France	49.8	28.9	21.4	50.6	30.6	18.8	31.6	48.2	20.2	38.4	43.4	18.2
Germany	45.1	27.6	27.3	52.8	36.1	11.2	26.0	50.0	24.0	51.7	42.9	5.4
Italy	47.7	27.5	24.9	52.8	26.6	20.6	22.9	57.2	19.9	44.5	40.5	15.0
Sweden	49.1	25.5	25.5	57.5	23.4	19.2	—[a]	—[a]	—[a]	—[a]	—[a]	—[a]
UK	41.1	31.9	27.1	64.0	21.3	14.7	39.0	39.8	21.1	61.2	27.2	11.6
USA	52.2	28.5	19.3	57.1	20.0	23.0	55.8	28.2	16.0	65.1	16.0	18.9

[a] Value not reported because the data refer to fewer than 30 observations.

Source: OECD (1996a: table 3.10).

Gosling *et al.* (1997) found that relatively few people from the bottom of the earnings distribution in the UK escape into the top half. Thus of British men who were in the bottom quarter of the earnings distribution in 1991, 50 per cent were still there in 1994 and a further 13 per cent were out of work altogether. Only 6 per cent made it into the top 50 per cent of the earnings distribution. In addition, the authors found that only 50 per cent of the persistence in low pay could be explained by individual characteristics. The remainder of the persistence remains unexplained. Furthermore, at least for the UK the highest probability of exit out of low pay occurs during the first year in low-paid employment and subsequent mobility is at an increasingly slower pace (Dickens 1997*b*). Stewart and Swaffield (1998) showed that the probability of exiting low pay is around twice as high in the first year as in the second, if individuals remained low paid over the first year. Dickens's (1997*b*) findings make a more depressing picture with respect to low-paid mobility. Using the New Earnings Survey (NES) he found that some 48 per cent of the bottom decile remain there one year later. However, similar with other studies, many of the movers leave employment altogether. Only 20 per cent move up the wage distribution and two-thirds of these make it only as far as the next decile. Similar results are reported when he uses the BHPS. Overall practically no low-paid employees moved beyond the median of the distribution. Lucifora (1997) finds that a similar pattern is observed for both Italy and France.

Who is Immobile? It also appears that upward movement is more difficult in countries with greater earnings inequality. Women, older, and less well-educated workers are likely to spend more time than other groups in low-paid employment, while the reverse is generally the case for younger workers. Consequently, these groups account for a larger share of those who have always been low paid than they do of those who have ever been low paid. Thus, OECD (1996*a*) and Keese, Puymoyen, and Swaim (1998) point out that, relative to the average for all workers, the risk of being in a low-paid job is particularly high for women in Belgium, Germany, Japan, and Switzerland, and exceptionally so for youths in Finland and for older workers in Japan and the UK. Furthermore, Asplund, Bingley, and Westergård-Nielsen (1998) adopt an error components framework in which three simultaneous equations are estimated: a mobility equation which describess the changes in rank; an attrition equation, which describes the probability that a respondent's wage is not observed in a period; and an origin equation, which determines the initial conditions of the mobility process. Thus, the authors estimate the year-to-year upward mobility of low-wage earners in Denmark and Finland and find that men in low-paid employment are more downwardly mobile than women, but acquiring occupation specific skills and other human capital tends to be related to upward mobility. However, Van Opstal, Waaijers, and Wiggers (1998) found that in Holland the accumulation of firm-specific human capital contributes far less to earnings upward mobility than does general experience. For the UK, Sloane and Theodossiou (1998) show that human capital endowments are important in assisting mobility into higher-paid jobs and Gosling *et al.* (1997) find that not only does human capital assist upward earnings mobility but also that the most important determinant of movement out of low pay is job tenure.

Another important issue highlighted by McKnight is the extent to which particular occupations are prone to low pay. She finds that the relationship between occupations and earnings and its apparent stability over long periods of time is such as to make occupation an appropriate proxy for low-paid employment when earnings data are not available. Arai, Asplund, and Barth (1998) similarly find that there are typical low-paid occupations. In a study of twenty-five occupational categories in three countries—Finland, Norway, and Sweden—occupation is revealed to be more important than an individual's human capital endowments or industrial affiliation. They also examine the extent to which workers appear to be trapped in these low-paid occupational groups. This appears to be the case for shop assistants, hotel and restaurant employees, textile workers, and cleaners, each of which has relatively flat age–wage profiles.

Institutions and low pay. A final issue concerns the extent to which institutional factors may influence the extent of earnings mobility. Lucifora (1999) argues that the presence of a 'safety net' designed to prevent earnings falling below a certain level may have a significant effect in reducing the incidence of low-paid employment. Such institutional arrangements include minimum wages, union strength, collective bargaining coverage, and unemployment benefits. In Italy small firms, a number of service industries, and workers on temporary or fixed-term contracts have not been subject to such protection and, therefore, have been more prone to low pay. DiNardo, Fortin, and Lemieux (1996) find for the USA clear evidence that the minimum wage compresses the lower tail of the density of wages, especially for women. Their kernel estimates suggest that changes in the minimum wage explain up to 25 per cent of the change in the standard deviation of the log of male earnings and up to 30 per cent of the corresponding change in female earnings.

Using an identical kernel density estimation approach, Bell and Pitt (1998) have examined the question of whether the decline in trade union membership and collective bargaining coverage can explain the widening in the distribution of earnings in the UK over the 1980s. The UK is a good laboratory for such an examination, as trade union membership declined substantially over this period and the gap between the top and bottom decile of male earnings had become larger by the late 1990s than at any time in the previous 100 years. While it is possible that unionization could widen the distribution of earnings because unions increase the pay of members relative to non-members, this effect in practice has been overridden because union membership is more prevalent among lower-paid workers and because unions tend to raise standard rates of pay. Bell and Pitt analyse a number of data sets, including the Family Expenditure Survey 1982–93, the National Child Development Survey 1981–91, and the General Household Survey/British Household Panel Survey 1983–91, and find that between 19.1 and 23.5 per cent of the rise in the standard deviation of male earnings is attributable, according to their kernel density estimates, to the decline in unionization. Therefore, labour market institutions can have a significant influence on changes in the distribution of earnings. Moreover, Lucifora (1999) concluded that for a number of OECD countries used in his study institutional arrangements in the labour market are able to explain a large part of the observed patterns in low-pay employment across countries. Union density, collective bargaining coverage, and centralization of bargaining negotiations all have significant influence on the incidence of low-pay employment.

3.2. Mobility for those not in Continuous Employment

Low pay to joblessness mobility. Evidence shows that much of the observed mobility out of low pay appears not to be into higher-paid jobs but out of full-time employment altogether. In fact, it appears that for many workers low-paid employment is a state of persistence and that low-pay incidence is shared by the same individuals over long periods of time. Indeed, though in several OECD countries a considerable movement out of low-paid employment occurred over the five-year period from 1986 to 1991, much of the movement was out of full-time wage and salary employment rather than into higher earnings. Thus, using the below 65 per cent of median earnings definition of low pay, 40.5 per cent of this group were no longer employed full-time in Germany, while the corresponding figures in the USA and Sweden were 39.2 and 31.6 per cent respectively. In addition, a large majority of those leaving low-paid employment left employment altogether, rather than moving into other employment states (OECD 1996a; Eriksson 1998; Sloane and Theodossiou 1998; Stewart 1998, 1999; Stewart and Swaffield 1998). Thus, in general, movement out of low pay is more likely to mean mobility out of employment altogether, rather than movement up the earnings distribution. Taking Stewart's analysis of the BHPS as an example, 14 per cent of those low paid at $t - 1$ are likely to be not working at t compared to 5 per cent of the higher paid. Further, 33 per cent of those not working at $t - 1$ who become employees at t are likely to be low paid compared to 8 per cent of those who were already in employment. While the cross-sectional relationship between low pay and poverty is not large, as most poor households do not contain any wage-earners, around half of those classified as 'permanent' low paid are in households below the poverty threshold.[4]

Unemployment and its effects on low-pay mobility. Gregory and Jukes (1998) highlighted a further important issue in the UK—namely, that previous unemployment has a detrimental effect on future earnings and thereby explains the incidence of low pay. The authors note that the earnings disadvantage for those who have experienced unemployment is clear and consistent, though the effect progressively decreases if the individual remains employed for more than two years. Long-term unemployment has

---

[4] The 'permanent' low-paid are defined by Stewart as those who were low-paid in at least one wave of the BHPS and higher paid in none—that is, in the waves in which they were not low paid they were not in employment. It should be recognized, however, that the permanent low-paid are a small, though not negligible, proportion of the total sample.

a long-lasting effect on the ability of individuals to earn higher wages. Importantly, the authors conclude that the market prospects of low-paid individuals are bleak. Their earnings are low, they bear a high risk of ending the low-pay employment spell by entering into joblessness, and when this occurs they remain out of work on average longer that their higher-paid counterparts. When the unemployment spell ends, they are again employed in a low-paid job, though the effect of the length of their prior unemployment on their current earnings appears to be weak.

Similarly, McKnight (1998), using British event history data, estimates by logistic regression the hazard rate of low-wage employment ending. If the exit probability declines as a consequence of an increasing duration of a spell of low-wage employment, this could be due to two factors: first, the sorting of individuals of lower ability into low-paid employment; second, true state dependence, whereby the experience of low-paid employment reduces the likelihood of an individual leaving low-paid employment as a direct result of experience of it. McKnight shows that for individuals in low-paid employment the number of spells in low-wage employment and the number and duration of spells in unemployment reduce the likelihood of exiting a spell of low-paid employment. The combination of the fact that low-wage people are more likely to move out of work and that those out of work are more likely to enter low-wage jobs produces a strong relationship between low-pay employment and joblessness. In effect, being in low-pay employment itself traps people in low pay. Such a pattern is also present in Italy. Lucifora (1999) shows that an important determinant of an individual's mobility into higher earnings is the initial position in the earnings distribution. Thus, individuals who start from the lower end of the earnings distribution are less likely to move higher up the earnings ladder compared to those who start from higher positions. Similar conclusions were reached by Stewart and Swaffield (1998) for the UK, who argued that those who have already been low paid for more than one period also find it difficult to move up the earnings ladder.

3.3. Long-Run Inequality and Cross-Section Inequality

The literature surveyed above can be summarized by highlighting the following issues. Although wage dispersion has increased in a number of countries, in some of them, notably the UK and the USA dramatically, there is only limited mobility from low-pay occupations to higher-paying ones for most countries. However, whether mobility is high or low is largely a subjective assessment. In terms of welfare implications, the important issue is whether mobility changes over time so as to match the increased wage inequality. In this case, given that there have been changes in the shape of the cross-section earnings distributions, it may be expected that there may also be some changes in the level of mobility, within the earnings distribution. The issue is to evaluate the extent to which the increased cross-sectional dispersion of earnings represents a widening of life-cycle earnings differentials. It is to be expected that the relationship between a rise in cross-sectional earnings differentials and long-run earnings dispersion depends on the rate at which individuals move through the earnings

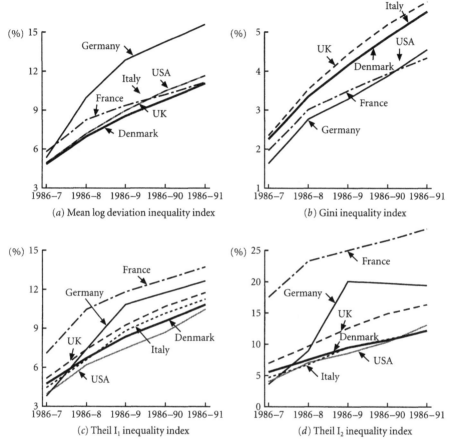

Fig. 4.2. Reduction in earnings inequality, 1986–1991

Note: A value zero indicates no equalizing effect from mobility, since earnings averaged over a multi-year period are no more equally distributed than a single year.

Source: OECD (1996a: chart 2.1). Copyright OECD 1996.

distribution over time. Thus, if earnings mobility has risen over the period, it is possible to argue that lifetime earnings dispersion has not increased in line with cross-sectional earnings dispersion.

The OECD (1997a) attempted to quantify the effect of earnings mobility over a period of time (1986–91) in reducing the cross-sectional inequality. It employed the methodology developed by Shorrocks (1978a,b), which involves comparing the distribution of average earnings over several years with that for a single year (Fig. 4.2). The choice of inequality index appears to matter, with the mean log deviation index and the Theil I index being most sensitive to inequality near the bottom of the earnings distribution. Country rankings with respect to the extent to which mobility reduces earnings inequality also depend on the inequality index selected. In general terms the evidence indicates that pay mobility over the period reduced cross-sectional inequality by 4 per cent to 30 per cent but most frequently by 10 per cent and that there are important cross-country differences.[5] However, this implies that the observed rise in cross-sectional inequality has almost been matched by the rise in the variance of lifetime pay.

Dickens (1997*b*), examining the behaviour of earnings mobility over the 1975–94 period for the UK, found that mobility decreased considerably over this period, with most of the decrease occurring in the early 1980s. The results from this analysis indicate that a large proportion of the cross-sectional difference displays a large degree of persistence and that, although these differences decrease over time, they take a long time to do so. The author concluded that at least half of the rise in the wage dispersion over the previous twenty years could be explained in terms of increasing permanent differences between individuals, and the remainder was accounted for by increases in the highly persistent transitory differences. Gottschalk and Moffitt (1994) report similar results for the USA, whereas for Italy Cappellari (1998) showed that the contribution of permanent differentials variance to the overall wage variance was just above 70 per cent over the period 1982 to 1993. Thus, the rise in cross-section inequality is reflective of increasing lifetime dispersion of earnings and, therefore, low pay appears not to be a transitory phenomenon.

4.   Conclusions

There is substantial earnings mobility in all countries, but this masks low-pay persistence for a substantial number of workers. While, however, earnings mobility has similar features across countries, the share of low-paid workers in the total workforce who remain low paid varies considerably. Thus, Keese, Puymoyen, and Swaim (1998) report that the proportion of the low paid remaining so over the period 1986–91 varied from 10 per cent in Denmark to just over 40 per cent in the USA. They conclude that the factors determining why some workers move into high-paid jobs while others do not is poorly understood, though the studies reported here indicate that education and job tenure play some role. Gender and age differences are also important. The fact that earnings mobility is significantly lower for women than for men can explain part of the gender earnings differential. The evidence for above average earnings mobility for young workers supports special consideration being given to this group in the setting of minimum wages.

Finally, returning to the questions raised at the beginning of this chapter, it appears that the longer workers remain in low-paid jobs, the more difficult it becomes to escape from them, and the longer one remains out of the low-pay category, the less likely one is to become low paid (that is, there is low-pay or high-pay persistence).

---

[5] The countries studies were for Denmark, France, Germany, Italy, the UK, and the USA.

This scarring effect of low pay may result either from the characteristics of individuals themselves (heterogeneity) or from the carry-over of the experience of low pay in one period to the next period(s) (structural dependence). The evidence suggests that the latter is much more important than the former, which has obvious policy implications. As well as having a higher probability of remaining low paid, the low paid are also more likely to experience moves out of employment (the low-pay/no-pay cycle), and this is true for both men and women, the young and the elderly, and the qualified and unqualified. Nor do low-pay paid jobs appear to act as stepping stones to higher-paid jobs. To some extent, therefore, for some workers at least, being in low pay traps them in low pay. Institutional arrangements in the labour market, including union membership and collective bargaining coverage, may moderate these effects by compressing the lower tail of the earnings distribution. Low pay also appears to be associated with long-run earnings inequality—that is, any tendency for the earnings distribution to widen is likely to have an adverse effect on the number of individuals who fall into the low-pay category. There is a clear role for public policy in identifying those most at risk of long-run low pay and providing a labour market framework in which the probability of low pay is minimized.

5   Low Pay and Household Poverty

BRIAN NOLAN AND IVE MARX

A number of major industrialized economies have seen earnings dispersion increase and the incidence of low-paid employment grow over the past two decades (OECD 1996*a*). Many have expressed their concern that, as a consequence, poverty in work has worsened. It is against this background that minimum wages, for example, have moved back into the spotlight. Much of the debate revolves around the question of whether and to what extent low-paid workers live in low-income households, and hence whether minimum wages are effective as a poverty alleviation device. At the same time, in-work benefits and/or tax credits are being introduced or existing programmes expanded, again with the aim of improving the living standards of low-paid workers. In continental Europe, where most countries have seen little or no increase in earnings inequality and where low-wage employment remains less widespread than in the Anglo-Saxon countries, the policy debate is somewhat different. There, prompted by the OECD, enhanced wage flexibility is being debated as a possible cure for persistent high unemployment. But there also exists a widespread perception that an expansion of low-wage employment would lead to a proliferation of the working poor. It is in this context that this chapter attempts to shed some light on the empirical relationship between low pay and poverty.

Low pay is conventionally measured in terms of the gross earnings of the individual, related to benchmarks derived from the distribution of earnings such as half or two-thirds of the median. Poverty status, on the other hand, is usually assessed on the basis of the disposable income of the household, adjusted for the size and composition of the household. The relationship between the two—low pay and poverty—is by no means straightforward, but improving our understanding of it is critical to policy formulation.

Here we draw on data from the Luxembourg Income Study (LIS) database and the European Community Household Panel (ECHP) to show what that relationship looks like empirically in industrialized countries. While most of the results are for full-time employees, the position of part-time employees is also considered. The extent of overlap between low pay and poverty is found to be rather more limited at an aggregate level than might generally be expected, but there is also a good deal of variation across countries. We discuss how this arises, and the factors influencing the extent to which the low paid are to be found in poor households. While these results are based on snapshots from cross-section data, the importance of a dynamic perspective in this context is then discussed. In the concluding section some of the policy implications and priorities for future research are explored.

1.   Measuring Low Pay and Poverty

A variety of approaches can be used to define and measure low pay (see e.g. CERC 1991; OECD 1996*a*). Significant choices have to be made first about the earnings measure to be employed—is it to be weekly or hourly, is it to be basic pay only or are other payments such as overtime to be included? The population of workers to be covered must also be decided—is it to include part-time as well as full-time employees, and is it to include those who work only part of the year? Finally, how is the low-pay benchmark itself to be derived—is some external standard to be sought or a purely relative benchmark based on a point in the earnings distribution itself to be used? If the latter, what point—for example, what proportion of the mean or median? Without rehearsing these issues in detail, probably the most commonly used approach has been to set the low-pay cut-off as a proportion of median gross earnings, most often two-thirds of the median. This has been the benchmark used by, for example, the OECD in recent comparative studies of low pay across countries. In order to avoid the complications of disentangling the impact of differences in wage rates from those of differences in hours worked in the week or weeks worked in the year, that OECD analysis has also concentrated on full-time full-year workers.

Turning to the measurement of household poverty, the definition of poverty that appears to be widely accepted in industrialized countries refers to exclusion from the ordinary life of the community owing to lack of resources. As Atkinson (1985, 1987) and Foster and Shorrocks (1988) emphasize, there is then a diversity of possible judgements about the specification of the poverty line and choice of poverty measure. However, the most common approach is to use relative income poverty lines, derived as proportions of mean or median household income. This is the approach employed *inter alia* in recent studies for the European Commission, Eurostat, and the OECD (ISSAS 1990; O'Higgins and Jenkins 1990; Förster 1994; Hagenaars, de Vos, and Zaidi 1994), and in cross-country comparisons based on the Luxembourg Income Study data such as Buhman *et al.* (1988). Unlike the low-pay literature, the mean is used more often than the median, though there are arguments in favour of each: the most common practice is to use 50 per cent of mean household income, adjusted for household size and composition using equivalence scales. The precise equivalence scales employed may have a significant impact on the size and composition of the group falling below the poverty line (Buhman *et al.* 1988; Coulter, Cowell, and Jenkins 1992), and no method of deriving such scales commands general support. The income concept used is disposable income, income of all household members from all sources minus income tax and social security contributions. Using the household as the recipient unit involves the conventional assumption that resources are shared within the household so as to equalize living standards.[1]

---

[1] For a further discussion of these issues, see e.g. Callan and Nolan (1991), and Van den Bosch *et al.* (1993), Atkinson (1995), Atkinson, Rainwater, and Smeeding (1995).

Table 5.1. The extent of poverty, low pay, and poverty among the low paid, based on LIS data, late 1980s–early 1990s

Country	% of working age population in poverty (below ¹/₂ mean) (1)	% of employees who are low paid (below ²/₃ median) (2)	% of low-paid employees who are in poor households (3)
Australia	12.5	14.5	7.6
Belgium	4.7	10.8	6.2
Canada	12.3	21.4	11.5
Finland	5.0	6.7	4.3
Germany	7.9	12.7	5.6
Netherlands	6.9	12.4	9.5
Sweden	6.6	11.2	5.5
UK	14.5	19.9	8.8
USA	19.1	26.4	24.0

Source: authors' analysis of LIS data.

2.   The Overlap between Low Pay and Poverty

We now look at the relationship between low pay and household poverty in a cross-section perspective, first drawing on the study by Marx and Verbist (1998), which used data from the LIS. The LIS figures refer to the late 1980s and early 1990s, the most recent data sets in the database available for most countries. The poverty status of the household is measured against an income poverty line set at half average disposable income, adjusted for household size and composition. The equivalence scale used to make this adjustment gives a value of 1 to the first adult in the household, 0.5 to each additional adult, and 0.3 to each child (commonly known as the 'modified OECD scale'). Household poverty has to be measured on the basis of disposable income over a whole year, since that is the accounting period for income used in the LIS (except for Belgium, where it is one month). Table 5.1 shows first the poverty rates for the population of working age in each of the countries to be covered. Poverty is highest in the USA, by a considerable margin, at 19 per cent. Australia, Canada, and the UK have the next highest rates, at 12–15 per cent, while the remaining countries have rates of between 5 and 8 per cent.

Given that income is being measured on an annual basis, it is necessary to define low pay in a manner consistent with that accounting period. The coverage of the analysis is therefore limited to full-year, full-time workers,[2] and low-paid workers are then

---

[2] Full-year, full-time workers are defined as those who worked forty-four weeks or more per year, and more than thirty-three hours per week.

defined as those earning less than two-thirds of the median gross wage of all full-year, full-time workers in that particular country. This means that low-paid temporary and part-time workers are not included in the analysis, and countries in the database for which there is no or insufficient information available on weeks and hours worked—namely Denmark, France, Italy, Norway, and Spain—had to be excluded. The incidence of low-wage employment this produces is shown in column (2) of Table 5.1.

We see that the USA again has the highest rate, with 26 per cent low paid, while Canada and the UK are next highest at about 20 per cent. Most of the other countries have about 11–14 per cent in low pay, but Finland is an outlier with only 7 per cent. While countries with relatively high poverty rates for those of working age generally have relatively high percentages in low pay, then, the correspondence is by no means exact. (These estimates of the extent of low pay are mostly broadly similar to those produced by OECD (1996a) and Keese and Swaim (1997), based on a similar definition of low pay.[3])

Column (3) of Table 5.1 then shows the percentage of the individuals categorized as low paid who are themselves living in poor households—our central focus of interest here. The overlap between low pay and poverty is greatest for the USA, where about a quarter of the low paid are in poor households. For Canada, Australia, the Netherlands, and the UK poverty rates for low-paid workers are about 10 per cent. For Belgium, Finland, Germany, and Sweden only about 5 per cent of low-paid full-time (full-year) employees are in poor households. These results suggest that for most countries there is only a limited—and often extremely limited—overlap between low pay and poverty.

We can see how robust this result is by turning to an alternative source of data on the relationship between low pay and poverty, the ECHP survey. The ECHP survey is a harmonized longitudinal survey of households and individuals carried out in the EU member states for Eurostat, the Statistical Office of the European Community. The first wave of the ECHP survey was conducted in 1994 in the then twelve member states. Income data in the survey refer to receipts in the previous calendar year. Eurostat has recently published summary results (Eurostat 1998b) of an analysis of low pay and household income based on data from the first wave, carried out in collaboration with the OECD, which has presented some related results (OECD 1998a). The OECD in addition includes results for the USA based on the Current Population Survey for 1996. Here we draw on these results to provide another set of 'observations' on the relationship between low pay at the level of the individual and poverty at the level of the household.

The Eurostat/OECD analysis also focuses on full-time, full-year wage- and salary-earners, once again to avoid the complications of disentangling the impact of differences in wage rates from those of differences in hours worked in the week or weeks

---

[3] The LIS-based estimates are higher for Belgium and Sweden, in part owing to the fact that the OECD figures use country-specific definitions of what constitutes full-year, full-time work, while the LIS-based estimates employ a single, relatively broad definition for all countries.

Table 5.2. The overlap between poverty and low pay, based on ECHP data, 1993

Country	% of employees who are low paid	% of low paid who are in households	
		Below ¹/₂ median income	Below ²/₃ median income
Belgium	9.1	7.3	17.2
Denmark	9.6	3.1	18.1
France	14.3	7.7	22.6
Germany	18.3	9.7	20.6
Greece	11.9	11.5	21.2
Ireland	18.9	3.3	7.1
Italy	11.7	18.4	28.8
Luxembourg	19.2	9.2	32.7
Netherlands	14.3	11.2	21.0
Portugal	15.4	13.7	23.2
Spain	16.8	10.6	21.8
UK	21.0	9.1	19.9
USA	26.3	22.1	38.4

Source: OECD (1998*a*: tables 2.7 and 2.8).

worked in the year. Low-paid individuals are again defined as those earning less than two-thirds of the median for full-time full-year employees. However, it appears that the earnings measure employed is net of tax and social security contributions rather than the more usual gross earnings concept generally employed in analysing low pay. Household poverty is again measured in terms of annual disposable household income adjusted for differences in size and composition.[4] However, two differences between this and the LIS-based poverty measure now arise: the equivalence scale calculates the number of equivalent adults as the square root of household size, and the poverty line is set at half the median rather than half the mean income.

Table 5.2 first shows the percentage of all full-time, full-year employees who are low paid in these results. Only five countries are included in both the LIS-based results reported earlier and in this Eurostat/OECD analysis—Belgium, Germany, Netherlands, the UK, and the USA. For these, the incidence of low pay is generally similar to that shown by the earlier LIS-based results, though it is now somewhat higher in Germany, presumably because of the inclusion of the east.

The table then shows the extent to which low-paid employees defined in this way are in poor households—that is, below half median equivalent income. The USA again has the highest proportion of its low paid living in poor households, at over 20 per cent. For most of the other countries, the proportion of the low paid in poor households is much lower than that. To assess the sensitivity of these results to the

---

[4] However the data for France relate to gross rather than disposable earnings and incomes.

Table 5.3. The probability of being low paid for employees in poor households, based on ECHP data, 1993

Country	% of employees in households below $^1/_2$ median income who are low paid
Belgium	64.9
Denmark	54.3
France	65.5
Germany	85.0
Greece	86.7
Ireland	89.9
Italy	73.4
Luxembourg	68.9
Netherlands	90.3
Portugal	61.6
Spain	88.0
UK	92.5
USA	87.2

Source: OECD (1998*a*: table 2.7).

location of the household poverty line, the percentage in households falling below two-thirds of the median is also shown. The degree of overlap is now somewhat higher, but in most countries it is still the case that less than one-quarter of the low paid are in these, what one might term 'poor or near-poor', households. The exception is again the USA, where 38 per cent of the low paid are in those households.

These results on the limited overlap between low pay and household poverty are consistent with earlier studies. For example, Layard, Piachaud, and Stewart (1978) and Bazen (1988) found that between 10 and 22 per cent of low-paid workers were in families below conventionally used poverty lines in the UK, while Burkhauser and Finegan (1989) reported about 8–18 per cent for the USA. However, such results have to be interpreted carefully. While most low-paid workers are not in poor households, most workers in poor households are themselves low paid. Table 5.3 shows that, in the results presented by the OECD, generally two-thirds or more of the workers living in households below the half-median income poverty line are in low pay. For many countries, then, only 10 per cent or less of the (full-time, full-year) employees in poor households are not low paid.

What explains this—at first sight curious—pattern whereby most low-paid employees are not in poor households but most employees in poor households are low paid? The crucial factor underlying it is the location in the household income distribution of all employees—whether low paid or not. Table 5.4, drawn from the results presented by Eurostat, shows that very few employees are in fact in households in the bottom part of the income distribution. In most countries, rather less than one in ten

Table 5.4. Location of employees in the household income distribution, based on
ECHP data, 1993

Country	% of employees who are in households located in		
	Bottom quintile	Second quintile	Quintiles 3–5
Belgium	3	11	86
Denmark	4	13	83
France	6	15	79
Germany	7	16	77
Greece	3	11	86
Ireland	1	8	91
Italy	5	13	82
Luxembourg	12	14	73
Netherlands	6	12	82
Portugal	4	14	82
Spain	4	12	83
UK	3	11	86

Source: Eurostat (1998*b*: table 9).

of all employees are in households located in the bottom quintile of the income
distribution. Over the twelve EU countries taken together, only 5 per cent of all employees are in such households. Indeed, less than 20 per cent of all employees in the
twelve countries are in households in the bottom two quintiles—80 per cent are in the
top 60 per cent of the household income distribution. In other words, employees
are not mostly to be found in households in poverty or towards the bottom of the
income distribution, for such households generally do not contain an employee.

It is not then so surprising that low pay is prevalent among employees in low
income households, but that such employees account for only a minority of the low
paid. Again drawing on the results presented by Eurostat, Table 5.5 shows where
low-paid employees are located in the household income distribution. We see that
generally about 60 per cent of the low paid are in the top 60 per cent of the income distribution, and a further one-quarter are in the second rather than the bottom quintile.
Less than one in five low-paid employees is in a household located in the bottom quintile of the income distribution. There is a good deal of variation across countries.
Ireland is a striking outlier in terms of very limited overlap, having only 5 per cent of
all low-paid employees in the bottom quintile. At the other extreme, Luxembourg has
the most pronounced overlap of the EU countries, with 32 per cent of the low paid in
the bottom quintile of the household distribution. The results presented by the OECD
for the USA and shown in Table 5.2, in terms of proportions below poverty lines rather
than in different quintiles, suggest that the overlap is even greater in that case. For

Table 5.5. Location of low-paid employees in the household income distribution, based on ECHP data, 1993

	% of low-paid employees who are in households located in		
	Bottom quintile	Second quintile	Quintiles 3–5
Belgium	10	17	73
Denmark	15	27	58
France	18	27	55
Germany	22	27	50
Greece	10	18	72
Ireland	5	11	84
Italy	18	17	65
Luxembourg	32	21	47
Netherlands	16	13	71
Portugal	13	23	63
Spain	16	18	66
UK	14	22	65

Source: Eurostat (1998*b*: table 10).

most of the countries covered, though, 10–15 per cent of the low paid are in households in the bottom quintile.

To conclude this section it is worth presenting some results focusing on Ireland, but measuring household poverty in a more comprehensive way than by income alone. Measuring income in household surveys is of course subject to error, and income from self-employment poses particular problems. In addition, in measuring poverty our primary focus is on exclusion owing to lack of resources, and income has limitations as the measure of living standards or control over resources. It is, therefore, worth going beyond income poverty lines also to employ non-monetary indicators of deprivation, available in two Irish surveys carried out in 1987 and 1994. A full description of these surveys, the indicators, and the way they have been used is given in Nolan and Whelan (1996). To focus on current basic exclusion owing to lack of resources, look at households that are both below relative income lines *and* experiencing deprivation of one or more of what have been identified as basic deprivation indicators— such as not being able to afford to heat one's house, buy adequate food, or have a second pair of shoes or warm overcoat. What we are primarily interested in here is whether this affects our assessment of the extent of overlap between low pay and poverty.

Drawing on Nolan (1998*a*), we measure low pay once again *vis-à-vis* a benchmark set at two-thirds of median gross earnings, and concentrate on full-time employees. The income concept being used is now current rather than annual, so we include all those who were full-time employees when surveyed, rather than only those who were

Table 5.6. The overlap between low pay and household poverty, Ireland, 1987 and 1994

% of low-paid individuals in poor households	1987	1994
Household below 50% of mean income	8.9	5.5
Household below 60% of mean income + experiencing basic deprivation	10.3	6.4

Source: Nolan (1998*a*: table 10).

also full-year employees. Table 5.6 first shows the percentage of these low-paid employees who were in households below the half average equivalent income poverty line. In either year, no more than 9 per cent were in households counted as poor by that measure. If the alternative poverty measure is applied, of a higher income line but also the condition that the household must have been experiencing basic deprivation, then the figure is only marginally higher. Even with this alternative poverty measure, then, only about 6–10 per cent of the low paid were in poor households. (Once again, most employees in poor households on this basis are themselves low paid.) While we saw earlier that Ireland appears to have an even smaller overlap between low pay and poverty than other EU countries, this does suggest that the limited overlap found more generally is not simply a reflection of the fact that the identification of poor households is based on income alone.

3.   Understanding the Results

The overlap between low pay and poverty is thus rather more limited than often assumed in policy debates, and this is primarily because in most countries most poor households do not contain an employee—whether low paid or not. In order to understand the observed pattern and tease out its implications, however, we want to know what distinguishes the minority of the low paid who are in poor households from the majority who are not. The LIS-based analysis of Marx and Verbist (1998) is of assistance here. With the same data and definitions as Table 5.1 above, Table 5.7 now looks at how the percentage in poverty varies among the low paid by gender and age.

We see that, as one would expect, the association between low pay and poverty is stronger for men than for women. Poverty rates for low-paid men are much higher than those for low-paid women in all the countries included in the analysis. In some, notably Belgium and Sweden, low-paid women are very unlikely indeed to be in poor households. As far as age is concerned, it is again in line with expectations that poverty rates for prime-aged low-paid workers tend to be higher than those for young people, although Sweden is an exception. (It should be noted that these poverty estimates by age and gender are based on relatively small numbers for some countries.)

Table 5.7. Poverty rates for low-paid individuals by age and gender, based on LIS data, late 1980s

Country	% of low paid in poverty by gender		% of low paid in poverty by age		
	Men	Women	Under 25	25–54	+55
Australia	10.2	5.3	4.6	12.2	7.7
Belgium	16.1	1.6	1.5	8.6	0.0
Canada	13.7	9.8	8.9	12.5	9.3
Finland	7.4	3.0	3.6	4.9	0.0
Germany	7.5	4.3	3.6	6.7	0.0
Netherlands	12.8	6.0	4.8	17.7	0.0
Sweden	10.8	2.2	12.4	3.7	1.8
UK	13.0	5.6	4.2	13.3	6.8
USA	32.2	18.3	21.7	25.4	17.8

Source: authors' analysis of LIS data.

Table 5.8. The distribution of low-paid workers by number of earners in the household, based on LIS data, late 1980s

Country	One earner	Two earners	Three or more earners
Australia	24.3	39.3	36.4
Belgium	34.8	53.5	11.7
Canada	21.7	48.8	29.5
Finland	27.0	54.3	18.7
Germany	33.8	42.7	23.5
Netherlands	24.6	52.5	22.8
Sweden	28.5	67.7	3.8
UK	22.1	43.6	34.3
USA	28.1	49.5	22.4

Source: authors' analysis of LIS data.

A crucial influence on the poverty status of households containing a low-paid employee is the extent to which the household is relying on those earnings. Analysis of the LIS data reported in Table 5.8 shows that most low-paid workers in fact live in households with more than one earner, and that this is particularly the case for low-paid women. The proportion of low-wage workers living in single-earner households varies from slightly over one in five in Canada and the UK to around one in three in

Table 5.9. Poverty rates and the impact of social transfers and taxes for low-paid household heads, couples with dependent children

Country	% in poor households	% in poor households before transfers and direct tax
Australia	33.3	38.5
Belgium	39.4	61.1
Canada	27.2	36.0
Germany	15.7	37.4
Sweden	5.7	34.7
UK	45.6	57.3
USA	55.5	57.1

Source: authors' analysis of LIS data.

Belgium and Germany. For the remainder, in a significant number of cases there are not just two but three earners in the household.

These low-paid individuals in multi-earner households are often married women or younger workers still living in the parental home. As a consequence, among low-paid workers, the percentage in poverty is particularly low for married women. Analysis of the LIS data suggests that only about 5 per cent of low-paid married women were in poor households in the UK and Canada and the figure was even lower in the other countries covered, except in the case of the USA. There the figure was 13 per cent—much higher than elsewhere but still low relative to other low-paid employees in the USA. Poverty rates for low-paid men with a partner but no dependent children are also relatively low in most countries, though in the UK about 10 per cent were in poor households and for the USA the figure was 20 per cent.

It is low-paid married men who are 'household heads' and have dependent children for whom the percentage in poverty is generally highest. The extent of cross-national variation here is striking, as shown in Table 5.9. The poverty rate for low-paid household heads with children was over 50 per cent in the USA, around 40–45 per cent for the UK, the Netherlands, and Belgium, around 30 per cent in Australia and Canada, and as low as 15 per cent for Germany, 10 for Finland, and 5 per cent for Sweden. Households having to make ends meet on low pay constitute a minority, but the financial hardship facing such households should not be neglected. A factor contributing to their poverty is that in many countries low-paid household heads are more likely to have a non-employed spouse, or one in temporary or part-time work, than heads in work who are not low paid (Marx and Verbist 1997). This presumably reflects the fact that, among other things, partners tend to have similar levels of education; it could in some instances also be affected by disincentives in tax/welfare systems.

The table also shows that the impact of social transfers and personal taxes on poverty rates may be a key factor explaining these differences. On a purely static basis, this shows for example that Australia, Canada, Germany, and Sweden would all have had poverty rates of about 35 per cent before transfers and direct tax. Hence, the fact that they had such different poverty rates is largely due to the differential impact of transfer and tax policies. For the UK and the USA, on the other hand, it is seen that their very high poverty rates reflect both very high pre-tax and transfer poverty rates and the limited—in the US case minimal—impact of transfers and taxes. (Note, however, that social security contributions, which are particularly important in continental Europe, are not taken into account in this analysis.)

Both the tax and transfer systems, and the role that low-paid earnings play in the income of the households in which the low paid live, will differ from country to country. To explain more comprehensively the variation we observe across countries in the degree of overlap between low pay and poverty, other factors obviously come into play. In general, one might expect those countries with relatively high poverty rates, and with a relatively high proportion of employees low paid, to have a greater overlap than others. This does seem the case more often that not, and the USA is, of course, the extreme case of a country with both high poverty and low pay rates and the greatest degree of overlap. However, the data from the two sources—the LIS and the ECHP survey—do not themselves give an entirely consistent picture of the way the degree of overlap actually varies across countries, and there are in any case counter-examples to the general rule just advanced. The most obvious is Ireland, which has high poverty and low pay rates but, as the OECD highlights, a very limited overlap between low pay and poverty.

The reasons why this comes about are instructive. Ireland had (in 1993) both a very high rate of unemployment (especially long-term unemployment), a large farming sector, and a level of support for the unemployed and pensioners that, compared to most richer EU member states, was relatively ungenerous. This meant that the—relatively large—population below relative income poverty lines was dominated by the unemployed, farm households, and those relying on state pensions. Since household poverty is being measured *vis-à-vis* relative income lines, then, the position of the low paid will depend not only on the income of their own households and how low-paid earnings contribute, but also on the position of other types of household relative to the average or median income. To understand the overlap between low pay and poverty fully, indeed, an in-depth analysis of the overall poverty profile in each country would be required.

4.   Complications

The results described so far show that in most EU countries only a minority of low-paid full-time employees are to be found in poor households, and that among the low paid it is those who are household heads with dependent children who are most likely to be poor. Before concluding that low pay is mostly not associated with poverty, however, a number of features of these analyses have to be emphasized, notably their limited coverage and focus and their cross-section perspective.

Table 5.10. Poverty for low-paid, full-time full-year workers versus all low paid, Netherlands, UK, and USA, 1993

Country	% of low paid in households below poverty line	
	Full-time, full-year workers	All workers
Netherlands	9.9	15.0
UK	3.9	9.7
USA	23.2	33.0

Source: OECD (1998*a*: table 2.10).

As far as coverage is concerned, both the LIS- and the ECHP-based analyses were confined to those employees who worked full-time, full-year. We know that those who are working part-time are more likely to be low paid than those working full-time, and those who worked only for part of the year are probably also more likely to be low paid when in work than those working for the full year. We might also expect that these subgroups among the low paid are more likely to be in poor households than low-paid full-time full-year workers. Analysis of the survey data for Ireland mentioned above shows that when part-time as well as full-time employees are included among the low paid (using an hourly earnings low-pay threshold), a substantially higher proportion of the part-timers are found to be in households below half average income (Nolan and Watson 1998). The same point is brought out by results presented by the OECD (1998*a*) for three countries only, separately for the low paid among full-time full-year workers and among all workers, as shown in Table 5.10. We see that when all low-paid employees, rather than just full-time full-year ones, are included, the proportion in households below half the median is again considerably higher in all three countries.

The focus of the analysis of the overlap between low pay and poverty is also limited in the sense that no account is taken of the role of the earnings of low-paid individuals in lifting and keeping their households out of poverty. The Irish data already mentioned can be used to illustrate the impact of the earnings of low-paid workers on the position of their households *vis-à-vis* the income poverty lines by a crude but revealing exercise. This involves simply deducting the net pay of the low-paid individual from the disposable income of the household, and then comparing that reduced income with the relative poverty lines. Table 5.11 shows how often this would bring the households containing low-paid individuals (below two-thirds of the median) below the 50 per cent income poverty line. We see that over one-third of all low-paid men and 22 per cent of all low-paid women are in households that are above the poverty line, but would be poor if the 'low pay' was not coming into the household. For low-paid women who are widowed, separated, or divorced, about half are in households that would fall below the income lines without their earnings.

Table 5.11. Poverty rates for households of low-paid employees in the absence of their earnings, Ireland, 1994

Status	% in households below poverty line without the earnings of the low-paid individual
Men	37.8
Women	22.2
Married	13.6
Widowed/separated/divorced	50.5
Single	24.3

Source: background data to Nolan (1998*a*).

The extent of overlap between low pay and household poverty at a point in time, as revealed by analysis of cross-section data, is also clearly only part of the story. From a dynamic perspective, the consequences of long-term low pay interspersed with periods of unemployment will clearly be much more serious than those of low pay experienced for a relatively short period, perhaps at an early stage in the working career. Dynamic analyses of earnings mobility and the relationship between earnings, unemployment, and poverty over time are increasingly becoming possible as suitable panel data become more widely available. The relationship between experiencing low pay and poverty that this reveals is a complex one, with that relationship appearing more or less pronounced than in static cross sections depending on the perspective one adopts.

This can be illustrated by the results of analysis carried out by the OECD (Keese 1998; OECD 1998*a*). Panel data for Germany, the Netherlands, the UK, and the USA allowed individuals who are low paid in a given year, in either of two years, and in any of five years to be identified. Table 5.12 shows the percentage of the full-time, full-year employees experiencing low pay who were in households below the half median income poverty line during the period in question. (In other words, with for example the five-year window, income over the five years is used to determine poverty status.) The results show that most employees experiencing low pay in a given year are once again not in poor households, and that when the time period is lengthened the degree of concentration in poor households falls. For example, in the case of Germany about 13 per cent of those low paid in 1993 were in poor households in that year, whereas only 8 per cent of those who were low paid in at least one year between 1989 and 1993 were in households with income over that whole period below half the median. (The UK is an exception here, with a slightly higher percentage in poor households when the five-year rather than the one-year window is used.) This pattern reflects the fact that, among other things, some of those who are low paid in a particular year will be in higher-paid employment in a later year.

While these results are illuminating, they focus on only one side of the coin: how poverty risk varies when we count all those who experience low pay at some point

Table 5.12. Percentage of employees experiencing low pay who are in poor households over different periods, Germany, Netherlands, UK, and USA

Country	Year	% in households below poverty line
Germany	1993	13.4
	1992–93	10.0
	1989–93	7.7
Netherlands	1993	9.9
	1992–93	6.7
	1989–93	4.8
UK	1993	3.9
	1992–93	5.4
	1989–93	5.8
USA	1993	23.2
	1992–93	22.5
	1989–93	21.3

Source: OECD (1998*a*: table 2.10).

during different periods. The other side of the coin is how the risk of being poor at some point varies with the duration of experience of low pay. The extent and nature of mobility over the earnings distribution and in/out of low pay have been the subject of considerable research in recent years (see e.g. Atkinson, Bourguignon, and Morrisson 1992; Gittleman and Joyce 1995; OECD 1996*a*). Again such studies show that how one reacts to the persistence/mobility with respect to low pay depends on one's prior expectations and the way one views the results. Sloane and Theodossiou (1996) report that, in the first and third waves of the British Household Panel Survey (BHPS), only 44 per cent of those who were low paid in 1991 were still low paid two years later. Stewart and Swaffield (1999) present results from the first four waves of that survey that provide a different perspective: of those who were low paid in 1991, 1992, 1993, and 1994, over two-thirds were also low paid in 1994. However, about 1.7 times as many people experienced low pay in at least one of the four years as are low paid in the first year.

From the point of view of impact on household poverty, it then matters a great deal precisely which types of low-paid individuals are and are not likely to move up the earnings distribution. Gregory and Elias (1994), using data for Britain from the New Earnings Survey, show that low pay (defined as being in the bottom quintile of the earnings distribution) is more persistent among prime age and older workers than young workers, and is much more marked for women. Few studies have looked directly at the relationship between persistence of low pay and household poverty, but Sloane and Theodossiou (1996) do report that when one focuses on those who remained in low-paid employment in both the first and third waves of the BHPS, less than 30 per cent were in households in the bottom three deciles of the income distribution.

A particularly important point in the context of low pay and poverty coming out of the research on earnings mobility is that the low paid can move out of low pay not simply by moving up the earnings distribution, but also by exiting from employment into unemployment, illness, or out of the labour force. Stewart and Swaffield (1998) note that in the British data such transitions out of employment are more likely for the low paid than the more highly paid, so restricting attention to those who are employees throughout overstates movement up the earnings distribution. They also conclude that those entering employment from a spell outside employment are more likely to be low paid, and those who had been low paid prior to being outside employment are more likely (than other entrants) to be low paid when they subsequently move back into employment. Such a cycle of low pay and joblessness is also found in Jensen and Verner's (1997) analysis of longitudinal data for Danish workers over a ten-year period. It is important to stress then that, among the low paid, it is not just those whom we see to be in persistent low pay over time whom we would expect to face a heightened risk of poverty.

Taking a life-cycle perspective, the impact of low pay, or of a cycle of low pay and joblessness, over a career is likely to have effects carrying over into retirement. As Atkinson (1973) emphasized, substantial experience of low pay and unemployment while at working age are linked to inadequate pension entitlement and poverty when elderly. This applies both to occupational and social insurance pensions. Hughes and Nolan (1998) show, for example, in the Irish case that occupational pension coverage is extremely low in what might be considered the secondary segments of the Irish labour market, and it is, of course, in precisely those sectors where low pay is most prevalent. With social insurance pension entitlement generally depending on a sustained record of contributions over one's career, a low-pay/out-of-employment cycle may lead to dependence in retirement on a means-tested social assistance pension safety net. In addition, of course, it minimizes one's chances of building up assets such as financial savings or housing, which can play a crucial role in influencing living standards in retirement.

A longitudinal perspective, not just over a number of years but over a working career and beyond, adds greatly to the depth and complexity of the relationship between low pay and poverty. However, what is most important about this type of dynamic analysis is the long-term causal connections it highlights, on which policy will ultimately have to focus if it is to be successful. The ECHP has already served as the basis for the cross-section analysis of the low-pay/poverty relationship discussed above. The longitudinal data to be available from this source will make possible dynamic analyses of earnings mobility and the relationship between low pay and poverty for a wide range of EU countries, which should be highly informative.

Before the implications of these results and the complexities that surround them are considered, one further complication must be mentioned. We have focused throughout on poverty measured at the level of the household, in contrast to low pay, which is of course at the level of the individual. This follows the conventional practice in the poverty measurement literature, but, as mentioned earlier, using the household as the recipient unit involves the critical assumption that resources are shared within the household so as to equalize living standards. If this does not in fact happen, there may be differences in poverty risk between individuals within a given household, which could have particularly important implications in the context of poverty and low pay. Suppose, for example, that some married women who do not work outside the home have a lower standard of living than their husbands, because the husband controls the resources coming into the household. Even with household income above the poverty line, some such women could have living standards as low as those in poor households. For them, working in a low-paid job might not be necessary to lift the household out of poverty, but it might allow the woman herself to escape poverty. The evidence on the extent of such inequalities within the household and of 'hidden poverty' is extremely limited, because the 'black box' of behaviour and distribution of power and resources within the household is such a complex area to investigate (see e.g. Jenkins 1991). Cantillon and Nolan (1998), for example, sought to measure differences between spouses in living standards via non-monetary indicators; the results did not suggest the existence of widespread poverty obscured by conventional measurement practices, but the limitations of the available measures were acknowledged and the need to improve on them stressed.

5.   Implications

The first and most obvious implication of these empirical findings on the limited overlap between low pay and poverty is that any policy aimed at improving the earnings of the low paid as a group will directly benefit only a minority of poor households. A valid response is that the same is true of any policy aimed at helping the working poor, simply because in most countries most poor households do not contain an employee: policies aimed at that subset must be judged on their effectiveness in benefiting that target group rather than their overall impact on poverty. This is true only up to a point, however: the limited (direct) impact that policies aimed at the working poor will have on poverty has to be kept in mind when considering their role in an overall anti-poverty strategy and the extent to which they can only complement other policies—notably those towards unemployment and pensions for the elderly. In this sense policies aimed at the low paid may be similar to those aimed at specific local areas with high poverty rates—commonly referred to as 'pockets of poverty' or 'black spots'. In a number of countries—notably Ireland and the UK again—such area-based policies have come to play a major part in the rhetoric and practice of anti-poverty action. The reality is, however, that most poor people do not live in such areas. An anti-poverty strategy that has as its central planks measures targeted towards the low paid and specific high-poverty areas—whatever their merits and attractions—will simply not assist the majority of the poor.

Unlike area-based policies, policies aimed at the low paid as a group will also have a very substantial spillover: much of the benefit will go to the non-poor. This applies, for example, to a minimum wage, even one that is highly effective in increasing the gross earnings of the low paid without adversely impacting on employment levels. Recent US studies suggest that even there, where the overlap between low pay and household poverty is greatest, increases in the minimum wage have relatively limited impact on poverty or income inequality and substantial spillover to the non-poor (see e.g. Horrigan and Mincey 1993; Mishel, Bernstein, and Rassell 1995; Neumark and Wascher 1997). This is particularly pertinent in the case of Ireland and the UK, which do not at present have national minimum wages but where in each case the current government has committed itself to the introduction of such a minimum. In the Irish case, an advisory Low Pay Commission has recently recommended that the minimum be set at about two-thirds of median earnings, whereas the corresponding UK Commission has recommended a somewhat lower rate. In both cases much of the debate has focused on the impact that a minimum wage in general, and one set at these recommended levels in particular, might have on employment. What tends to be somewhat neglected—by both proponents and opponents of the minimum wage—is the limited direct effect one would expect a minimum wage on its own to have on household poverty. Even in the absence of negative effects on employment, most of the benefits would go to non-poor households, simply because that is where most of the low paid are to be found (see e.g. Gosling 1996 and Sutherland 1997 for the UK, and Nolan 1998a for Ireland). Where any disemployment effects would be felt is also important, of course, but it is far from clear whether the low paid in poor households are likely to be more or less vulnerable than those in non-poor households.

This limited impact on poverty is not in itself an argument against the introduction of a minimum wage, and the overlap between low pay and poverty appears to be a good deal greater in the UK than in Ireland. It is also important to be clear that the pattern in any one country can change substantially over time, as evidenced by the increase in the numbers of 'working poor' in the UK in recent years. As Gosling (1996) puts it in the UK context, a minimum wage is not a good way to redistribute income from the rich to the poor, but it would be more distributive there now than in the past. In either country, a substantial proportion of the working poor would indeed benefit from a minimum wage—but it is necessary to caution against unrealistic expectations. In doing so, of course, objectives other than poverty alleviation—notably promotion of greater equality in earnings between men and women—must also be given full weight.

From the point of view of poverty and policies aimed at reducing it, though, the central role of unemployment in the case of most EU countries must be stressed. As debates about the minimum wage illustrate most sharply, the potential impact of alternative strategies on not just the low paid but on low earnings and unemployment taken together must therefore be the focus of attention. It is important to note in that context that introducing or increasing the minimum wage may also have an indirect effect on poverty in the sense that it could help to draw people depending on benefits, particularly on social assistance, back into work. (This is particularly important if there is more upward income mobility from low-paid jobs than from long-term dependence.) Also, increasing minimum wages could in some instances affect the scope for increasing benefit levels, where the latter are constrained by the level of the statutory minimum wage. This is, for example, the case in Belgium, where it is an accepted principle that the maximum unemployment benefit level should not exceed the minimum wage. Because of this link, an increase in the minimum wage could indirectly benefit the non-employed living on benefits, particularly the unemployed.

The interface between tax, social security, and low pay is a key area for policy, in terms of the potential both for direct impact of reforms on poverty and for ensuring that dynamic behavioural responses enhance rather than erode that direct impact. The tax and welfare systems offer ways of targeting the low paid who are in poor households, and this can look attractive as a way of minimizing spillover and concentrating on the subset of the low paid who are in poor or near-poor households (Scholz 1996; Whitehouse 1996). Indeed, in several countries a minimum wage policy is now complemented with in-work benefits, with the aim of raising work incentives and alleviating in-work poverty. Since its expansion after 1993, the Earned Income Tax Credit (EITC), which supplements the incomes of low-wage working parents, has become a major anti-poverty programme in the USA. The direct impact of EITC on poverty appears to have been quite substantial, especially in terms of reducing child poverty (CEA 1998). There is also evidence that EITC has raised work effort among single women—a remarkable upsurge in work activity of single mothers closely tracks the expansion of EITC after 1993 (Eissa and Liebman 1996).

However, even where such measures do reach their intended target—which may not happen, owing, for example, to problems of non-take-up of benefits[5]—this generally comes at a high cost in terms of disincentive effects. In-work benefits encourage labour participation because in-work incomes are made relatively higher than out-of-work incomes. Also, in the phase-in range, marginal tax rates will tend to fall, providing increased work incentives for those already in work. But the labour supply effects may not be unambiguously positive because in-work benefits are gradually reduced once a certain earnings limit is reached. If the phase-out range is wider than the phase-in region and if more people fall within the phase-out range (which may well be the case), then more people may in fact face increased marginal tax rates. In the case of the EITC, however, this effect does not seem to have dominated the positive effects for other groups (Blank, Card, and Robins 1999).

In-work cash transfers aimed at the low paid may be seen as complements rather than substitutes for the minimum wage. Indeed, a substantial minimum wage may be a prerequisite for in-work benefit programmes to be efficient in the longer run. For example, if low-wage supplements are available, low-pay workers may have less of an

---

[5] Scholz (1996) estimates that a relatively high fraction of families eligible for the EITC—about 81–6 per cent in 1990—have claimed the benefit. The participation rate of the less-generous UK Family Credit is estimated at around 50 per cent.

incentive to bargain for higher wages. They might even put up with even lower pay (Freeman 1996a). As the discussion in Keese (1998) and OECD (1998a) brings out, whether they operate effectively as such depends on the level of the minimum wage and the extent and nature of the in-work benefits themselves. Other factors matter too, such as the shape of the earnings distribution, or the cost and availability of childcare. And there are likely to be important interactions with the other parts of tax/benefit system. All this makes it difficult to evaluate the net effects of a combined policy of in-work benefits and minimum wages. Simulations for the USA, which focus on the EITC, suggest that there are strong complementary effects (OECD 1998a). However, Sutherland's (1997) simulation analysis for the UK brings out the potential for serious disincentive effects and poverty traps. Indeed, withdrawal of benefits or increases in tax and social security contributions as earnings rise may mean that it is precisely the low paid in poor households who fail to benefit from a minimum wage.

This focuses attention on the broader range of policies aimed at helping families with children, including introducing or increasing universal cash transfers (Child Benefit). This can have a more immediate impact on poverty among both those depending on earnings and those on social welfare, without adversely affecting work incentives, but at significant exchequer cost. To give another example, availability of good-quality childcare may be critical in reducing the disincentive to work for lone parents and women married to low-paid men in receipt of in-work benefits. Particularly when one takes the implications of the dynamic perspective seriously, it is clear that, to be effective, policies aimed at the working poor will have to fit within a broad-based anti-poverty strategy, rather than focus narrowly on a specific subset of the low paid at a point in time. This also applies to policies aimed at making labour markets—and particularly wage setting—more flexible in response to persistent, and in some countries rising, female and youth unemployment. A general expansion in low-wage employment is sometimes advanced as a way to tackle poverty by promoting the employment prospects of potential second earners in low-income households. However, countries where low pay is most prevalent are also currently the ones where means-testing in social protection is most important, and they in fact have relatively high poverty rates both among the low paid and among workless households. The context in which low-paid employment occurs is crucial for its impact on poverty, and the same will be true for an expansion in low-paid employment.

6 Minimum Wages and Low-Wage Employment

STEPHEN BAZEN

The role of minimum wages and the analysis of their labour market impact changed in the 1990s. This was partly due to new research in the USA that undermined the apparent consensus that had emerged in the early 1980s. However, it was also due to the lack of convincing evidence that minimum wages are responsible for the high unemployment rates in Europe. These developments led in many quarters to a change of attitude towards minimum wage setting. Instead of being regarded as harming those they are intended to help owing to their assumed negative effect on employment, minimum wages came to be regarded by many as a protective measure for vulnerable workers, and an element of the level playing field for competition among firms. Evidence of such a change is present in the First Report of the Low Pay Commission, which recommended the initial level for the national minimum wage that was introduced in the UK in April 1999.

From a European perspective, during the 1980s the dominance of free market economics, which involved increased emphasis on the role of labour market flexibility, the rise and persistence of the unemployment rates for young persons and low-skill workers, and the shift in the balance of power towards employers and away from workers, led to minimum wages being called into question as a device for setting the wages of the lowest paid. Yet such research that was cited at the time came mainly from the USA, and the few studies for European countries provided very mixed results. Negative employment effects where they were found concerned only young persons.

In this chapter, the basis of the change of position in the USA is re-examined and its relevance for the debate in Europe is assessed. The implications go well beyond the existence and size of any effect on employment and concern a number of issues relevant to the future of research on the effects of minimum wages. These involve the statistical methods used in analyses and the interpretation given to the results obtained—that is, the appropriate theoretical framework for analysing low-wage labour markets—for it is on each of these fronts that the so-called new economics of the minimum wage is distinct from earlier research in the USA.

In many ways research on the effects of minimum wages in Europe has lagged behind research in the USA. This is due to a number of factors. Until the late 1970s, minimum wages were widely regarded as part of the industrial relations landscape and were not subject to the kind of heated debate that has traditionally accompanied plans to uprate the minimum wage in the USA. Furthermore, research into the economic effects has been restricted by the existence and access to the kind of data that are required. However, with the passing of time, more data have been generated and are more widely available. Studies can now take into account the experience of the 1980s and 1990s, and increasingly government statistical agencies have given researchers access to microdata. European initiatives underway will lead to internationally comparable micro- and panel data sets being made more widely accessible.

In order to set the scene, the chapter begins with a brief review of the theoretical mechanisms that describe how minima can be expected to affect the labour market. This is followed by a review of the 'new' economics of the minimum wage in the USA, and then an examination of what is known about the impact of minimum wages in Europe in the light of the US experience. The chapter ends with a consideration of where further research is needed and the form that future research might take.

1.   The Economics of Minimum Wages

The introduction of a minimum wage potentially yields a large number of benefits. It provides protection for the lowest-paid workers; it reduces wage and income inequality; it reduces pay discrimination; it reduces poverty among working families; it improves incentives to work for the unemployed; and it could have positive effects on investment, consumption, economic growth, and government finances (Freeman 1996*a*).

However, the realization of these benefits depends on the minimum having no substantial adverse effects on the economy, in general, and on employment, in particular. If the result of raising the wages of the lowest paid is to leave a large number of them without jobs, then the minimum wage will fall into the category of policy measures that harm those they are intended to help. If, on the other hand, there are only limited effects on employment, the potential advantages will be real advantages.

It is difficult to present a single, representative account of what will happen in theory when a minimum wage is introduced. On the other hand, it is possible to provide an overview of the theoretical reasoning underlying the argument made *against* a minimum wage on the basis that it will harm those it is intended to help by reducing their employment. It is clear that this is a rather extreme view of what kind of reactions can be expected, but nevertheless it underlies much of the case against having minimum wages.

The neoclassical argument against a minimum wage is that it artificially raises the wages of the lowest paid above the market level. The latter corresponds to the situation where firms' labour requirements are identical to households' desire to work. Firms are prepared to hire all persons wishing to work at the market wage and the market wage is sufficient reward for those individuals who wish to work rather than remain outside the labour market. If this situation is altered by government (or any other type of intervention in wage setting) by raising the wage above the market level, profits will be reduced and firms will respond by reducing employment levels. This occurs for two basic reasons, both concerned with competitiveness. First, as a factor of production, low-wage labour becomes less competitive than machines or higher-paid labour. To the extent that firms can replace low-wage workers by machines or by other workers, they will reduce the employment of those workers whose wages have been pushed up by the minimum wage. Secondly, the goods and services produced by firms employing workers affected by the minimum wage will cost more. As a consequence, firms will reduce the scale of their operations, and, in order to limit the reduction in profits, employment in general will be reduced, as will the use of machinery. Certain firms may even find it necessary to close down. In short, the introduction of a minimum wage reduces the employment of the low paid because their labour becomes less competitive compared to other workers or to machines, and because what they produce becomes less competitive compared to substitutable goods or services.

This is an extreme view of how the labour market operates. It precludes a number of adjustment mechanisms through a series of questionable assumptions. One such assumption is that, without a minimum wage, all individuals wishing to work at going wage rates can find work, so that any unemployment is deemed to be voluntary (that is, an individual is voluntarily unemployed if he is not prepared to work at going wage rates and a job is available). More relevant in the case of the impact of introducing a minimum wage is that this theoretical account assumes that firms can sell all they wish at current market prices and that to produce more goods or services would be uneconomic (the cost of increasing output would be greater than the revenue from the extra sales at current market prices). This situation rarely occurs in reality—the vast majority of firms could increase output without needing to increase their prices.

A further weakness in this account of the functioning of the labour market is that it presupposes that firms are constrained by market forces to pay a given market wage. Any firm that tried to pay less would, according to this theory, see all its workers leave to go to other firms. Likewise, a firm that paid above the going market rate would have queues of workers at its gates. In this context, the minimum wage makes firms pay more than they wish for the current level of employment, so that they produce and sell less with higher costs, and profits are reduced.

In the more realistic context in which firms are not constrained, in the absence of a minimum wage, to pay a prevailing market wage, the effect of introducing a minimum wage will still be to reduce profits but need not necessarily entail a reduction in employment levels. Affected firms could react in a number of ways. First, they could simply accept that their profit margins, where these are based on the ability to pay low wages, are squeezed. Secondly, selling and producing less at a given price may not be the most profitable thing to do following the introduction of a minimum wage. There may even be situations, within this narrow theoretical context, in which, once this unrealistic assumption concerning the necessity of having to pay the going market wage rate is dropped, the highest profits are attained at even higher employment levels than before the introduction of the minimum wage (as in the monopsony case). Thirdly, firms could attempt to offset the reduction in profits by raising prices—although the extent to which this is possible will depend on the degree of competition in product markets. Fourthly, at the time of its introduction, a minimum wage could lead to a revision of management practices, the adoption of different, skill-biased technologies, and improvements in the organization of work that improve productivity, reduce unit labour costs, and offset the increase in costs brought about by the minimum wage. This is often referred to as the 'shock' effect.

Once it is recognized that the theoretical reasoning underlying the criticisms of introducing a minimum wage is based on some rather questionable foundations, the conclusion that employment will be reduced substantially has to be diluted. What is clear though, and this is correctly predicted by the neoclassical theory, is that firms' profits will be reduced. One possible reaction is to reduce employment, and, even if this occurs, the crucial issue is the size of any employment effect in both the short term and the long term.

Within this narrow theoretical framework, then, the undisputed consequence of the introduction of a national minimum wage will be to raise a certain number of workers' earnings above what they would otherwise have been and to reduce the profits of the firms that employ them. Furthermore, even if there is a negative employment effect associated with its introduction and this is not large, the income of low-paid workers as a group will rise. The introduction of a national minimum wage will, therefore, transfer money away from those persons whose income derives from the profits of firms affected towards families containing low-paid workers (Freeman 1996a). This is, in turn, will alter spending patterns.

As there are gainers and losers in income terms, losers will possibly reduce their expenditure on consumption goods whereas gainers will certainly increase their spending on goods and services. The reason is clear. Persons deriving income from the profits of firms employing low-paid workers will be households in the middle- and high-income groups—either as proprietors of firms or as shareholders. Such households generally spend a small proportion of their current income on goods and services, and have high savings rates. The low paid, on the other hand, are found mostly in low- to middle-income groups and typically spend a high proportion of their current income on goods and services. It is, therefore, clear that, unless there are substantial employment effects, the introduction of a national minimum wage will increase total consumers' expenditure as the increase in expenditure of households containing low-paid workers will far outweigh any reduction in richer households' expenditure. This modification of the structure and size of consumers' expenditure will have beneficial effects on the economy to the extent that firms will face increased product demand from consumers. Although general in nature, this increase in overall consumers' expenditure will to some extent offset, among those affected by the introduction of the minimum wage, the reduced competitiveness of their goods and services. This is a factor not taken into account in the standard neoclassical framework that is used to show that minimum wages lead to reduced employment.

In addition, one of the consequences for low-paying firms of a minimum wage is that they will have a greater incentive to invest. This occurs first as a result of the incentive to replace low-paid workers with machines that are now relatively cheaper to use, and, secondly, because a minimum wage closes the option of competing purely on the basis of the ability to pay low wages. Firms will have to look at other ways of competing that will probably involve investment. If this is the case, initially firms producing capital goods will expand their output and possibly create jobs. Furthermore, the growth potential of the economy will improve, and possibly lead to higher employment in the future. Again this will mean that any initial detrimental impact on employment may be offset to a large extent over time.

As far as workers are concerned, over time the existence of a minimum wage may mean that employment opportunities are limited, and that firms become more selective when recruiting. As a consequence, those already in work will be less inclined to search for alternative employment and will remain with an employer longer than would otherwise have been the case, and, as a result, labour turnover will be reduced. For those without work, there will be a greater incentive to acquire skills in order to increase the likelihood of finding stable employment. These two consequences will over time improve the supply side of the economy, and enable the economy to grow faster. While it is not possible to know to what extent these longer-run mechanisms can offset any initial, adverse effect on employment, it is clear that the long-run, net effects of introducing a minimum wage could be much smaller than the initial impact and possibly compensate for it in full.

Thus from the basic premiss of a rise in the wages of the lowest-paid workers and the consequent reduction in firms' profits, a number of reactions to the introduction of a minimum wage are theoretically possible. Some of these entail reductions in employment, others may leave employment unaffected or even increase it. Given the absence of a single clear-cut conclusion, the issue will need to be resolved through empirical analysis.

2.   The 'New' Economics of the Minimum Wage in the United States

For a long time, the US experience was cited as evidence that minimum wages reduce employment. Introduced under the Roosevelt presidency in 1936, the national or, to give it its real title, federal minimum wage has been a political football. This is because there is no indexation mechanism, so that increases have to be made by Congress, and this requires the passage of a bill. Each time the matter is raised, there is a lot of debate, with business interests often mounting vigorous campaigns against raising the federal minimum. When a bill manages to get through, it often contains a number of increases programmed over two or three years. This means that increases in the federal minimum wage are irregular, that it sometimes remains unchanged for a number of years (under Ronald Reagan it remained unchanged between 1981 and 1989), and that it often declines in real terms. Graphs of the nominal, real, and relative levels of the federal minimum wage are presented in Fig. 6.1.

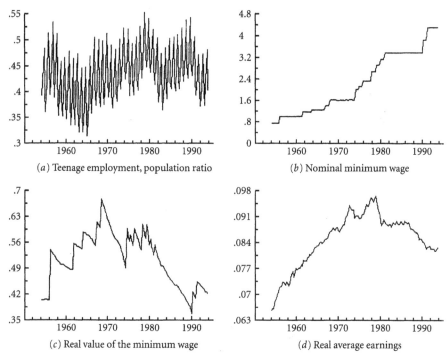

Fig. 6.1. Minimum wages and youth employment in the USA
Source: Bazen and Marimoutou (1997).

Alongside this, there is also a system of state-level minimum wages that sometimes diverge from the federal minimum. Thus local government may have different views from Congress and raise the state's minimum wage above the federal minimum. Furthermore, the federal legislation excludes certain workers and occupations from its scope and individual state legislation sometimes fills these holes.

2.1. *Recent Studies of its Impact*

The labour market in the USA is viewed by the majority of economists, businessmen, and politicians as operating along the neoclassical lines described earlier. Intervention in wage determination is regarded as harmful a priori, and thus the majority of economists and businessmen are against minimum wages. Such a view, however, would need to be supported by evidence that minimum wages have actually been harmful.

The results of the earliest studies gave rise to no clear-cut conclusions. However, following a number of studies of the effects of the federal minimum wage, a consensus emerged among economists at the end of the 1970s. Increases in the federal minimum were found to have a small, but statistically significant, negative impact on the employment of teenagers but apparently no effect on the employment of other demographic groups. A 10 per cent increase in the minimum wage (with prices or adult earnings held constant) reduces the employment of teenagers by between 1 and 3 per cent below what it would otherwise have been (Brown, Gilroy, and Kohen 1982). Teenagers comprise around 40 per cent of workers earning the minimum. *In any terms these effects are small* and may well be worth accepting as a small cost for having minimum wage protection. However, the events of the 1980s and 1990s have since undermined this consensus.

The federal minimum wage was frozen at $3.35 for the period 1981 to 1989, before being raised to $3.80 in 1990 and $4.25 in 1991 (see Fig. 6.1*b*). On the basis of the consensus view, youth employment should have risen substantially after 1981, as the minimum wage fell both in real terms (by 25 per cent) and relative to adult earnings (by 15 per cent). In other words, teenagers became more attractive to employ. However, while youth employment did rise, it did not rise to the extent implied by the studies of the effect of the minimum wage. That is, if a 10 per cent increase in real terms in the minimum wage reduces employment by 1 per cent, then a 10 per cent reduction in real terms should raise employment by 1 per cent. In fact when the experience of the 1980s was incorporated in the study of the employment effects of minimum wages, the impact of the minimum wage was found to be much smaller and not statistically significant.

When minimum wages were raised at both federal and state levels in 1990 and 1991, the studies undertaken for the period prior to 1980 suggested that youth employment should fall relative to what it would otherwise have been. Recent work by David Card and Alan Krueger (1995) in particular, suggests that employment did not fall following the increase in the federal minimum wage, and may have risen in certain states. In fact, the Princeton economists undertook a series of studies of the impact of increases in minimum wages in the early 1990s, and this work has provoked a very heated debate. It is rare for economic research to attract so much attention among politicians and economists alike. Yet the results of Card and Krueger's evaluation of the rises in minimum wages that were implemented at the early 1990s provoked the kind of reaction that 'might be expected by the friends of and defenders of child-molesters', according to their Princeton colleague Angus Deaton (1997).

2.2. The Work of Card and Krueger

The most interesting and widely quoted part of their work was a study of the effect of the increase in the state minimum wage on employment in fast-food restaurants in New Jersey. In April 1992 the minimum wage in New Jersey was raised from the federal level of $4.25 to $5.05 an hour. Such a large increase (of some 19 per cent) ought, according to the neoclassical model of the labour market, to reduce employment below what it would otherwise have been for the affected group of workers. In order to examine this hypothesis, Card and Krueger examined how employment varied in fast-food restaurants (Burger King, Wendy's, Roy Rogers, Kentucky Fried Chicken) between the first and final quarters of 1992. What makes their results so striking is that they used an approach normally reserved for the natural sciences.

In order to assess the effect on employment in New Jersey, Card and Krueger surveyed the same chains of fast-food restaurants in the neighbouring state of Pennsylvania, where the minimum wage remained unchanged at the federal level over the period. In this way, Card and Krueger were able to use restaurants in Pennsylvania as a control group against which they could evaluate the impact of the rise in the minimum wage in New Jersey, given that the groups they studied were in the same sector of the economy in the same region of the USA. Any difference in employment between the two states should therefore have been due to the minimum wage. If employment had declined in the New Jersey restaurants relative to the Pennsylvania restaurants, the American political and academic establishment would not have been at all surprised.

However, whichever way they measured differential employment changes, Card and Krueger could not find any evidence of a negative impact on employment associated with the rise in the New Jersey minimum wage. First, they found that, between the first and last quarters of 1992, more than 53 per cent of restaurants in Pennsylvania had reduced their employment levels compared to 44 per cent in New Jersey. Furthermore, the proportions of restaurants where employment had increased were 41 per cent and 51 per cent respectively. This is the opposite of what would have been expected if the labour market had operated along neoclassical lines. Secondly, the pattern of change was reflected in average employment levels. Employment fell by 9 per cent in fast-food restaurants in Pennsylvania and rose by 2.8 per cent in restaurants in New Jersey. It is difficult, therefore, to conclude that the rise in the New Jersey minimum wage reduced employment in fast-food restaurants. If anything, it appears to have increased it.

2.3. Are their Conclusions Sound?

The results of Card and Krueger's study are in stark contrast to the predictions of the neoclassical and hitherto dominant approach (at least in the USA) to the operation of the labour market. Employment is supposed to fall as a result of such a large increase in the minimum wage. Naturally, some economists and a number of employers' organizations have challenged their work on a number of grounds. The main criticism concerns the quality of the data collection and the representativeness of the sample. The main data used were collected by telephone questionnaire with the restaurant manager before and after the rise in the New Jersey minimum wage. (Card and Krueger incidentally have made freely available all the data, along with the computer programs used to analyse the data, on the Internet.) Employer-sponsored research has sought to discredit this by providing payroll records for fast-food restaurants in New Jersey and Pennsylvania to other researchers that purport to show that the employment did fall more in New Jersey as a result of the minimum wage. However, it turns out that the records do not constitute a random sample, nor do they correspond to the restaurants investigated by Card and Krueger. In fact, the relevant payroll records confirm the result that employment was not reduced (Card and Krueger 1998).

However, moving away from the political aspect of the debate, there is always the nagging question in any kind of survey that the information obtained is subject to errors. In particular, restaurant managers may not give accurate answers to the questions posed, especially when the interviewer is not physically present. However, Card and Krueger go to great lengths to examine the robustness of their findings given the possibility of measurement and other problems with the data. In view of this, and given the sheer number of restaurants that increased employment in New Jersey, it is highly unlikely that their results are simply the outcome of erroneous data.

Other criticisms relate to possible reasons why employment increased and no reductions in employment in New Jersey due to the minimum wage were observed in the Card and Krueger study, reasons that would leave the conventional wisdom intact. One is that it would take time for the impact to be observed and that the period studied (eight months after the rise in the minimum) was too short to observe the kind of negative employment effect predicted by the neoclassical theory. This may be true in terms of the kind of change of technology that involves the replacement of minimum-wage workers with machines. However, the competitiveness effect—the increased costs involving lower sales volumes—should have been observable. After all, the results are measured against the benchmark of what happened in Pennsylvania and thus take into account seasonal variations in consumption and other demand-side movements common to both states. And, as Card and Krueger point out, an employer seeking to reduce employment in the long run because of the higher minimum wage would hardly increase it in the short run, which is clearly what some employers did.

Others have pointed out that the reason for no negative impact on employment being observed is that the increase in the minimum wage had been debated and announced well in advance of its implementation. Firms may already have reduced employment before Card and Krueger's study began (by not replacing people who left, by not renewing temporary contracts, and so forth). There may be some truth in this argument, but it is not sufficient to discount the results obtained. Turnover is very high in fast-food restaurants, and employment could be reduced quite quickly in response to market conditions. As Card and Krueger point out, it is unlikely that an employer seeking to reduce employment as a result of a rise in the minimum wage would need to reduce employment more than three months in advance of its implementation (the first wave of the study took place in February and March 1992; the minimum was increased on 1 April).

2.4. Putting it into Perspective

Card and Krueger's results do stand up to outside scrutiny and there has been no convincing refutation of them. What is more, when they looked at increases in minimum wages in other states and the increases in the federal minimum wage implemented under George Bush's presidency, they were still unable to find evidence of any significant negative effects on employment. This begs the question of how the rise in the minimum wage led to increased employment in New Jersey, and why no significant reduction in employment is observed elsewhere when the minimum wage is raised. Such conclusions are not generally compatible with the neoclassical view of the operation of the labour market.

The conclusion that employment increased is found for fast-food restaurants. *It is not a conclusion found for the whole economy or for a particular group of workers such as young persons.* One explanation is that young persons in all sectors benefit from minimum wage increases (even if there are limited employment reductions), and they spend some of their extra income in fast-food restaurants. This would account for a positive link between the rise in the minimum wage and employment. A second possibility is that employers were able to pass on higher costs as price increases and these did not deter customers. This alone would not account for a rise in employment. A third reason advanced is that employers have power in the labour market and, in the absence of an effective minimum wage, are able to keep wages down. An increase in the minimum wage reduces the scope of their wage-setting power, thereby reducing profits. In certain circumstances (the monopsony situation), the highest profits in the presence of a minimum wage involve the employer expanding employment and output. (Profits are lower than before the increase in the minimum wage, but are higher than those corresponding to previous output and employment levels.)

While employment was found to increase in fast-food restaurants, Card and Krueger find no significant negative effects on employment in other contexts in the USA as a result of recent increases in minimum wages. This conclusion is less difficult to account for and is less contentious than the results of the study of fast-food restaurants. What this evidence does not imply is that the minimum wage can be raised without limit or that a higher minimum wage might not have significant negative employment effects. As the graphs in Fig. 6.1 above show, the US minimum wage after the upratings of the beginning of the 1990s was at a lower level relative to average earnings than it was in 1981 and was lower in real terms than it was in 1960, 1970, or 1980. A minimum wage that does not really bite cannot do much damage.

Subsequent studies find mixed results. For example, Schmitt and Bernstein (1998) present three different tests of the impact of the increase in the federal minimum wage that occurred in October 1996, when the federal minimum was raised from $4.25 to $4.75. Their evidence concerns the whole of the USA and not particular states or sectors, and suggests that there was little effect on employment, with most estimates being statistically insignificant at conventional levels. There is some evidence of small, but statistically significant negative effects on the employment of teenagers. Bazen and Marimoutou (1997), using time series data, find results that are similar to the earlier findings summarized in Brown, Gilroy, and Kohen (1982). The advantage of using time series data is that, if the impact of minimum wages occurs with a lag, this will be detected in the estimated model. The reason that studies since 1982 do not identify any effect of minimum wages on teenage employment is that they fail to take account of the seasonality and underlying trends in teenage employment in a statistically satisfactory manner. In a study using quarterly data for the period 1956–93, Bazen and Marimoutou find that a 10 per cent increase (decrease) in the real value of the minimum wage will reduce (increase) teenage employment by 1 per cent in the short run, and by 2 per cent in the long run, other things being equal. Thus, the main findings of Card and Krueger may be limited to particular sectors and states they studied or perhaps concern only the short-run impact. Nevertheless, neither of the above-mentioned studies (Bazen and Marimoutou 1997; Schmitt and Bernstein 1998) finds evidence of large employment effects.

3.   The Economics of Minimum Wages in Europe

In terms of the analysis of the labour market impact of minimum wages, the US experience is of limited scope. The minimum wage is low relative to average earnings, it is not indexed to prices or earnings, it is uprated irregularly at the will of Congress, and it does not cover all of the workforce. This is the opposite of what happens in those European economies where minimum wages exist. A possible exception is the case of the now defunct Wages Councils system in the UK.

3.1. The United Kingdom

At the time of their abolition in August 1993, the Wages Councils set legal minimum wage rates in a limited number (twenty-six) of sectors. In many ways, Wages Councils were a form of surrogate collective bargaining, and operated in sectors where the normal pay bargaining process was underdeveloped or insufficiently effective. The main difference was their tripartite nature. Each council consisted of equal numbers of employer and employee representatives and up to three independent members nominated by the Secretary of State for Employment. From 1986 onwards, each council set a single minimum wage for its sector and a rate for overtime work, along with provisions for holidays and other working conditions. The council would meet each year to fix the minimum wage, and, once set, the minimum wage was a legal minimum. The level of the minimum wage in each sector was determined in a similar way to collective bargaining, with the exception that, where no agreement could be reached, the independent members would adjudicate. As in the USA, the rates set were low and only a minority of the 2.5 million workers covered were actually paid the minimum— the vast majority earned more.

There were a number of lacunae in the protection afforded by the Wages Councils. Firstly, from 1986 onwards, the minimum wage rates applied only to workers aged 21 or over. Secondly, a significant number of firms underpaid workers even with these very low wage rates. In theory, a Wages Inspectorate existed to enforce payment of the legal minimum wage rates set by the Wages Councils. In practice, prosecution was rare and the fines involved were negligible. For example, in the period 1979–91, more than 100,000 firms were found to be underpaying their workers, and only eighty-two were prosecuted. Thirdly, the Wages Councils system had not evolved to cover emerging low-paying sectors such as contract cleaning and security. These limitations combined with the setting of relatively low minimum wage rates meant that the effectiveness of the Wages Councils as a system of minimum wage protection was limited.

At the time of their abolition, relatively few studies had examined their impact on employment. An internal Department of Employment study found that male employment in the clothing sector had been reduced by Wages Councils minimum wage rates, and Kaufman (1989) found a very small, negative impact on female employment in a group of Wages Councils sectors over a number of periods. More recently, a number of other studies using more reliable data (and for a longer period of time) found no evidence that employment had been reduced by the Wages Councils. Machin and Manning (1994) and Dickens, Machin, and Manning (1994) found that, if anything, employment was increased by minimum wages in these sectors (although the effect is not generally statistically significant). These latter results are thus similar to those found by Card and Krueger.

The UK experience of minimum wage legislation, however, is not representative of European practice in that the Wages Councils fixed a variety of relatively low minimum rates in a limited number of sectors and suffered a good deal of non-compliance. Where statutory minimum wages exist in Europe, they are applicable nationally at a single rate (though with lower rates for young persons), and, unlike the United States, in the main, they are regularly uprated. In the remainder of this section we review the experience of France and a number of other European countries.

3.2. France

In France the minimum wage is set at a much higher level relative to average earnings, has risen constantly in real terms since the 1960s, is indexed on prices and partially on earnings, and affects all workers. What makes the French minimum wage system particularly interesting as a case study is that, once the minimum wage is increased, it cannot be reduced in real terms. In other words, any increase is locked in and it would require a major change of legislation simply in order to freeze the minimum wage. It is the opposite situation to that in the USA, where legislation is required simply to increase the minimum wage. This is because the legislation introduced in 1970 (which modified the original minimum wage legislation of 1950) requires that: (a) the minimum wage be increased fully in line with prices every time the monthly retail price index rises by 2 per cent since the last uprating, so that in times of high inflation there may be five or six rises a year; (b) the minimum wage must be increased by at least half the growth of real average manual workers' earnings (as measured by a monthly earnings index) for the twelve months up to 1 July of each year.

Therefore, if the minimum indexation requirements are observed, the minimum wage will rise fully in line with inflation and to some extent in line with real earnings growth. In relative terms, the minimum wage will decline as a proportion of average earnings (being only partially indexed on manual workers' earnings). In fact, the minimum wage increased relative to average earnings after 1970, feel back slightly in relative terms over the latter half of the 1980s, and stabilized during the 1990s. These types of movement occur because the minimum wage can also be increased on a discretionary basis and such increases have been the rule rather than the exception. In the period 1970–80, discretionary increases were implemented in every year except for 1986–8 and 1993–5. Sometimes these were sufficient to raise the relative value of the minimum wage, and occasionally these discretionary increases made the overall annual increase substantial (the minimum wage was increased by 10 per cent in June 1981 following the election of François Mitterrand).

Unemployment in France grew steadily over the 1980s and 1990s, especially among the young and unskilled. Furthermore, and in contrast to the UK during this period, the rate of unemployment among women was as high as for men. In the light of this high rate of unemployment and the specific groups affected, the OECD among others argued that the minimum wage was one of the main causes, particularly as the minimum was increased relative to average earnings during the early half of the 1980s when unemployment took off and then increased steadily in real terms during the 1990s. Youth employment in particular declined over the 1980s and 1990s, and young persons are one of the main groups directly affected by the minimum wage.

However, while it may be tempting to conclude on a theoretical basis that the rise in unemployment in France is associated with the rise in the minimum wage, there is little empirical evidence that minimum wages have had adverse effects on employment. Recall that it is necessary to control for other influences on employment when attempting to measure the impact of the minimum wage. The first studies using data up to 1979 found very mixed results and the most reliable of these found no evidence of significant effects on employment (Martin 1983). When the data for the 1980s became available (a period in which the minimum wage was increased substantially), three studies independently found that young persons' employment had been reduced as a result of the rise in the minimum wage, but that this effect was small in size (Benhayoun 1990; Bazen and Martin 1991; Ducos and Plassard 1991). It could account for only a small fraction of the decline in youth employment and no effect was identified on adult employment. (Since then one of the studies has been repeated using the latest revised data and this has led to the robustness of the previous findings being questioned—see Benhayoun 1994.) Research undertaken since then, however, has reinforced the basic finding that young persons' employment may have been reduced to a limited extent especially in the first half of the 1980s by the rise in the minimum wage in sectors that are most concerned by the minimum wage (Bazen and Skourias 1997).

Whichever dimension of the impact on employment is examined, the overall conclusion is that the minimum wage in France may have reduced employment to a limited extent for young persons and in certain low-paying sectors (Bazen and Benhayoun 1995; Bazen, Benhayoun, and Skourias 1995). There is no possible way that the minimum wage can be held responsible for the rise in unemployment that occurred during the 1980s and 1990s on the basis of any of the studies.

3.3. The Experience of Greece, the Netherlands, Portugal, and Spain

There are far fewer studies for other European countries. Koutsogeorgopoulou (1994) finds evidence of small negative effects on young persons' employment and industrial employment in Greece, and Ribeiro (1995) finds some evidence that minimum wages reduce the employment of young women in Portugal. However, as is clear from the review of studies for the USA, the UK, and France, more evidence is required for these conclusions to be regarded as robust. In the Netherlands, for example, there have been a number of studies undertaken, but the results are very mixed. Van Soest (1989, 1994) finds evidence of negative effects on the employment of young persons, whereas Salverda (1992) concludes that there is no significant effect.

A recent study presents the results of four different tests of the effect that minimum wages have had on employment in Spain (Dolado, Felgueroso, and Jimeno 1998). Teenage employment is found to be reduced in a similar way (sign and magnitude) to that which is found using time series data for France and the USA. Using cross-section data, it is found that teenage employment declined more noticeably between 1990 and 1994 in regions where a large proportion of workers are low paid and therefore paid close to the minimum wage. Thus, while more work on these and other European countries is needed, it is difficult to avoid the conclusion that in Europe minimum wages have a small, but nevertheless negative effect on the employment of young persons.

4.   The Impact of Minimum Wages on the Distribution of Earnings

One of the most striking features of the US labour market since the early 1980s is the substantial widening of the distribution of earnings. Two recent studies have attributed part or all of the widening at the bottom end to the decline in the real value of the minimum wage (DiNardo, Fortin, and Lemieux 1996; Teulings 1998). In Europe, however, apart from the UK, earnings distributions have not widened in the same way and this may be due to the manner in which minimum wages have been set. As with previous examples, the experience of the UK is similar, though on a smaller scale, to the situation in the USA. For example, Machin (1997) finds that the decline in Wages Councils minimum rates and the erosion of collective bargaining coverage contributed to the rise in earnings inequality in the UK.

4.1. Minimum Wages and Earnings Differentials

The introduction of a minimum wage, depending on its level, will affect different types of employee. This is because the distribution of wages has, at least in the relevant

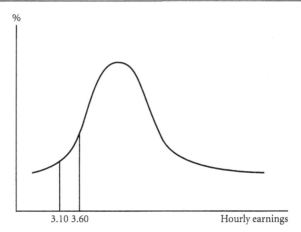

Fig. 6.2. Minimum wages and the distribution of earnings

range, a bell shape (see Fig. 6.2). There are relatively few people earning substantially less than the minimum wage, but a relatively large number earning just below it. So, while some workers will see their wages rise substantially (from less than £3 to £3.60), many will have more modest rises of less than 10 per cent. The first impact of a minimum wage is to raise the pay of affected workers up to the minimum wage. If there are no further effects, this creates a pile-up of workers or spike at that point in the distribution of earnings. If there are substantial employment effects, the size of the spike will be smaller as workers laid off disappear from the distribution and enter unemployment. If differentials among the lowest paid are restored to any extent, the spike will be smaller as some workers pass into the zone above the minimum wage. Such a spike is observed in almost all earnings distributions where minimum wages are set. This is evidence of the compression of differentials at least in the short run.

There will in general be further, indirect effects because wage differentials do not simply represent the relative scarcity of different types of worker. Wage rates are often negotiated or determined within a company wages policy to reflect notions of fairness, to reward loyalty and the taking of responsibility, to provide incentives, and so forth. A minimum wage, by altering the lowest layer of differentials, will therefore generate wage increases for workers not directly affected. Some differentials will need to be maintained and thus the overall increase in firms' wage bills will be larger than the direct effect. At the same time, firms will want to limit the extent of any knock-on effects so that, unless a large proportion of a firm's workforce is directly affected, the extent to which differentials are restored will be limited to the lower part of the pay ladder (see below). The notion, therefore, of a single category of workers in a labour market with a single market wage rate being perturbed by the introduction of a minimum wage is a dangerous simplification. Even a large number of distinct labour markets each with its own market-determined equilibrium wage rate is likely to misrepresent what happens when a minimum wage is introduced or uprated.

In order to have an inequality-reducing effect on the distribution of earnings, a minimum wage must represent an effective floor in terms of coverage and compliance. Over time, it will need to be uprated regularly in order to remain effective. Bazen, Gregory, and Salverda (1998a) examine the evolution of the earnings distributions for the UK, France, and the Netherlands over the period running from the middle of the 1970s to the middle of the 1990s. In the former country the distribution of earnings widens considerably, whereas in the latter two the distribution becomes more compressed. When the overall effect is analysed in terms of the upper and lower halves of the distribution, there is a clear difference between the UK, where the lowest decile declines substantially relative to median earnings, and the other two countries, where it remains fairly stable over the period taken as a whole. These evolutions can be linked to the role that the minimum wage plays in providing a floor to the earnings distribution and the way in which France pursued an 'active' minimum wage policy whereas in the Netherlands the minimum wage and the structure of youth differential rates was manipulated in order to give firms an incentive to employ low-paid workers.

4.2. Minimum Wages and Collective Bargaining

One of the most striking and well-established findings concerning the minimum wage in France is its effect on wage differentials. As pointed out above, the minimum creates a spike at that point in the distribution of earnings. If differentials among the lowest paid are restored to any extent, the spike will be smaller as some workers pass into the zone above the minimum wage. In France there is clear evidence of the minimum wage having relatively limited knock-on effects and a small impact on youth employment, so that the spike is clearly observable. In fact, the rise in the minimum wage at the beginning of the 1980s caused the proportion of workers earning less than two-thirds of median earnings to fall from 17 to 13 per cent between 1979 and 1985 and to remain stable at that level thereafter. Furthermore, unlike in the UK, because of the minimum wage the position of the workers 10 per cent from the bottom of the earnings distribution relative to the worker in the middle—the ratio of the lowest decile to median earnings—did not fall away under the pressure of rising unemployment.

One unintended outcome of minimum wage policy in France in the 1980s was that it caught up with and overtook the wage rates set in collective agreements. By 1990, out of the 164 major collective agreements, 134 contained wage rates that were lower than the national minimum wage. This occurred because, in the face of high unemployment and a tight macroeconomic policy stance aimed at controlling inflation, employers were able to negotiate very low wage increases, generally lower than the rate of growth of productivity. For the lowest paid, the national minimum wage became the determinant of wage increases.

While the collectively agreed basic wage may be below the national minimum wage in France, employers are legally obliged to pay the latter. This gave rise to problems of maintaining differentials among workers, and also meant that some workers who would have normally moved up the collectively determined wage scale were remaining on the national minimum wage for a number of years. In 1989, the minimum wage as a proportion of average earnings stood at 45 per cent, the same relative level as in 1978, but affected twice as many workers. This situation caused the French government to request specifically that the social partners renegotiate the lower segments of basic wage scales, which they duly did. The proportion of workers earning the national minimum wage fell substantially between 1989 and 1994. However, the problem had not been resolved, since many collective agreements were only partially renegotiated, so that when, following the election of President Chirac, the national minimum wage was raised by 4 per cent, the proportion of minimum-wage workers went back up to its 1989 level.

Thus, while there is evidence of only a limited impact on employment, the minimum wage in France appears to create problems for collective bargaining when employers have the upper hand in negotiations and the government pursues an active minimum wage policy. Knock-on effects owing to the restoration of differentials are limited to the lower segment of the earnings distribution precisely because employers resist them.

5.   The Future of Minimum Wage Research

The conclusion that emerges from existing research—when expressed in the simplest terms—is that minimum wages have a small, verging on negligible, impact on employment but a marked effect on the distribution of earnings. This conclusion, which may itself be modified by future research, is based mainly on the US experience and to a lesser extent that of the UK and France. While the small amount of research on other countries will need to be developed, further research is also required on the UK and France. The research that constitutes the so-called 'new' economics of the minimum wage is based on new approaches with mainly cross-section data, with a natural experiment based approach.

What kind of data are required? It is important to bear in mind that the workers affected by minimum wages do not constitute a homogeneous group. It is true that young workers, women, and immigrants are disproportionately present, but there are also some prime-age males. Thus, for any given minimum wage target, the population affected will be heterogeneous—some workers will have their pay increased by a lot, others by a few per cent. Affected workers will be spread across different sectors, work in firms of different sizes, and undertake different types of work. They will come from various age groups and have different levels of experience. A country's statistical services do not and cannot collect data on employment and earnings that correspond to the concept of a labour market adopted in orthodox theoretical analysis.

Cross-section and panel data have the advantage of taking account of the hetero-geneity of the population that is affected by minimum wages. The variation in the earnings and employment of the affected population following a rise in the minimum wage is directly observable. However, even when there are data for a number of suc-cessive years, only the short-run impact of minimum wage increases can be detected from this information base. Firms may change technology, adopt a medium-term strategy of reducing their reliance on minimum wage workers, or adjust the size of their labour forces only slowly.

On the other hand, aggregate time series data are able to detect effects in both the short and long runs, albeit at the expense of having to use variables corresponding to a group of workers. A further complication arises in that, when seeking to establish the impact of minimum wages on employment, for example, over a period of time, it is necessary to recall that many factors other than wages affect employment such as macroeconomic policies, technological changes, interest rates, the price of raw mater-ials, and so forth. Thus, if employment falls at the same time that the minimum wage is introduced or updated, it does not necessarily mean that the minimum wage has destroyed jobs. In order to isolate the effect of the minimum wage on employment, it is critical that the effect of these other factors be taken account of and somehow dis-sociated. The impact has to be measured against the benchmark of the level of employ-ment that would have occurred without the minimum wage. Traditionally this has been achieved by using observations on employment, the minimum wage, and other likely influences for a number of years, and estimating the effect of an increase in the minimum wage on employment holding other influences constant. The latter effect is identified on the assumption that, in periods when the minimum wage increased substantially, the employment effect should be more pronounced.

One of the factors that will influence the use of the various types of data is their availability. Individual data are more widely available and more surveys are under-taken. Panel data sets are also becoming more frequent and European initiatives to provide access to researchers to harmonized panel data should enable both the deepening and widening of minimum wage research. As far as time series data are concerned, for many European countries, data on young persons' employment exist for a relatively short period—typically less than thirty years—and are sometimes of variable quality, being subject to revisions based on population censuses and modified owing to changes in policy measures aimed at reducing unemployment. Nevertheless, as time goes on, more data will be generated and the opportunities for doing min-imum wage research should improve.

How should we analyse the data? The work of Card and Krueger used predominantly a 'natural experiment' type approach to analysing the impact of the minimum wage. The basic premiss is to emulate the experimental approach used in natural sciences such as chemistry and biology by examining what happens to the employment and earnings of workers affected (the 'treatment' group) relative to otherwise similar workers who are not affected by the minimum wage (the 'control' group). The impact of the minimum wage is, therefore, assessed against the benchmark of what happens to the control group. The main conditions for a reliable analysis are that the control and treatment groups be as similar as possible and that there is no systematic 'sorting' of workers into the groups. This has the advantage of comparing outcomes and thus not having to specify a priori a structural model of labour market behaviour. However, this approach may be appropriate to the situation in the USA where state minimum wage laws operate independently of the federal legislation, but it is difficult to apply in Europe.

A national minimum wage does not discriminate among similar workers, since it applies equally to all low-paid workers. The approach can be sensibly applied only where minimum wages legally exclude certain low-paid workers, allowing a 'control' group. This is partly the case in the USA at the federal level, but is particularly appropriate in the context of state minimum wages where an increase can occur in one state but not in adjacent ones. In this case, low-paid workers in adjacent states can serve as control groups against which the employment of the same workers in the state under consideration can be gauged. Secondly, in order to identify differential treatment of otherwise similar groups, it really requires a large, discrete increase in the minimum wage rather than a small, indexation-based increase of a couple of percentage points. This again limits the applicability of this type of method in that, apart from going back to the date at which it was introduced, increases in an effective, continually binding minimum wage are unlikely to be adapted to this kind of approach. The introduction of a national minimum wage in the UK, however, provides the right kind of framework.

The introduction of a national minimum wage of £3.60 an hour in April 1999 provides an excellent opportunity for testing the labour market impact of minimum wages for a number of reasons. First, there had been no minimum wage legislation outside agriculture since 1993, and so it is in many ways a unique opportunity, since it is rare to be able to study the impact at the moment of its introduction. Secondly, employment and wages had been determined relatively freely since then, and the UK labour market has come to be regarded as one of the most flexible in Europe. Thirdly, the minimum wage affected a non-negligible proportion of the labour force. The Low Pay Commission (1998) estimated that just under two million workers were directly affected, of whom about 70 per cent are part-time workers and three-quarters are female. Fourthly, there are a large number of data sets that can be used and no doubt case studies have been undertaken. These can be used in conjunction with the methods similar to those mentioned above, but not a strict 'natural experiment', as used for the state minimum wage legislation in the USA.

In the absence of a natural experiment type of situation, research can proceed on two bases. In the first economic theory is used to derive a structural model, the estimated parameters of which enable the impact of minimum wages to be determined. This is a difficult exercise in that the data generation process may well be at odds with the structural model if the latter is derived strictly from economic theory. Further-more, assumptions made when deriving the model can often constrain the nature of the impact of minimum wages. A second alternative lies in between the theory-free natural experiment type approach and the theory-dominated structural approach. This involves specifying a loose and fairly general reduced-form relationship as a starting point and then testing this against the properties of the data. The data will then determine the nature and size of the effects of minimum wages. A problem often encountered with this approach is that the outcome is dependent to a large extent on the quality of the data, and, as was mentioned above, existing data sets do not always provide the kind of information that is required to undertake the exercise properly.

How should we interpret the results? The research findings presented above do not sit well with the standard neoclassical approach to the labour market outlined earlier. Firms can apparently increase the wages of the lowest-paid workers and, by and large, continue to employ them. What does this imply about the operation of the low-wage labour market? A number of possibilities have been suggested. Following the work of Card and Krueger, and Dickens, Machin, and Manning, a variant of the monopsony case has been suggested as an explanation for the observation that employment is seen to rise following an increase in the minimum wage. Individual firms are assumed to face upward-sloping labour supply curves. A minimum wage, if set in the relevant range, can result in an increase in employment. The applicability of this view is still a matter of debate. It does explain the observed outcome and it is well grounded theoretically—firms maximize profit, workers behave rationally and there is a point of equilibrium. On the other hand, in order to recruit an additional worker, do firms really have to increase the wage offered not only to the worker but also to existing workers?

A second approach is based on the notion that there are wider effects that are not taken into account. Theoretically, the effects of minimum wages are usually presented in a partial equilibrium approach. However, minimum wage workers are found in many sectors of the economy and wage changes will have effects on the pattern of product demand. An increase in the minimum wage will alter not only the cost of goods produced by minimum wage workers but will also lead to an increase in the demand for products purchased by the workers concerned. For example, if the elasticity of demand for youth employment with respect to the minimum wage is −0.1, a 10 per cent increase in minimum wage will reduce employment by 1 per cent. However, it will also raise the income of youths as a group, and reduce firms' profits. If youths have a greater propensity to spend out of income than the recipients of profits, total spending will increase, with positive effects on employment. This does not, of course, guarantee that the partial equilibrium effects will be fully attenuated nor that employment creation will affect minimum wage workers.

A third possibility is that the tools of demand analysis are not appropriate to this segment of the labour market. If wages are the outcome of bargaining and employers have the upper hand, then, in the absence of minimum wages, wages can be kept low and profits are higher as a result. Such a situation can persist only if workers have no effective alternative and will probably be associated with high turnover. A minimum wage limits employer bargaining power. When it is introduced or increased, firms simply give up the profits that were obtained through being able to depress wages. Over time employment could be reduced, but a number of reactions are possible. This kind of explanation is often evoked, but as an avenue of research it is underdeveloped. In order to compete with more orthodox approaches, its theoretical basis and conclusions need to be fully articulated.

6.   Conclusions

This review suggests that minimum wages can and do have a marked effect in low-wage labour markets, but not of the type emphasized so often in policy debates. The pronounced effect on the distribution of earnings is not generally associated with significant reductions in employment. This conclusion is based on the results of the most recent research in the USA and the lesser-known results of studies of the European experience. The divergence of these conclusions from the arguments on which the policy recommendations that emanate from certain economists and a number of international organizations are based will mean that those recommendations will have to be reviewed. Nevertheless, it should also be stressed that these relatively optimistic conclusions are based on current practice, and do not imply that the same would be true if minimum wages were set at much higher levels.

7 The French Experience of Youth Employment Programmes and Payroll Tax Exemptions

FRANCIS KRAMARZ

It may seem ironic for a French person to give opinions or advice on youth employment programmes and tax exemptions in view of the fact that the level of unemployment in France is over 11 per cent and around 25 per cent among young workers. Of course, it is always difficult to resist the opportunity to give your views on the world. So, I seize this possibility with great pleasure.

The outline of the chapter will be as follows. I will mostly give a summary of recent research by colleagues of mine or myself. I will start with the motivation for the discussion, then I will present the basic measures that constitute employment policy in France, in particular showing you the number of beneficiaries and levels of expenditure for the different programmes. Using recent research articles, I will try to assess the impact of these programmes on youth employment, as well as the impact of payroll tax exemptions on the employment of minimum wage workers. Finally, I will present some conclusions.

1. Employment Policy in France

France is supposed to have a very active labour market policy. State interventions are multiple. It must be emphasized that programmes are directed not only to young workers but also towards older ones. As I mentioned earlier, the unemployment rate for young workers is around 25 per cent, and a lot of research has been carried out to try to evaluate the impact of these policies on the young. But we have almost no information for older workers, an issue to which I will return. You will see that the interventions affecting older workers are the most expensive and among the most important labour market interventions in France. I am sure the same applies in other countries, although no one has worked on this topic. Such policies may have strong macroeconomic effects. Another important intervention is the relatively high minimum wage, which is uprated automatically by law. In France, the minimum wage is very different from the US minimum wage studied by David Card and Alan Krueger. Minimum wages in France and the USA are closely similar in terms of purchasing

Table 7.1. Employment policy in France: number of beneficiaries, by programme type, 1994

Programme type	Number of beneficiaries
All programmes	2,425,000
Subsidized employment	1,548,500
In the private sector	1,148,800
Specific exemption programmes	781,400
Help for firm start-ups	36,500
Exemption for part-time jobs	243,200
Others	92,200
In the public sector	399,700
Vocational training	380,500
Programmes for young workers	95,400
Programmes for adult workers	211,900
Help for firm restructuring	73,300
Early retirement	496,500
Early retirement for ages 55–9	203,800
Exempted from job search	284,300

Source: Direction de l'Animation, de la Recherche, et des Études Statistiques du Ministère du Travail (DARES).

power parity; in France, however, payroll taxes add another 80 per cent to cost, while in the USA payroll taxes at these wage rates are quite low.

Let us focus now on employment policies in France. Table 7.1 presents the various types of programme and their number of beneficiaries for 1994. Roughly 10 per cent of the workforce was benefited from a programme of some form.

The first type of programme, labelled 'subsidized employment', can be found in both the public and the private sectors, but mostly in the private sector. In the private sector one finds specific programmes involving tax exemptions, such as apprenticeship programmes. Less well known is the support for firm creation—the grant of public money to create new firms. This programme is mostly focused on people who were previously unemployed; basically they receive a lump sum to start up a firm. In the private sector, beginning in the 1990s, tax exemptions were introduced for part-time jobs in order to promote part-time work, which is less common in France than in other developed countries such as the USA or the UK. In the public sector around 400,000 employees benefited from subsidized employment in 1994.

'Vocational training' constitutes the second main type of active employment policy in France. The principles that govern training in France are quite original and are included in all books describing employment policy in France, even though we may not necessarily think of it in this context. Some of these programmes are targeted on

Table 7.2. Employment policy in France: expenditure by programme type, 1994

Programme type	Expenditure		Beneficiaries
	FFr billion	Share (%)	Share (%)
All programmes	107.4		
Subsidized employment	48.1	44.8	64.3
In the private sector	28.9	26.9	47.9
Specific exemption programmes	21.7	20.2	32.4
Help for firm start-ups	2.5	2.3	1.5
Exemption for part-time jobs	1.6	1.5	10.1
Others	3.1	2.9	3.8
In the public sector	19.2	17.9	17.6
Vocational training	35.1	32.7	15.1
Programmes for young workers	5.6	5.2	4.0
Programmes for adult workers	20.7	19.3	8.8
Help for firm restructuring	7.7	7.1	2.1
Early retirement	24.2	22.5	20.6

Source: DARES.

young workers. We will come back to them, because they apparently have a lot of appeal. But we see that programmes for adult workers involve many more workers: 211,900 to be precise. This is the result of the laws on continuing training that were implemented in the 1970s and have been expanded progressively over the period. Firms in France are required to spend a certain amount on continuing training. The level of spending is defined as a fraction of the wage bill; this was equal to 1 per cent in the 1970s, and has increased steadily, until now it is approximately 2 per cent. This law on vocational training is mandatory on all types of firm. In addition, the money must be spent on courses, or paid over to institutions that train workers. It cannot be devoted to on-the-job training. Related to this is assistance to firms for restructuring. This is not the only French institution that interacts with the death process. Its result is to prevent some firms from dying and to invest money in firms with little future. These programmes to assist firms in restructuring involved 73,000 workers in 1994.

The final type of programme is 'early retirement'. These programmes are very extensive, involving 500,000 people in 1994. In particular, early retirement for those aged 55–60 involved over 200,000 people. Older workers may also be exempted from job search, possibly from as early as age 52. Fewer and fewer persons aged between 50 and 60 are now in work in France (see Card, Kramarz, and Lemieux 1999 for evidence on this point). It is difficult to know what these people do, but roughly 20 per cent of the workforce are involved—a potentially devastating situation.

Table 7.2 presents expenditure on these programmes for the same year, 1994. The table gives each programme's share of total expenditure, as well as its fraction of the beneficiaries. This allows us to compare programmes that are costly with programmes that are relatively cheap.

Total expenditure was FFr107 billion (1994 rates, approximately $17 billion). Spending on the various employment policies overall is very similar to what is observed in other countries. At close to 1 per cent of GDP (the numbers are not exactly comparable to the numbers that I give here), it places France in the middle of the pack. Northern countries tend to spend more.

If we examine expenditure by type of programme, we see that subsidized employment in the private sector accounted for 45 per cent of expenditure and 64 per cent of beneficiaries. In the public sector, the equivalent numbers are 17.9 per cent and 17.6 per cent respectively. These programmes are relatively cheap. Notice, in particular, the small amount that is spent on part-time work, 1.5 per cent of expenditure, compared to the proportion of beneficiaries, 10.1 per cent, which is quite large. Expenditure on support for firm creation amounted to FFr2.5 billion, 2.3 per cent of the total, and helped 1.5 per cent of beneficiaries. This means that we slightly overspend on help for firm creation relative to other programmes. To give other examples of programmes involving subsidized employment in the private sector, let us suppose that you have just established a firm and want to hire an employee. You will not pay payroll taxes for this person for some years. Help is also available when you hire your second and even your third employee. One of the crucial difficulties lies in the increasing complexity of the potential help currently available. The whole structure is so intricate that it is almost impossible to have a clear picture of what is going on. This is the style of French policy: layers and layers of rules, with new ones added regularly.

Vocational training is very important, with more than FFr35 billions devoted to it. Notice that, in terms of relative expenditure, training is even more crucial: 32.7 per cent of expenditure is allocated for 15 per cent of beneficiaries. Furthermore, most of the money goes to adult workers who are already in a job, generally under a long-term contract. From one perspective, this is excellent. The law on training has a long history, starting in the 1970s, with the objective of promoting continuing training and providing incentives to those who did not receive further education and therefore started at the bottom of the career ladder. But from other perspectives it may not be. First, evidence shows that most of the workers who benefit from continuing training were already well trained, in terms of formal education. Secondly, those firms that might benefit most from training to boost their knowledge base seldom use the money that has to be spent on training. Hence, the law acts mostly as a taxing device (see Delame and Kramarz 1997). Assistance to firms' restructuring is also quite expensive.

This is also true for all expenses related to early retirement. One of the most important facts to note is that in France we devote a huge amount of money to programmes that basically tell workers 'go back home, don't work any more'. Such programmes are expensive, and we do not know whether they are helpful or not. It may be that the macro effects of such policies are extremely bad. But, unfortunately, other countries seem to be following the same route, with the idea that, by sending old workers back home, young workers are enabled to find jobs more easily. It does not seem to work exactly this way, at least in France. But we do not know much about these retirement policies and their impact on the functioning of the French labour market.

2.   Do Youth Employment Programmes Help?

In this section, I will review two articles that have studied these youth employment programmes. The first is an article in the *Review of Economic Studies* in 1997 by Liliane Bonnal, Denis Fougère, and Anne Sérandon. These authors have studied the period of the mid-1980s. We first review the programmes that existed at that time, which were not very different from those in existence now. The first three rows in Table 7.3 (their table 1.1) represent programmes in operation in the private sector that provide a large amount of training—the apprenticeship contract, qualification contract, and adaptation contract. One would expect them to be the best, because of the training component. To give an example of how they function: workers on apprenticeship contracts receive 30 per cent of the minimum wage in the first year, a share that increases in both the second and the third years. At the end of the three years they are receiving 80 per cent of the minimum wage. Thereafter they work at normal wage rates. Qualification contracts are temporary employment contracts, of up to twenty-four months' duration, in which workers receive a fair amount of training. In addition, employers benefit from tax exemptions. (In France, there are two types of employment contract. A *contract de durée determinée (CDD)*, a short-term contract for temporary employment, that can last up to twenty-four months, while a normal contract, a *contract de durée indeterminée (CDI)*, has indefinite duration.) In 1998, 90 per cent of hiring was made on short-term *CDD* contracts. Mandatory severance pay has to be paid at the end of these, a *précarité* bonus, of 6 per cent of the contract. Roughly one-third of these contracts are transformed into long-term *CDI* contracts (see Abowd, Corbel, and Kramarz 1999).

Other types of programme shown in the table involve little training. The *stage d'insertion à la vie professionnelle (SIVP)* was designed to prepare young people for work. The training given by government centres is sometimes considered to be of poor quality. Community jobs *travaux d'utilité collective (TUC)*, which were created in 1984, resemble these programmes. As at 2000, this type of programme has had a continuous existence, albeit in different forms. Recently, the government created youth employment contracts, which were supposed to be for both the private sector and the public sector. Unfortunately, they were not implemented in the former and exist only in the latter. In the late 1990s they constituted a new type of contract. We will see that the results for these community jobs are not good. Hence, given the close resemblance between the new contracts and these community jobs, the prospects for young people employed on those new programmes are not very good.

First, Bonnal, Fougère, and Sérandon estimate transition models between six states: unemployment, *CDI, CDD*, public employment programmes, out of the labour force,

Table 7.3. Main programmes for youth employment in France, 1986–1988

Programmes	Durations	Objectives	Eligible workers	Potential employers	Amount of training	Wage levels	Employer incentives
Apprenticeship contracts	Temporary employment contracts (between 1 and 3 years)	To provide specific training leading on completion to a formal qualification or to entry to national diploma examinations	Young people without any diploma or without any formal qualification	All private firms in craft, trade, and industrial sectors	At least 400 hours of training for non-college graduates; at least 1,500 hours of training for college graduates	The apprentice is paid by the firm, the wage depends on age and seniority in the contract (between 17 and 75% of the legal minimum wage)	Firms are exempted from paying social security contributions
Qualification contracts	Temporary employment contracts (between 6 and 24 months)	As above	As above	All private firms	At least one-quarter of the contract duration	As above	Firms are exempted from paying social security contributions and the employer training tax
Adaptation contracts	Either temporary employment contracts (from 6 to 12 months) or permanent employment contracts	To provide a specific training (adapted to the job occupied)	Young people with a formal qualification but who have difficulties to find a job	As above	At least 200 hours in the case of a temporary contract; for permanent employment contracts, it depends both	The wage is paid by the firm; it is at least equal to the legal minimum wage	Firms are exempted from paying the employer training tax, but have to pay social security contributions (since July 1987)

Courses for preparation to the working life (SIVP)	Non-renewable temporary contracts	To give a formal qualification (adapted to existing jobs)	Young people with no work experience or unemployed for more than one year	As above	on the job and on the young worker's qualification Training provided either by the firm or by a government training centre	Trainees receive a lump sum from the state and a complementary allowance from the firm	Firms are exempted from paying social security contributions
Community jobs (TUC)	Non-renewable temporary employment contracts (from 3 to 12 months or 24 months since 1987)	To help young people to find a regular job	Young workers between 16 and 21 years old or long-term unemployed between 22 and 25 years old	State or local administration, public institutions, non-profit making associations, and so on	No formal or specific training	Trainees are paid by the state and receive a fixed payment (about FFr1,250) and sometimes an allowance from the firm	
Training courses for 16–25 year olds	Courses with a duration between 6 and 9 months	To facilitate social and professional integration	Young people leaving the educational system without any qualification	Courses take place in state training centres	Between 550 and 700 hours of training	Trainees receive a lump sum from the state	

Source: Bonnal, Fougère, and Sérandon (1997: table 1.1).

and attrition. They also distinguish four youth programmes for the states held previous to the start of the analysis: qualification programme or apprenticeship, containing a lot of training; community jobs; courses in preparation for working life (*SIVP*), and all other courses. Furthermore, and crucially, they introduce unobserved heterogeneity into the estimation. Even though estimation becomes more difficult, the results are changed dramatically. I will now review the results.

The first message that emerges from the analysis is that training matters. Participation in work training programmes in the private sector increases the rate of transition from unemployment to *CDI* for low-education workers. But this effect is present only for the low educated. It has no effect on people who have higher qualifications, or holders of technical school certificates. On the other hand, participation in work programmes such as community jobs has exactly the reverse effect. It has no impact on low-education workers. They do not exit faster from unemployment to stable employment. For high-education workers, on the other hand, exits from unemployment to *CDI* are reduced. This programme was designed basically for low-education workers. However, many of the slots on it—in particular in the new programmes recently established—have been filled by high-education workers, some with university education. If we accept this result, it is not going to have a positive effect for these workers. In fact, participation in such programmes seems to act as a negative signal. More generally, workplace schemes seem to induce more stability in long-term contract employment than workfare, and seem to end less frequently in a transition to unemployment. This is another strong result that we get from this study.

The next important result is that observed and unobserved heterogeneity matter. This is hardly surprising. The programmes are extremely selective. That is one of the consequences of participation depending on education level, as we noted above. Finally, and maybe surprisingly, entitlement to unemployment insurance does not necessarily increase the duration of unemployment spells. Low-education workers enter programmes even when they still qualify for unemployment insurance. As we will see in the next study, people want to work but it does not seem to be easy for them to do so.

I turn now to Thierry Magnac's study (Magnac 1997). This looks at more recent programmes, from 1990 to 1992, using Labour Force Survey data. Magnac uses a Chamberlain-style transition model—that is, a logit with both unobserved heterogeneity and state dependence of order one or two (that is, up to two previous states). This analysis is made possible by the monthly nature of the data. Although there are almost no time-varying covariates, transitions can be studied at the monthly level or aggregated up to the quarter, for instance.

Magnac distinguishes the same states as Bonnal, Fougère, and Sérandon: *CDI*, *CDD*, state-provided training, schooling, unemployment, and non-participation. The findings are slightly different from those of Bonnal and her colleagues, since the latter introduce only one dimension of unobserved heterogeneity. Magnac allows for as many dimensions of unobserved heterogeneity as there are states. Hence one can look at the correlation between the various unobserved heterogeneity components in the different states. So what are the results? Once more, they show that unobserved heterogeneity matters. Omitting unobserved heterogeneity biases all coefficient upwards. Conditioning on unobserved heterogeneity, low-education people are less mobile than in the absence of conditioning. Magnac also shows that few young workers go back to education after leaving school. This result may be quite specific to France, where almost no one goes back to education after being in work for some time. Indeed, the French education system seems to be designed to prevent situations in which people work and then go back to education. More importantly, the results show that workers in stable employment have long employment durations, even after controlling for unobserved heterogeneity. In addition, workers employed on short-term contracts seem to get one such contract after another. In other words, once employed on *CDD*, you are more likely to have another *CDD* contract. An identical result holds for training schemes. People seem to get accustomed to training schemes. While employed on these programmes, you accumulate information on them, which may favour future re-employment on such schemes. A discouraging finding to emerge from Magnac's results is that training schemes are not ladders to stable employment.

As in Bonnal, Fougère, and Sérandon, controlling for unobserved heterogeneity changes the estimation results dramatically. In addition, Magnac looks at the determinants of heterogeneity. This is rather difficult, so he expands the econometric framework, using simulated maximum likelihood. He is able to show, for instance, that women or those with a father of non-European origin are less likely to start the period with a stable employment contract. When examining the fixed effects, Magnac shows that men are less likely to have *CDD* or *CDI* contracts, but are as likely as women to be on training schemes, in unemployment, or in further education. I think that the most interesting aspect here is the correlation across states of the fixed effects. These correlations can be computed and they show that short-term contracts, long-term contracts, and schooling are complements, while training schemes and unemployment are close substitutes. So it seems better to be employed on a short-term contract because, as I said above, one-third of these workers become employed on a long-term contract. But training schemes do not appear to be very effective, and they are very close to unemployment in those terms.

Finally, Thierry Magnac simulated the suppression of all training schemes to estimate the change in unemployment that would result from such a policy experiment. In contrast to the results above, his results here contain some encouraging aspects. More precisely, training schemes are not substitutes for non-participation, which is to say that young workers really want to enter the labour market. Those who use such training schemes want to have a job. If you suppress training schemes, employment probability increases, which means that people would stay longer in education to avoid an unemployment spell. But also training schemes appear to be substitutes for jobs that firms would offer. What Magnac finds is that young people would stay longer in their jobs in the absence of training schemes. In fact, training schemes, because of their specified and compulsory duration, induce firms to have more workers than they otherwise would.

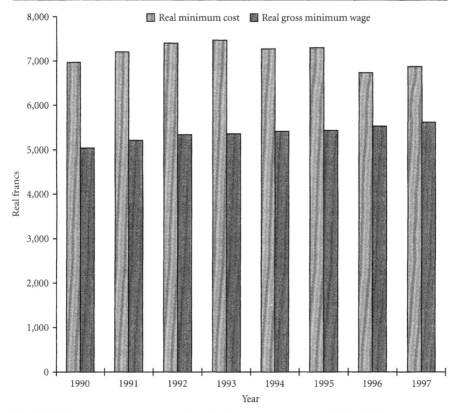

Fig. 7.1. The mimimum wage and real mimimum wage cost, 1990–1997
Source: Kramarz and Philippon (1998).

3.   The Impact of Tax Exemptions on Minimum Wage Workers

Until now, we have examined the impact of programmes on young workers based on results from French colleagues. Now, I will focus on my own results (Kramarz and Philippon 1998), which examine the impact of payroll tax exemptions implemented in the mid-1990s for workers paid around the minimum wage. First, let us examine what happened in France in the 1990s. Fig. 7.1 shows the real gross minimum wage, excluding employer-paid social security contributions, and the real minimum cost, which includes these employer-paid contributions. (In France the definition of the minimum wage is given in terms of the wage inclusive of employee-paid contributions and excluding employer-paid contributions.) There are various points to note here. First, the minimum wage was increased regularly over the period. But the pattern is

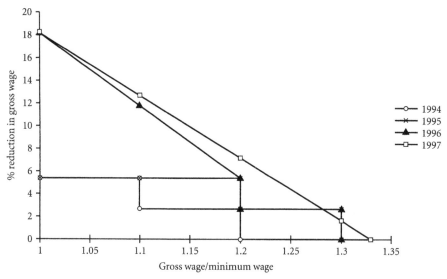

Fig. 7.2. Reduction in employer-paid payroll taxes

Source: Kramarz and Philippon (1998).

different for the minimum cost. For those paid at the minimum wage, there was a substantial reduction in payroll taxes of 18 per cent of the gross wage between 1995 and 1996 (Holland has similar programmes). As shown in Fig. 7.2, this exemption is applicable for workers paid up to 1.33 times the minimum wage (in 1997).

This is considered a very expensive programme, so it is of interest to evaluate its effects. Fig. 7.3 shows two wage distributions, for 1992 and 1996. The distribution of costs is shown on the same figure. This exemption appears to be manna from heaven. Even more clearly, in Fig. 7.4 we see that, apparently, more people are displaced to lower wages. This is clear if you compare the distribution of costs of 1996 with the costs in 1996 using 1992 wages. One can see that slightly more people are paid at the minimum wage where tax exemptions are maximal and slightly less people are paid just above. In addition, some low-wage workers may see their wage kept down in order for the employer to benefit from the exemptions. Fig. 7.5 provides more evidence. On one axis, we give the various years, while on the other, we have sliced the distribution into its different components in terms of the ratio of the cost of the minimum. The first slice goes from 1.0 to 1.03, the next from 1.03 to 1.05, and so on. What is illustrated is based on the use of panel data and represents the probability of transiting from employment to unemployment. Everybody here is employed in year t. If we consider year t as 1990 and 1991 as $t + 1$, we see that roughly 20 per cent of people employed in 1990 around the minimum wage lost their jobs in 1991, and the numbers are something like 5 per cent for people far away from the minimum wage. But, for $t = 1995$, the year after which payroll taxes decreased strongly, we observe a significant switch.

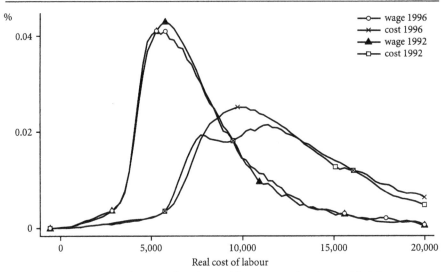

Fig. 7.3. Empirical distribution of real monthly wage and real monthly labour cost, 1992 and 1996

Source: Kramarz and Philippon (1998).

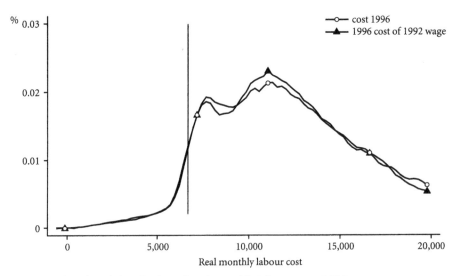

Fig. 7.4. Simulated distribution of real monthly labour cost, 1996

Source: Kramarz and Philippon (1998).

Prob (Employment $(t+1)$ = 0/Employment (t) = 1)

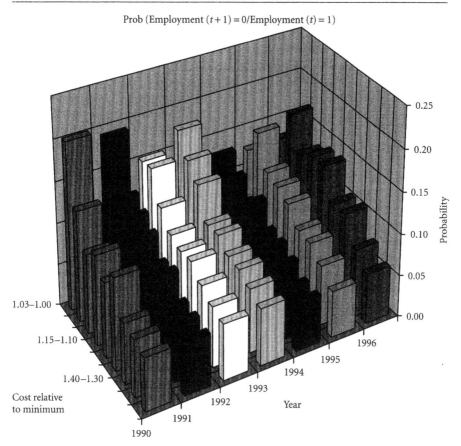

Fig. 7.5. Probability of disemployment, 1990–1996

Source: Kramarz and Philippon (1998).

Those workers who benefit less from the tax exemptions—that is, those with slightly higher wages—lose their jobs more often than those who benefit fully from the tax exemptions. This can be made more formal in an econometric sense. The methodology is described now.

Consider all workers who are employed in year t. As shown above, divide the distribution of wages according to position with respect to the minimum wage. Because there is still unobserved heterogeneity, you cannot focus on those workers paid at the minimum wage without examining what happens to other workers, because you do not have adequate controls for this unobserved heterogeneity. Assume now that there is an increase in the minimum cost. There are many workers whose cost of employment lies between the minimum cost in year t and the minimum cost in year $t + 1$. The question is: are they going to lose their jobs because they have been caught by the increase in the minimum cost? Of course, some of these low-wage workers are going to lose their jobs anyway, because their qualities are low, or they are more likely to change jobs, and so on. But, to control for these unobserved components, they must be compared with a group that is not directly affected by the increase in the minimum wage but that closely resembles these minimum wage workers—that is, workers whose cost is just above the new minimum cost. This marginal group should be as small as possible to give good control in terms of unobserved heterogeneity. All effects are identified by this restriction: marginal workers are not affected in their transition probabilities by the cost increase, but their unobserved characteristics are close, even identical, to those affected. What Kramarz and Philippon have found is that a 1 per cent increase in the minimum wage implies a 1.5 per cent increased probability of losing one's job for those minimum wage workers. Even though they constitute a small group, less than 3 per cent of the population, there is a sizeable elasticity here and all numbers are significantly different from zero.

The same exercise can be carried out for a decrease in the minimum cost, just thinking the other way around. Assume a perfectly competitive labour market—few people believe this assumption, but let us believe it for a second. Then, workers with low productivity (lower than the old minimum cost) will enter the market. In econometric terms, the question is: do people come from non-employment more often who are liberated by the cost decrease than those who are paid slightly more? In fact, we find that there is no strong difference, hardly significant (maybe at the 10 per cent level) between the treated and the control group. To understand this last result, one thing does matter. What are the employers' expectations? Do they believe that this 18 per cent exemption will last? If they believe that the government will eliminate this exemption in, say, three years' time, why should they hire someone using this rebate? Indeed, employers would have to pay the firing costs three years from now. These firing costs are high. Abowd and Kramarz (1998) provide estimates of firing costs amounting to approximately one year's pay for workers who are fired. Of course, these costs depend on the seniority, and hence would be much smaller for three years seniority. Maybe employers are not willing to benefit from the 18 per cent exemption and pay these firing costs three years later. So the question is: will these exemptions last and will the promises that they will last be credible?

4.   Conclusion

The conclusion will consist of four points.

First, as researchers we have to study early retirement schemes and their macroeconomic impact. Nobody has worked on what is happening to older workers. I think this is crucial. There is a lot of money involved, and a lot of countries are adopting schemes that resemble those existing in France. It may be a very bad idea to do this.

Second, training may not matter as much as we would like, even though it seems to matter.

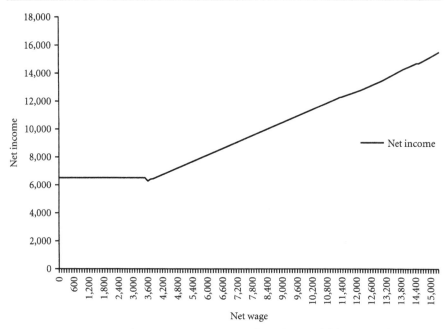

Fig. 7.6. Net income relative to net wage, couple with two children (5 and 10 years old; one adult employed)

Source: Laroque and Salanié (1999).

Third, if you think that a policy should be implemented, you have to think of all the policies already in place and evaluate them together. Let me give you a nice example of such a situation for France, giving rise to what economists call a poverty trap. Fig. 7.6 is drawn from research conducted by Guy Laroque and Bernard Salanié. Indeed, nobody appears to know the facts that I am going to show you now, which is a shame because they are troublesome. We consider a situation with one wage-earner in a couple with two children. They benefit from various allowances and benefits that have been implemented one after another (for a family of two children, housing, and so on). They also benefit potentially from the *revenu minimum d'insertion* (*RMI*), the French minimum income. First, consider what the situation would be if no one in the family worked. They receive approximately FFr6,500 per month, just from the income support plus family and housing allowances. Assume now that the head of the family works part-time and gets FFr2,000 francs or even FFr4,000. You see their income does not change because the *RMI* decreases as the people get money from work. If they start working more, their income decreases because of the law on housing allowances, so instead of losing one franc for every franc coming from work, the household loses FFr1.2. If the worker receives the minimum wage from work (approximately 5,000 francs), the income of the family is increased by FFr1,000. If work is rewarded at 1.5

times the minimum wage, the income will increase by FFr2,900 when compared to the non-work situation. Of course, this calculation does not include the various expenses that would be associated with working, such as childcare, transport, and similar expenses. So basically you have to work for a wage considerably larger than the minimum wage really to benefit from the same income as you would have received without working. The accumulation of various layers of legal arrangements were responsible for this situation.

Finally, we do not know why young workers do not get jobs in France while they find them easily in Germany and the USA. There may be multiple reasons for this situation: the education system, the minimum wage, the demography of firms could all play a role. In general, labour demand has focused on demand by skills. Very little is known about the age pattern of firms' demand, in particular for jobs in the lower part of the wage distribution. A future, and crucial, research agenda must include such an analysis together with the possible substitutions between young and old workers, in particular in the low-education group. Substitutions within the wage distribution at its bottom end have to be better understood. We now have the matched employer–employee data sets that are necessary to examine such issues.

8 Low-Wage Services: Interpreting the US–German Difference

RICHARD B. FREEMAN AND RONALD SCHETTKAT

Services are the main sector of employment growth in advanced countries, and the principal area of difference between US and West European employment. Between 1970 and 1995 the USA increased the ratio of service employment to adult population by 15 percentage points while manufacturing employment per adult fell. In Germany (West) manufacturing employment relative to the population also fell, while service sector employment per adult rose. Employment in service sector jobs per adult increased by about 9 percentage points in Germany—6 points less than in the USA. The 6 point difference in the growth of service sector jobs per adult accounts for about 75 per cent of the 1980–95 increased gap between the German and US employment/population ratios. Since Germany and the USA had similar employment/population rates in 1970, the service sector difference also explains roughly three-quarters of the actual 1995 US–German difference in employment/population ratios overall. Thus, service industries are crucial for any explanation of the US–German differentials in employment trends.

The part of the service sector that has attracted most attention in discussions of German unemployment are low-wage service industries, where many low-skill workers who make up a disproportionate share of the unemployed might seek work. Analysts have argued that more flexibility in both supply and demand at the low-wage end of the labour market would increase employment in Germany and in the EU more broadly (e.g. Siebert 1997). Welfare state arrangements in Germany, like social assistance, may create reservation wages for low-skilled workers above the wages in low-paid jobs. On the demand side, collectively bargained wages may set a wage floor, which pushes costs for low-skilled services to a level prohibitive for private service demand, particularly when combined with non-wage labour costs like social security contributions. Reductions in social assistance and in labour costs would presumably generate more low-wage service employment, and thus lower German and EU unemployment.

Despite much policy discussion, there is little detailed empirical work comparing US and German low-wage services. Analyses have been either highly aggregative or based on a priori thinking, rather than quantitative estimates of the key differences

Ernest Berkhout provided invaluable research assistance for this paper.

between low-wage services in the USA and Germany, much less of the relevant elasticities of demand or supply that might explain these differences. As a result, there is some confusion about the basic facts regarding employment and wages in low-wage service sectors in the two countries, and little hard evidence about the nature and causes of differences.

- How much, in fact, does employment differ in low-wage service sectors between the USA and Germany?
- Are the same sectors low wage in both countries, and, if so, how far are they below average pay in each country?
- Do the service sectors use similar proportions of low-wage or low-skill labour or do they employ different skill mixes in the two countries?
- What explains any low-wage service sector jobs 'deficit' in Germany relative to the USA? High reservation wages? High labour costs? Or other differences between the two economies?

This chapter seeks to provide facts to answer these questions and to clarify the debate about the contribution of the low-wage service sector to the German employment problem. We find that:

1. Germany has a smaller low-wage service sector than the USA, though the ratio of low-wage service employment to population rose in Germany relative to the USA from 1980 to 1995.
2. Low-wage service industries are further below the national average in wages in Germany than in the USA. Adding to this difference, low-wage service industries employ proportionately more skilled workers in Germany than in the USA, though women workers make up a much larger share of employees in these areas in Germany.
3. A majority of low-wage workers in Germany are found in a limited number of low-wage service sector industries and in a few low-paying occupations. By contrast, low-wage workers are found throughout the US job market.

In short, we find little support for the notion that the German–US deficit in low-wage services is due to excessively high wages in those industries in Germany. Given the existence of open unemployment, we also see little support for the claim that low-wage services face a labour shortage owing to high reservation wages in Germany. The difference in sectoral employment must thus lie in some other differences between the economies, on which we offer some speculations.

1.   The Service Sector Employment Difference

The starting point for our analysis is the basic fact that Germany has a smaller service sector than the USA. In Germany shares of national production, consumption, and employment in services fall below the equivalent shares in the USA (see Table 8.1).

Differences in shares, however, have no clear implications for employment, since, by definition, a smaller share in one sector implies a larger share in another. In this case the lower share of services in Germany implies that the country has relatively higher output and employment in manufacturing than in the USA.

To analyse the link between levels of employment and sector, we calculated the ratio of employment in a sector to adult population: the number of workers employed in that sector per person of working age. Since sectoral employment/ population ratios add up to the total employment/population ratio, they provide the appropriate statistic to assess the contribution of sectors to aggregate employment. These statistics, also given in Table 8.1, show that Germany has a *somewhat* higher manufacturing employment to population ratio than the USA but a *much* lower service sector employment ratio. As noted in the opening paragraph, it is this difference that accounts for the decline and gap in the employment/population ratio in Germany relative to the USA.

Where do the Low-Wage Service Industries Fit into this Picture? To answer this question and provide a more detailed analysis of low-wage services in Germany and the USA we use data from a new micro-based data set, the Comparable German–American Sectoral Database (CGAS). The CGAS classifies workers in the two countries into comparable detailed occupations (about ninety-five) and industries (about sixty-five) for the period 1970 to 1995. Within industry and occupation it contains cells based on wages, occupation, industry, age, sex, and nationality, rather than observations on individuals (which we could not get for Germany). Theoretically the data allow for differentiation of about 1.2 million cells per year. The underlying sources of the data for the CGAS database are the US Census of Population, the Current Population Survey, the German *Mikrozensus*, and German social security data (*Beschaeftigtenstatistik*). Combining these data files provides us with hundreds of thousands of cells, which allow for the detailed analysis of international employment growth differentials after controlling for educational variables, gender, age, and so on (for more details, see Freeman and Schettkat 1999).

The first step in our analysis was to identify the major low-wage services. We rank-ordered industries in the CGAS by mean level of pay within Germany and the USA. Table 8.2 lists the fifteen industries at the low end of the distribution and gives their share of employment and employment to population ratios in 1989 and 1995. The upper panel uses the US wage structure to order the industries. The lower panel uses the German wage structure. Both wage structures place essentially the same industries at the bottom. Twelve out of the fifteen lowest paying industries are identical, and six of the seven low-paying service sector industries are the same. The key low-wage services in terms of number of employees are (in order) eating, drinking, and care facilities; non-food retail trade; food retail trade. The other low-wage services are private households, personal services, services to dwellings, business services, and other repair services. The figures on the share in overall employment show that the service industries dominate the low-wage sector.

Table 8.1. The sectoral distribution of the German and US economies

Country and year	Employment to population (ratio)			Shares in overall employment			Shares in GDP (current prices)			Shares in GDP (constant 1990 prices)			Shares in Final Demand (constant 1982–5 prices)		
	Total	Manufacturing	Services	Agriculture	Manufacturing	Services	Agriculture	Manufacturing	Services	Agriculture	Manufacturing	Services	Agriculture	Manufacturing	Services
USA															
1960	61.0	21.5	34.3	8.49	35.27	56.24	4.45	42.46	53.09	3.72	41.31	54.97	n.a.	n.a.	n.a.
1970	61.9	21.3	37.9	4.53	34.35	61.11	3.23	39.66	57.11	2.58	39.28	58.14	1.0	47.0	51.0
1980	65.9	20.1	43.4	3.55	30.53	65.92	2.86	37.98	59.16	1.94	34.07	63.98	1.0	45.0	57.0
1989	71.8	19.1	50.6	2.88	26.66	70.46	2.29	32.07	65.64	2.15	31.71	66.13	1.0	43.0	56.0
1995	72.6	17.4	52.9	2.82	23.85	73.34	1.95	29.27	68.77	2.37	30.71	66.91	n.a.	n.a.	n.a.
Germany															
1960	68.8	32.3	26.9	13.96	46.97	39.07	6.41	58.36	35.23	2.82	56.39	40.79	n.a.	n.a.	n.a.
1970	67.8	33.4	28.5	8.64	49.33	42.03	3.80	58.20	38.00	2.08	57.33	40.59	n.a.	n.a.	n.a.
1980	65.0	28.4	33.1	5.29	43.70	51.02	2.52	51.54	45.94	1.85	52.38	45.76	1.0	58.0	41.0
1989	63.0	25.1	35.5	3.76	39.81	56.43	2.00	46.79	51.21	1.84	46.85	51.30	1.0	58.0	41.0
1995	64.2	24.3	38.2	3.34	37.54	59.12	1.26	41.10	57.64	1.80	41.71	56.49	n.a.	n.a.	n.a.

Sources: computations based on OECD Labour Force Statistics (CD-ROM), International Structural Data Base (CD-ROM); final demand categories computed with data from the OECD Input–Output database, constant prices 1982 for the USA, 1985 for Germany, exact years: 1972, 1982, 1990 for the USA, 1978, 1990 for Germany (Russo and Schettkat 1998).

Table 8.2. Employment in the fifteen lowest-paying industries in the USA and Germany (shares and employment/population ratios, working age population 15–65)

Industry	Classification[a]	Shares in overall employment				Employment/population ratio (15–65)			
		USA		Germany		USA		Germany	
		1989	1995	1989	1995	1989	1995	1989	1995
Ranking according to US wages 1989									
Private households (88)	s	1.04	0.77	0.27	0.41	0.66	0.46	0.15	0.23
Agriculture	a	1.45	1.19	0.78	0.95	0.92	0.71	0.44	0.54
Eating, drinking & care facilities	s	7.40	7.70	3.50	4.94	4.66	4.60	1.98	2.79
Apparel etc.	m	1.28	1.03	0.98	0.42	0.81	0.62	0.56	0.24
Personal services	s	1.16	1.01	0.90	1.74	0.73	0.60	0.51	0.98
Services to dwellings etc.	s	0.55	0.54	0.55	0.66	0.34	0.32	0.31	0.37
Retail trade, food	s	3.02	2.92	2.46	1.97	1.91	1.74	1.39	1.11
Meat products	m	0.43	0.42	0.66	0.56	0.27	0.25	0.37	0.32
Leather, leather products	m	0.14	0.13	0.28	0.17	0.09	0.08	0.16	0.10
Retail trade, non-food	s	7.22	7.54	5.73	6.93	4.55	4.51	3.24	3.92
Fishing	a	0.03	0.03	0.01	0.01	0.02	0.02	0.01	0.01
Business services	s	1.08	2.34	0.41	0.32	0.68	1.40	0.23	0.18
Carpets and rugs	m	0.47	0.46	1.08	0.91	0.30	0.27	0.61	0.51
Lumber and wood products	m	1.28	1.21	1.61	1.65	0.81	0.72	0.91	0.93
Toys, amusement, sporting good	m	0.12	0.14	0.32	0.20	0.08	0.09	0.18	0.11
Total manufacturing		3.72	3.39	4.92	3.91	2.35	2.03	2.79	2.21
Total services		21.47	22.82	13.82	16.98	13.53	13.64	7.82	9.59
Overall		26.68	27.43	19.53	21.84	16.82	16.40	11.05	12.34

Table 8.2. (cont'd)

Industry	Classification[a]	Shares in overall employment				Employment/population ratio (15–65)			
		USA		Germany		USA		Germany	
		1989	1995	1989	1995	1989	1995	1989	1995
Ranking according to German wages 1989									
Private households (88)	s	1.04	0.77	0.27	0.41	0.66	0.46	0.15	0.23
Agriculture	a	1.45	1.19	0.78	0.95	0.92	0.71	0.44	0.54
Personal services	s	1.16	1.01	0.90	1.74	0.73	0.60	0.51	0.98
Retail trade, food	s	3.02	2.92	2.46	1.97	1.91	1.74	1.39	1.11
Eating, drinking & care facilities	s	7.40	7.70	3.50	4.94	4.66	4.60	1.98	2.79
Services to dwellings etc.	s	0.55	0.54	0.55	0.66	0.34	0.32	0.31	0.37
Retail trade, non-food	s	7.22	7.54	5.73	6.93	4.55	4.51	3.24	3.92
Meat products	m	0.43	0.42	0.66	0.56	0.27	0.25	0.37	0.32
Fishing	a	0.03	0.03	0.01	0.01	0.02	0.02	0.01	0.01
Other repair services	s	0.39	0.39	0.13	0.07	0.25	0.23	0.07	0.04
Paper and allied products	m	0.72	0.66	0.72	0.62	0.45	0.39	0.41	0.35
Wholesale trade, nondurable	s	0.90	0.91	0.63	0.65	0.57	0.54	0.35	0.37
Apparel etc.	m	1.28	1.03	0.98	0.42	0.81	0.62	0.56	0.24
Leather, leather products	m	0.14	0.13	0.28	0.17	0.09	0.08	0.16	0.10
Business services	s	1.08	2.34	0.41	0.32	0.68	1.40	0.23	0.18
Total manufacturing		2.57	2.24	2.63	1.78	1.62	1.34	1.49	1.01
Total services		22.76	24.12	14.57	17.69	14.35	14.42	8.25	10.00
Overall		26.82	27.58	17.99	20.43	16.90	16.49	10.18	11.55

[a] a = agriculture, m = manufacturing, s = services.

Note: according to German wages, industries ranked 11 and 14 exist only in Germany and were dropped.

Looking across countries, the share of workers in the low-paying industries in over-all employment is substantially higher in the USA (27 per cent upper panel, 28 per cent lower panel) than in Germany (22 per cent upper panel, 20 per cent lower panel), independent of the US or German ranking. The difference is almost entirely due to low-wage services. In particular, the USA employs a higher share of workers in 'eating, drinking, care facilities' (7.7 per cent compared to 4.9 per cent in Germany), 'retail trade' (10.5 per cent in food and non-food retail trade compared to 9 per cent in Germany), and 'business services' (2.3 per cent compared to 0.3 per cent in Germany). In 'personal services' relatively more persons are employed in Germany (1.7 per cent) than in the USA (1.0 per cent).

From 1989 to 1990, however, the employment to population rate for low-wage service sectors in the USA barely changed, while the rate rose by about 2 percentage points in Germany. This reduced the gap or deficit with the USA by about one-third. In 1989, the USA had 6 per cent more adults employed in low-wage services than Germany. In 1995, the USA had about 4 per cent more adults employed in low-wage services than Germany. Put differently, during the period of rising joblessness in Germany, low-wage services expanded more than in the USA.

2.   Low-Paying Services in the Industry Wage Structure

One possible reason for Germany having fewer workers in the low-paying service sector than the USA is that wages in this 'low-pay' area are higher relative to average pay than in the USA. Given that Germany has a much narrower distribution of wages overall than the USA, this would seem to be a reasonable possibility. If true, higher relative pay in German low-wage services would provide some support for a demand-side interpretation of the German low-wage service employment deficit: the workers cost too much.

Surprisingly, the 'wage difference' story turns out to be false. Table 8.3 displays industry-specific wages relative to the mean wage in the USA and Germany respect-ively. These data show that relative wages of low-pay industries are strikingly similar in the two countries. Indeed, in 1995 the seven lowest-paying service sectors have an average pay that is 67 per cent of mean wages in the USA and 61 per cent of mean wages in Germany. The lowest paying service, private households, pays about 45 per cent of the overall mean wage in both sectors, while pay in retail trade, both food and non-food, is 9 percentage points closer to the average in the USA than in Germany. It is hard to argue, on the basis of this evidence, that German low-wage services are paying such relatively high wages as greatly to reduce demand for these services, and thus that high wages in those sectors explains the lack of employment.

The similarity in the position of low-wage services in the industry wage structure between the USA and Germany seems to conflict with the well-established fact that the USA has a much wider distribution of wages overall than does Germany and that the bottom deciles of the US wage distribution are much further from the median than the bottom deciles of the German wage distribution (OECD 1993).

Table 8.3. Wages in low-paying industries (ranked according to US 1989 wages)

Industry	Classification[a]	USA 1989 Wage relative to mean	Standard deviation	Wage rank	USA 1995 Wage relative to mean	Standard deviation	Wage rank	Germany 1989 Wage relative to mean	Standard deviation	Wage rank	Germany 1995 Wage relative to mean	Standard deviation	Wage rank
Private households	s	0.41	0.38	1	0.45	0.36	1	0.45	0.39	1	0.51	0.34	1
Agriculture	a	0.57	0.29	2	0.58	0.33	2	0.50	0.34	2	0.52	0.35	2
Eating, drinking, and care facilities	s	0.62	0.37	3	0.66	0.40	4	0.63	0.33	5	0.67	0.31	6
Apparel, etc.	m	0.64	0.37	4	0.68	0.42	6	0.76	0.30	15	0.76	0.30	16
Personal services	s	0.66	0.37	5	0.66	0.37	5	0.52	0.40	3	0.73	0.43	11
Services to dwellings, etc.	s	0.66	0.34	6	0.65	0.35	3	0.66	0.29	6	0.65	0.32	5
Retail trade, food	s	0.70	0.36	7	0.69	0.38	8	0.60	0.35	4	0.60	0.32	4
Meat products	m	0.70	0.36	8	0.68	0.37	7	0.69	0.25	8	0.71	0.25	9
Leather and leather products	m	0.71	0.45	9	0.75	0.44	10	0.77	0.34	16	0.81	0.31	23
Retail trade, non-food	s	0.73	0.36	10	0.75	0.37	11	0.66	0.34	7	0.68	0.33	7
Fishing	a	0.73	0.58	11	0.74	0.71	9	0.70	0.28	9	0.73	0.26	12
Business services	s	0.81	0.42	12	0.86	0.45	15	0.78	0.26	17	0.81	0.23	24
Carpets and rugs	m	0.81	0.35	13	0.81	0.42	13	0.87	0.28	26	0.92	0.26	32
Lumber and wood products	m	0.82	0.35	14	0.81	0.39	12	0.94	0.20	30	0.94	0.19	35
Toys, amusement, and sporting goods	m	0.83	0.52	15	0.91	0.56	18	0.90	0.27	29	0.92	0.26	33
Other repair services	s	0.90	0.39	22	0.92	0.45	20	0.72	0.28	10	0.68	0.26	8
Wholesale trade, nondurable	s	0.96	0.39	27	0.95	0.43	25	0.75	0.30	13	0.75	0.28	14
Paper and allied products	m	1.14	0.41	41	1.10	0.43	41	0.75	0.33	12	0.80	0.31	19

[a] a = agriculture, m = manufacturing, s = services.

Note: According to German wages, industries ranked 11 and 14 exist only in Germany and were dropped.

The explanation that reconciles the difference between the distribution of wages among industries and the overall distribution of wages is that the USA has much greater intra-industry dispersion in wages (Freeman and Schettkat 1999). Table 8.3 records the standard deviation of log wages among cells within the sectors. Taking the low-pay industries, the average (unweighted) standard deviation of log wages among cells within industry is about 0.4 in the USA compared to 0.3 in Germany for the fifteen lowest-paying industries ranked by US wages. The main differences in the within-industry differentials occur at the higher end of the low-paying industries rather than at the low end.

The similarity in the difference in pay by industry in the USA and Germany also seems in conflict with the fact that the distribution of wages by occupation is wider in the USA than in Germany (Freeman and Schettkat 1999). The explanation that reconciles similarity in the distribution of wages among industries and differences in the distribution of wages among occupations is partly arithmetic. Consider pay in an industry that employs two types of workers, high-wage and low-wage workers. In the country with the wider skill structure for wages (the USA), let high-paid workers receive 1.50 while the low-paid workers receive 0.50. Then an industry that employs high- and low-wage workers in equal proportions will pay 1.00 on average. Compare this to the pay in a country (Germany) where high-skill occupations are paid 1.10 and low skill occupations are paid 0.90. Here, too, the industry average pay will be 1.00. More broadly, by mixing high- and low-paid workers, a country with a highly unequal skill structure can produce the same industrial wage structure as a country with a more narrow distribution of wages overall.

3.   Occupations in Low-Wage Services

Do low-wage services in the USA and Germany use the same types of workers (as in the preceding example) or does their employment composition differ in response to differences in the skill structure of pay or relative supplies of workers with different skill attributes?

Labour demand analysis suggests that, faced with differences in relative wages, the same industry should employ different skill mixes of workers. The industry in the high-skill premium country should economize on skilled workers and hire disproportionately fewer skilled workers than the industry in the low-skill premium country. This would reduce average pay in the industry in the high-skill premium country, though it would not necessarily lower pay relative to other industries, which would face a similar incentive to substitute less skilled for more skilled workers. In any case, substitution in response to differences in the structure of pay across skill groups should produce differences in the composition of workers in low-paid services in Germany rather than in the USA.

Table 8.4 presents evidence that suggests considerable substitution of workers within sectors. It records the proportions of workers working in low-paying occuptions

Table 8.4. Intra-industry wage distribution

Industry	Classification	Relative industry wage	Low paying		High paying	
			Wage relative to industry mean	Share in industry employment	Wage relative to industry mean	Share in industry employment
USA						
Occupations						
Private households	s	0.41	0.93	86.66	1.63	13.34
Agriculture	a	0.57	0.91	81.64	1.45	18.36
Eating, drinking, and care facilities	s	0.62	0.81	66.96	1.31	33.04
Apparel, etc.	m	0.64	0.88	74.14	1.51	25.86
Personal services	s	0.66	0.90	74.70	1.35	25.30
to dwellings, etc.	s	0.66	0.93	77.90	1.30	22.10
Retail trade, food	s	0.70	0.85	80.20	1.26	19.80
Meat products	m	0.70	0.83	75.67	1.41	24.33
Leather and leather products	m	0.71	0.92	77.87	1.56	22.13
Retail trade, non-food	s	0.73	0.92	84.92	1.38	15.08
Fishing	a	0.73	0.69	21.57	1.08	78.43
Business services	s	0.81	0.78	60.14	1.32	39.86
Carpets and rugs	m	0.81	0.83	72.07	1.42	27.93
Lumber and wood products	m	0.82	0.88	75.62	1.36	24.38
Toys, amusement, and sporting goods	m	0.83	0.78	71.99	1.49	28.01
Cells						
Private households	s	0.41	0.79	67.58	1.44	32.42
Agriculture	a	0.57	0.85	76.43	1.48	23.57
Eating, drinking, and care facilities	s	0.62	0.76	71.83	1.47	28.17
Apparel, etc.	m	0.64	0.78	76.79	1.70	23.21
Personal services	s	0.66	0.76	66.64	1.44	33.36
Services to dwellings, etc.	s	0.66	0.80	72.83	1.46	27.17
Retail trade, food	s	0.70	0.76	68.37	1.39	31.63
Meat products	m	0.70	0.77	68.37	1.44	31.63
Leather and leather products	m	0.71	0.74	71.98	1.63	28.02
Retail trade, non-food	s	0.73	0.76	69.27	1.42	30.73
Fishing	a	0.73	0.61	54.51	1.43	45.49

Business services	s	0.81	0.72	67.15	1.54	32.85
Carpets and rugs	m	0.81	0.78	70.38	1.49	29.62
Lumber and wood products	m	0.82	0.78	64.87	1.39	35.13
Toys, amusement, and sporting goods	m	0.83	0.69	72.55	1.75	27.45

GERMANY

Occupations

Private households	s	0.45	0.87	66.46	1.18	33.54
Agriculture	a	0.50	0.92	75.64	1.25	24.36
Eating, drinking, and care facilities	s	0.63	0.87	60.41	1.18	39.59
Apparel, etc.	m	0.76	0.87	75.38	1.35	24.62
Personal services	s	0.52	0.80	59.51	1.32	40.49
Services to dwellings, etc.	s	0.66	0.92	84.59	1.29	15.41
Retail trade, food	s	0.60	0.85	67.86	1.29	32.14
Meat products	m	0.69	0.85	50.14	1.13	49.86
Leather and leather products	m	0.77	0.87	70.84	1.29	29.16
Retail trade, non-food	s	0.66	0.82	56.49	1.21	43.51
Fishing	a	0.70	0.90	61.14	1.17	38.86
Business services	s	0.78	0.92	76.34	1.27	23.66
Carpets and rugs	m	0.87	0.88	66.60	1.22	33.40
Lumber and wood products	m	0.94	0.94	67.61	1.13	32.39
Toys, amusement, and sporting goods	m	0.90	0.89	64.39	1.18	35.61

Cells

Private households	s	0.45	0.77	53.77	1.26	46.23
Agriculture	a	0.50	0.77	51.70	1.25	48.30
Eating, drinking, and care facilities	s	0.63	0.75	50.14	1.25	49.86
Apparel, etc.	m	0.76	0.79	60.74	1.31	39.26
Personal services	s	0.52	0.73	59.65	1.41	40.35
Services to dwellings, etc.	s	0.66	0.78	59.72	1.25	40.28
Retail trade, food	s	0.60	0.74	54.71	1.28	45.29
Meat products	m	0.69	0.81	53.81	1.20	46.19
Leather and leather products	m	0.77	0.75	55.45	1.28	44.55
Retail trade, non-food	s	0.66	0.75	55.68	1.28	44.32
Fishing	a	0.70	0.78	44.41	1.15	55.59
Business services	s	0.78	0.83	59.30	1.23	40.70
Carpets and rugs	m	0.87	0.79	53.45	1.23	46.55
Lumber and wood products	m	0.94	0.86	54.06	1.16	45.94
Toys, amusement, and sporting goods	m	0.90	0.80	53.08	1.21	46.92

Source: computations based on CGAS.

and high-wage occupations and the proportions with the characteristics (age, sex, education, and occupation) that would make them high or low paid. Consistent with substitution, German low-paying services have proportionately more high-wage workers defined by occupation or detailed characteristics than American low-paying services. For example, in the large eating, drinking, and care facilities category, 40 per cent of Germans compared to 33 per cent of Americans are in high-paying occupations, and 50 per cent of Germans compared to 28 per cent of Americans are in high-paying cells.

4.   Low-Wage Workers versus Low-Wage Services

To what extent are low-wage workers concentrated in low-wage service industries or in particular low-wage service-type occupations rather than being dispersed throughout the economy? How important are low-wage services in the employment of low-wage workers in the USA and Germany?

Defining low pay as wages below two-thirds of the mean wage, about 15 per cent of workers in the CGAS are in cells with a wage below two-thirds of the German mean wage (below median wage: 15 per cent) in Germany. In the USA the proportion with wages below two-thirds of the mean is about 30 per cent (while those with wages two-thirds below the median is 24 per cent).[1] The share of low-wage workers is thus twice as high in the USA as in Germany.

Who are these workers, and where do they work? Table 8.5 presents information on their demographic characteristics and their concentration among sectors. The most striking difference in demography is that women workers are more highly represented among low-wage employees in Germany than in the USA. Given male–female wage gaps, this may help explain why relative wages in low-pay services are further below the average wage in Germany compared to the USA.

To examine the concentration of employment of low-wage workers among sectors, we calculated Herfindahl indices by industry and occupation. A larger Herfindahl implies a greater concentration of employment in a limited number of sectors. The Herfindahls in Table 8.5 show a striking difference between Germany and the USA in the concentration of low-wage workers by industry and occupation. In the USA low-wage workers are widely distributed across the economy. In Germany low-wage workers are highly concentrated in low-pay industries and occupations. Fully 70 per cent of low-wage workers work in the fifteen lowest-paying industries. This contrasts to 58 per cent of low-wage workers in the USA employed in the fifteen lowest-paying industries. The situation with respect to occupations is even more

---

[1] These shares are a bit higher if one computes the share of German workers who are below two-thirds of the US mean wage. Using OECD-PPPs for 1989 (1 PPP $ = 2.104 DM), we find 19% of German workers below the two-thirds limit.

Table 8.5. Characteristics of low-wage workers (data for 1989)

Characteristic	USA	Germany
Mean low wage divided by overall mean	0.521	0.517
Age	32.8	33.7
Education (mean years of schooling)	11.8	10.9
Share of women	0.63	0.86
Industry concentration	0.0754	0.0924
Occupational concentration	0.0531	0.1199

Note: industry concentration: Herfindahl index, industry shares among low-wage workers; occupational concentration: Herfindahl index, industry shares among low-wage workers.

Source: computations based on CGAS.

striking: 37 per cent of low-wage Americans work in the fifteen lowest-paying occupations, whereas 63 per cent of low-wage Germans work in the fifteen lowest-paying occupations.

Table 8.6 displays the industries and occupations that have shares of low-wage workers above the economy's average. By themselves, the major low-paying services —eating, drinking facilities; retail trade food; retail trade non-food, and personal services—account for over half of Germany's low-wage workers, and for around 40 per cent of US low-wage workers. Nearly 30 per cent of all low-wage German workers are in sales, which is nearly twice the contribution of sales to low-wage work in the USA.

The underlying reason for these differences is the very different within-industry or within-occupation dispersions of wages in the two countries. A wide within-sector dispersion of wages translates into low-wage workers throughout the economy, while a narrow within-sector dispersion translates into a concentration of low-wage workers in low-wage industries and occupations.

5.   Skill and the Low-Wage Services

The analysis thus far has treated workers within the low-wage sectors in Germany and the USA as comparably skilled. A worker in an eating or drinking facility in Germany is similar to one in the USA. While this is a defensible proposition for at least some activities—the hamburger flipper does pretty much the same task in a German McDonald's as in an American McDonald's—it is also a proposition that is probably wrong for other activities. The bottom tail of Germans on educational tests is invariably closer to the German mean than the bottom tail of Americans is to the American mean, and the German mean score on tests usually exceeds the American

Table 8.6. Industry distribution of low-wage workers, 1989 (industries with an above average share of low-wage workers, %)

Industry	Share of low-wage workers in industry employment	Industry share in total low-wage employment
USA		
Private households	91.5	3.1
Agriculture	85.2	4.0
Eating, drinking, and care facilities	76.7	18.2
Apparel, etc.	78.6	3.2
Personal services	74.1	2.7
Services to dwellings, etc.	72.8	1.3
Retail trade, food	65.7	6.4
Meat products	66.2	0.9
Leather and leather products	64.8	0.3
Retail trade, non-food	61.5	14.2
Fishing	40.9	0.0
Business services	49.9	1.7
Carpets and rugs	44.2	0.7
Lumber and wood products	38.3	1.6
Toys, amusement, and sporting goods	53.3	0.2
Fifteen lowest-paying industries		58.4
Forestry	42.3	0.1
Rubber and misc. plastics	33.1	0.8
Pottery and related products	46.1	0.0
Miscellaneous manufacturing	47.6	0.5
Wholesale trade, misc.	31.5	0.5
Entertainment, sports	47.5	2.0
Membership organizations	35.8	1.4
Germany		
Private households	93.2	1.7
Agriculture	87.3	4.6
Personal services	79.0	4.8
Retail trade, food	69.3	11.6
Eating, drinking, and care facilities	56.9	13.5
Services to dwellings, etc.	59.7	2.2
Retail trade, non-food	56.4	21.9
Meat products	45.5	2.0
Fishing	44.4	0.0
Other repair services	39.4	0.3
Paper and allied products	34.8	1.7
Wholesale trade, non-durable	36.6	1.6

Table 8.6. (cont'd)

Industry	Share of low-wage workers in industry employment	Industry share in total low-wage employment
Apparel, etc.	42.7	2.8
Leather and leather products	40.9	0.8
Business services	27.5	0.8
Fifteen lowest-paying industries		70.4
Unspecified leasing	45.1	0.1
Trade mediation	36.1	1.1
Food industries	29.7	3.1
Carpets and rugs	20.1	1.5
Toys, amusement, and sporting goods	14.8	0.3
Wholesale trade, durable	19.9	0.4
Wholesale trade, misc.	31.4	1.5
Wholesale trade, misc.	37.3	0.5
Legal, management, accountancy, PR	22.5	1.7
Other services not defined	19.8	0.3

Source: computations based on CGAS.

mean.[2] This suggests that one important reason why the USA has a higher share of low-wage workers within services and a higher share of low-wage service employment per adult in the population may simply be that the USA has more less skilled workers.

Comparing skills across countries is difficult. The standard measure of skills are inputs such as years of schooling or the highest degree achieved, which differ depending on the institutional features of educational systems. In addition, if the quality of education differs, even well-chosen comparisons of educational levels may be misleading. The fact that the US educational system is based at a local level, with relatively little national or even state control, implies moreover that, to a greater extent than in most countries, a year of schooling has different meaning within the country.

[2] The International Adult Literacy Survey shows the following distribution for three different skills on a scale from 0 to 500:

Country	Prose			Document			Quantitative		
	Fifth percentile	Mean	Ninety-fifth percentile	Fifth percentile	Mean	Ninety-fifth percentile	Fifth percentile	Mean	Ninety-fifth percentile
USA	140	270	375	125	260	370	150	280	375
Germany	210	275	350	210	290	360	225	300	370

Source: OECD (1997b).

Level	Authors' classification scheme			Green–Steedman classification scheme		
	USA	Years of schooling	Germany	USA	Years of schooling	Germany
I	9th grade	9–	No certificate Hauptschule	High-school Graduate	9–	Hauptschule
	10th grade	10	Realschule		10	Realschule,
	11th grade	11			11	Apprentice of less than 3 years
	High-school graduate	12	Hauptschule + Apprenticeship		12	Abitur, Fachhochschulreife
II	Some college, no degree	13	Realschule + Apprenticeship; Abitur	Some college	13	Apprentice 3 years or more
	Associate degree	14	Hauptschule + Meister	Associate degree and equivalent qualifications	14	All Meister and Techniker
		15	Realschule + Meister		15	
III	Bachelor's degree	16	Fachhochschule	All 4-year Bachelors' degrees and higher	16	All first and higher degrees
		17	Abitur + Fachhochschule		17	
IV	Master or higher	18+	University degrees		18+	

Fig. 8.1. Equivalent skill levels

Sources: authors' estimates and Green and Steedman (1997).

Still, difficulties notwithstanding, we want to assess the extent to which US–German differences in low-wage employment can be attributed to differences in the distribution of skills between the countries. In the following analysis we use two different classifications of skill: one that we have derived that seeks to transform German and US schooling levels into comparable measures on the CGAS; and one based on Green–Steedman, who have developed another such comparison (see Fig. 8.1).

We begin with years of schooling as derived from the national data sets. Then we develop a comparable classification scheme, which accounts for differences in skill levels attached to years. We distinguish four levels in which to classify workers into equivalent skill groups. Hillary Steedman and Andy Green developed a somewhat different classification scheme, based on 'detailed scrutiny of syllabuses, examination papers and assessment procedures' (Green and Steedman 1997: 2) that provides a useful alternative to ours. Green and Steedman correct for the difference in actual skill levels by shifting the German scale up across the entire skill levels—that is, the German educational system is estimated to produce higher skill levels in general. Our classification scheme shifts the German scale up only at the lower end of the

Table 8.7. Wages, wage dispersion, and skill distributions according to different classification schemes, 1989

Skill level	Authors' classification scheme			Green–Steedman classification scheme		
	Log wage	Standard deviation	Share in employment	Log wage	Standard deviation	Share in employment
USA						
Level 1	2.08	0.40	45	2.08	0.40	45
Level 2	2.29	0.42	30	2.20	0.42	21
Level 3	2.57	0.38	17	2.33	0.41	8
Level 4	2.79	0.39	8	2.64	0.39	25
Germany						
Level 1	2.71	0.37	16	2.7	0.37	13
Level 2	2.98	0.30	69	2.75	0.36	2
Level 3	3.32	0.19	7	2.96	0.29	58
Level 4	3.32	0.15	8	3.25	0.22	26

Source: computations based on CGAS.

schedule.[3] We do not regard years of schooling in Germany at the higher levels to be superior to the American schooling. Since this chapter focuses on the lower end of the scale, the two systems of contrasting education should yield roughly comparable results in terms of explaining differences in employment.

Table 8.7 shows the share of employment in the four levels of education by the two categorizations. For the lowest level the two systems give comparable employment and log wages. Our categorization puts more US workers in the second and third lowest levels and fewer in the highest level than does Green–Steedman. For Germany, our scheme gives more weight to the second level and much less to the third and fourth level, whereas in the Green–Steedman scheme level III covers almost 60 per cent of the workforce and level IV constitutes 25 per cent of the workforce. Our top group consists of Masters' degrees and above, whereas their top group consists of all Bachelors' degrees and above, on the US schooling. If one takes the standard deviation of log wages as a measure for the quality of the classification schemes—the lower the standard deviation for wages within a grouping the better the grouping—there is no difference between the two schemes for the USA, but our scheme produces substantially lower standard deviations for Germany.

Whether the skill distribution is based on the Green–Steedman or on our classification does not make a difference in the USA. The fifteen lowest-paying industries in the USA are also low-skill industries (see Table 8.8). In many industries about 80 per

---

[3] This may be justified by the fact that in the International Adult Literacy Survey (OECD 1997*b*) among the low-educated adults (those who had not completed upper secondary education) about 50% of Germans scored at level 3 or better (out of 5) on the document reading scale but only about 18% of the Americans.

Table 8.8. Skill distribution within the fifteen lowest-paying industries, 1989

Industry		Skill level							
		USA				Germany			
		I	II	III	IV	I	II	III	IV
1001	Authors	0.80	0.13	0.05	0.02	0.29	0.66	0.03	0.02
	G–St	0.80	0.05	0.08	0.07	0.28	0.02	0.56	0.15
1004	Authors	0.73	0.13	0.12	0.02	0.15	0.85	0	0
	G–St	0.73	0.01	0.12	0.14	0.15	0	0.78	0.07
1010	Authors	0.89	0.07	0.04	0.01	0.23	0.77	0.00	0.01
	G–St	0.89	0.02	0.04	0.05	0.21	0.02	0.68	0.09
1020	Authors	0.86	0.08	0.05	0.01	0.31	0.66	0.02	0.01
	G–St	0.86	0.03	0.05	0.06	0.28	0.02	0.60	0.09
1022	Authors	0.81	0.11	0.07	0.01	0.39	0.58	0.02	0.01
	G–St	0.81	0.05	0.06	0.08	0.37	0.02	0.51	0.10
1030	Authors	0.83	0.09	0.08	0.00	0.41	0.56	0.01	0.02
	G–St	0.83	0.04	0.05	0.09	0.40	0.02	0.51	0.08
1031	Authors	0.81	0.12	0.06	0.01	0.21	0.77	0.02	0.01
	G–St	0.81	0.05	0.07	0.07	0.20	0.01	0.69	0.10
1049	Authors	0.73	0.19	0.07	0.00	0.27	0.68	0.04	0.01
	G–St	0.73	0.07	0.12	0.08	0.25	0.02	0.61	0.12
1065	Authors	0.62	0.24	0.12	0.02	0.13	0.82	0.02	0.03
	G–St	0.62	0.10	0.15	0.13	0.11	0.02	0.74	0.13
1068	Authors	0.75	0.19	0.05	0.01	0.20	0.78	0.01	0.01
	G–St	0.75	0.09	0.10	0.05	0.18	0.02	0.74	0.06
1075	Authors	0.68	0.20	0.09	0.02	0.32	0.63	0.03	0.02
	G–St	0.68	0.08	0.12	0.12	0.29	0.03	0.55	0.13
1086	Authors	0.79	0.16	0.05	0.01	0.55	0.44	0.01	0.01
	G–St	0.79	0.07	0.09	0.05	0.53	0.02	0.39	0.06
1087	Authors	0.54	0.26	0.16	0.04	0.22	0.70	0.05	0.03
	G–St	0.54	0.10	0.16	0.20	0.19	0.03	0.60	0.17
1095	Authors	0.86	0.10	0.03	0.01	0.48	0.51	0.01	0.00
	G–St	0.86	0.04	0.06	0.04	0.44	0.03	0.49	0.03
1096	Authors	0.76	0.17	0.07	0.01	0.20	0.78	0.01	0.01
	G–St	0.76	0.07	0.09	0.08	0.18	0.02	0.70	0.10
Total, fifteen lowest-paying industries	Authors	0.71	0.19	0.08	0.02	0.24	0.72	0.02	0.02
	G–St	0.71	0.08	0.11	0.10	0.22	0.02	0.65	0.11
Total, all industries	Authors	0.56	0.22	0.16	0.07	0.18	0.69	0.06	0.07
	G–St	0.56	0.08	0.14	0.23	0.16	0.03	0.60	0.22

Source: computations based on CGAS.

cent of all workers are in the lowest skill level. For Germany, however, the distribution differs strongly between the Green–Steedman and our skill classification. In general, skill level I has a much lower share in Germany than in the USA and our classification puts a high share on skill level II. According to skill classification, the low-paying industries would be low skill in the sense that the lion's share of workers in these industries is in skill level II or below. Using the Green–Steedman classification, however, would make these industries high skill, which we feel is probably inappropriate.

6.   Conclusion: Wages or Wedges or What?

This chapter has documented that Germany does indeed have fewer workers in low-wage service industries than the USA and that this difference is closely linked to Germany's overall lower employment to population rate compared to the USA.

There are four possible reasons why Germany has fewer workers in the low-wage service sector. The first is that the cost of labour in Germany for those sectors is sufficiently high as to produce high prices that discourage consumer purchases. This chapter finds little evidence in support of this proposition in terms of wages. Still, the fact that our data relate to the hourly wage 'normally paid' leaves open the possibility that non-wage costs or charges may contribute to lower service sector employment. Labour costs include paid vacation time, which adds additional costs of 4 per cent in the USA and about 12 per cent in Germany. This difference would eliminate the lower relative wages found in several low-wage services in Germany in Table 8.3. Social security contributions are an additional 7.5 per cent of employer costs in the USA but 20 per cent in Germany. If we assume that the incidence falls largely on employers and consumers, this would create a sizeable labour cost gap, but the higher labour costs would be found in all industries in Germany. Any impact on demand for low-wage services would require that low-wage services have higher labour shares in gross output (so that the same change in cost would produce a greater change in prices) than other sectors and/or higher elasticities of demand for the product. There are a lot of dubious assumptions for this explanation to fly.

The second explanation is that high social assistance payments reduce the supply of workers to low-wage industries in Germany. In Germany, workers have to pay social security contributions and income taxes, which reduces their take-home pay to about 64 per cent in Germany, compared to about 76 per cent of gross earnings in the USA. But the fact that Americans purchase their health care at the workplace or at home and must buy other services that taxes pay for in Germany would reduce this differential. In any case, our analysis of the German benefit structure (Freeman and Schettkat 1999: table 9) suggests that this is an improbable explanation as well.

The third explanation is that Germany's workforce is too skilled for low-wage service jobs. The evidence that Germany uses more skilled occupations and workers in low-wage services than the USA raises doubts about this explanation, though we have not finished our analysis of this issue.

The fourth explanation is a more subtle one, regarding the interrelation between other aspects of the German economy and life style and demand for low-wage services. Germans work shorter hours and they may substitute service consumption by 'do-it-yourself'. This reasoning would fit the desire of Germans to work less and Americans to work more (Bell and Freeman 1996). For it to stand up, however, we would need time-use data showing that low-wage services are purchased disproportionately by workers who put in many hours and that the specific services bought in the market in the USA are in fact produced in the home in Germany.

9 Trade or Technological Change? Which is Working against the Low Skilled?

MARY GREGORY AND STEPHEN MACHIN

Across the advanced economies the last twenty years of the twentieth century saw a sustained decline in the relative demand for low-skilled workers. Within the EU the persistent high levels of unemployment that characterized most member states in the 1980s and 1990s in substantial part reflect the poor employment prospects of the low skilled. The effects of this, in the marked deterioration in the position of low-skilled workers in the labour market, are now widely documented (Glyn and Salverda, this volume). Throughout the EU unemployment rates for low-skilled workers are several times greater than for the higher skilled, and the low skilled predominate among the long-term unemployed (Nickell and Bell 1995). Worse, these unemployment rates seriously understate the marginalization of the low skilled. Falling employment rates and growing non-participation in the labour force, even among prime-age men, indicate a degree of exclusion from work that may be as large again as overt unemployment among the low skilled. Developments in the relative wage position of the low skilled are less clear-cut. In a number of countries, notably within the EU, the earnings distribution has remained relatively stable; in others, however, the shift in the employment structure has been accompanied by growing wage inequality, as relative earnings for the high skilled have increased while those for the low skilled have declined. The USA presents the most extreme case, with real earnings for workers in the lowest deciles of the distribution declining markedly, in absolute as well as relative terms, between the 1970s and the mid-1990s. In the UK, although wages for workers at the bottom of the distribution have not fallen in real terms, none the less growth has been much slower for low-wage workers than for higher earners, and wage inequality has widened (Machin 1996a, 1998, 1999).

While the fact of falling demand for low-skilled workers is widely acknowledged, its causes remain in dispute. Many economists' first guess, viewing the job losses in much of manufacturing industry, was that it must have been brought about by increased exposure to international competition. This view has found considerable populist political resonance, particularly in the USA. In more substantial academic vein, the debate on the sources of this shift in demand against the low skilled was given major impetus by the work of Wood (1994, 1995). In Wood's analysis the diagnosis is clear. Increasingly from the 1960s the newly industrializing countries emerged as significant exporters of manufactures, claiming a sharply rising share of imports and of the domestic market for manufactures among the OECD economies. These imports of low-skill intensive manufactures replaced output and jobs in the advanced economies, displacing significant numbers of low-skilled workers. The emergence of these new trading nations brought a major shift in global patterns of comparative advantage, in which lower-skilled workers in the advanced economies were the losers (Freeman 1995).

Persuasive empirical evidence in support of important effects of trade on the demand for low-skilled workers has, however, proved elusive. Researchers spurred to investigate the impact of trade on employment structures and/or relative wages have typically found the effects to be small, sometimes indiscernible. Moreover, other suspects have been put forward, with empirical support claimed for their role. The most prominent of these is skill-bias in technological change. New technologies, most commonly identified with the microchip and the introduction of computers at the workplace, require more skilled workers to implement them, raising the demand for skills (see, *inter alia*, Krueger 1993; Berman, Bound, and Griliches 1994; Berman, Bound, and Machin, 1998). On the other hand, the work of the less skilled is more readily automated, and tends to be superseded by technological advances.

This chapter reviews the main lines of analysis around this theme, drawing in particular on work by each author. This will relate to the OECD economies in general and to the UK more specifically.

1.   Why Trade may Hurt Low-Skilled Workers:
The Heckscher–Ohlin Approach

The argument that the emergence of the newly industrializing countries into the international trading arena has been detrimental to the economic status of low-skilled workers in the advanced economies starts from the well-known Heckscher–Ohlin model. This explains a country's trade patterns in terms of its factor endowments. In the basic Heckscher–Ohlin model a country that is well endowed with skilled labour can produce skill-intensive goods at lower relative cost than economies that are less well endowed. These countries therefore focus their production activities on skill-intensive goods, exporting these in exchange for goods whose production makes intensive use of the scarce factor, unskilled labour. Similarly, countries abundant in low-skilled labour will export commodities whose production makes intensive use of this. Trade in the skill-intensive good will take place when its world price exceeds the price that would prevail in the home market in the absence of trade. The export of these goods, therefore, embodying the services of the abundant factor, increases the demand for it. This increase in demand through exports raises the relative price of the abundant factor. Moreover, any increase in the price of the exported good will increase the wage return to the factor used intensively in its production—skilled labour in the case of the advanced economies—and thereby decrease the relative wage return to their scarce factor, low-skilled labour. In this way, the relative wages for scarce and abundant factors are seen within the Heckscher–Ohlin framework as determined through product prices on world markets.

A major feature of the last quarter of the twentieth century was the rise in productivity in low-skilled manufacturing activities in the newly industrializing countries. This had many sources, including the massive expansion of basic and secondary education in these countries over the previous generation, and the international transfer of technology and capital, in part through the activities of multinational corporations. The same period saw reductions in trade barriers through the various rounds of negotiations under the GATT and WTO, coinciding with the falling real costs of transport and communications. This set of factors led to a major increase in the supply from the newly industrializing countries of those goods whose production is intensive in low-skilled labour, with a concomitant fall in their world prices. In the advanced countries this fall in the prices of low-skilled intensive goods has led to a fall in the demand for low-skilled labour. In terms of the Stolper–Samuelson theorem, the fall in world prices for low-skilled intensive goods (equivalent, from the perspective of an advanced country, to the reduction in a protective tariff on its imports) reduces the reward to the locally scarce factor, low-skilled labour. The increased supplies of low-skilled workers to world trade depress the wage of unskilled workers in skill-abundant countries, increasing the skill differential in wages, w_s/w_u. In this way the expansion of trade with countries in the industrializing world, where low-skilled labour is relatively abundant, leads to a deteriorating position of the less skilled in the skill-intensive, advanced countries.

The Heckscher–Ohlin and Stolper–Samuelson models predict relative wage changes, where wages for skilled and unskilled workers adjust to absorb the changes in demand for their services. It is easy to extend the models to allow part of the labour market adjustment to occur in terms of employment. If the wage for low-skilled workers is relatively fixed, either through institutional constraints, such as mimimum wage regulation, or because of a reservation wage floor below which people will not work, then the result will be falling employment rates of the less skilled in the skill-abundant country.

The expansion of trade from economies with abundant supplies of low-skilled labour therefore has clear implications for wage structures and relative labour demand in the advanced economies. A number of methods have been developed to test for the relevance and size of these effects. We will concentrate on two. The first works directly within the Heckscher–Ohlin framework, looking at the OECD economies and their trade with non–OECD countries. The second will evaluate the relative impacts of trade and technology more generally for the skill structure of employment in the UK.

2.   Testing for Heckscher–Ohlin Effects: Within-Industry Skill Shifts

Since skilled labour is the abundant factor throughout the advanced economies while low-skilled labour is scarce, the clear prediction of the Heckscher–Ohlin approach is that the wage premium to skills should widen in the advanced economies as trade with the newly industrializing countries expands. An immediate difficulty in trying to measure the role of trade directly by this route is that, while the skill premium has clearly widened in some advanced economies, notably the USA and the UK, this has not universally been the case. In countries where wage structures have been relatively stable, as in parts of continental Europe, any effect of trade in widening the skill differential must be being offset by other influences, such as the role of trade unions or coverage extension in maintaining a compressed wage distribution, or minimum wages setting a wage floor (Lucifora, this volume). This indicates that a sharper test is likely to be required, to counter these influences.

Continuing with the Heckscher–Ohlin line of argument, to the extent that wage differentials rise in response to the increase in international trade, this should lead to substitution away from the employment of skilled labour, now more expensive, in favour of relatively cheaper low-skilled workers. The share of skilled employment within each industry should fall. However, the expansion of trade also shifts production towards high-skilled sectors and away from low-skilled sectors. This 'between-industry' reallocation works in favour of the employment of skilled workers. The effect on the share of skilled employment overall is, therefore, ambiguous.

A range of empirical tests of the orthodox trade hypothesis is presented in Desjonqueres, Machin, and Van Reenen (1999). These tests vary from looking at cross-country patterns of changes in wage and employment structure, to disaggregated analysis of what has happened in specific industries.

The analysis by Desjonqueres, Machin, and Van Reenen first separates 'within-industry' and 'between-industry' changes in wage and employment structures, using the by now familiar decomposition developed by Berman, Bound and Griliches (1994). If S_j is the share of workers of skill type j in aggregate employment, then we can decompose the change in the share of j-skill workers in total employment into two components, one due to the reallocation of employment *between* industries characterized by different proportions of skilled workers, and the second due to changes in the proportion of skilled workers *within* individual industries:

$$\Delta S_j = \sum_i \Delta E_i \bar{S}_{ji} + \sum_i \Delta S_{ji} \bar{E}_i$$

where E_i denotes the employment share of industry i in aggregate employment and an overstrike indicates the average share over the period.

Figs. 9.1–9.4 report the results of carrying out this decomposition for a range of advanced economies. Two measures of skill often adopted in this context are reported, as available: the numbers of non-production and production workers (white collar and blue collar), and the numbers with a graduate education. While these

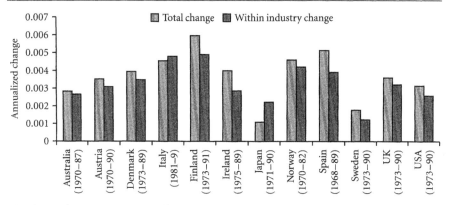

Fig. 9.1. Changes in non-production/production employment shares in manufacturing

Source: Desjonqueres, Machin, and Van Reenen (1999: fig. 1).

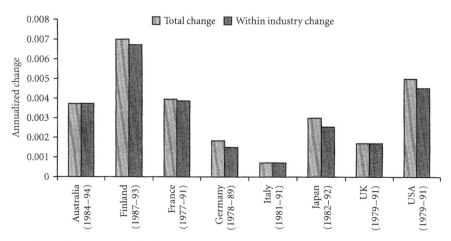

Fig. 9.2. Changes in high-education employment shares in manufacturing

Source: Desjonqueres, Machin, and Van Reenen (1999: fig. 2).

classifications, particularly the level of education, will differ across countries, the focus is on the decomposition of the change in the employment structure *within* each country. Manufacturing and non-manufacturing are reported separately, proxying the traded and non-traded sectors. The pattern is very clear. The manufacturing sectors of all the countries considered show a major shift towards the increased use of skilled workers. This within-industry shift makes up by far the largest component of the overall increase in the use of skills. This is true equally of comparisons for manufacturing based on non-production/production workers (Fig. 9.1) or on the education-based definition of skill (Fig. 9.2). This feature is evident, irrespective of the changes in

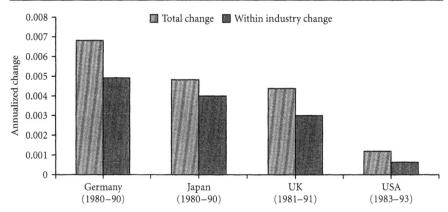

Fig. 9.3. Changes in non-production/production employment shares in non-manufacturing

Source: Desjonqueres, Machin, and Van Reenen (1999: fig. 3).

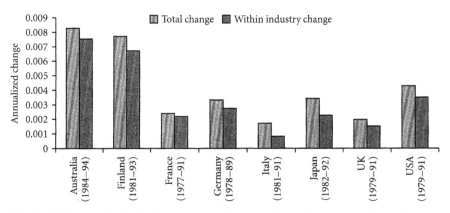

Fig. 9.4. Changes in high-education employment shares in non-manufacturing

Source: Desjonqueres, Machin, and Van Reenen (1999: fig. 4).

wage differentials that the country may or may not have experienced. Following the argument above, Figs. 9.3 and 9.4 repeat the analysis for non-manufacturing. This shows essentially a similar pattern. If one takes the trade model as presented earlier at face value, then its prediction that the within-industry share of skilled employment will fall with the growth of trade with low-skilled countries is clearly not supported by the data.

In spite of the clarity of these results, an obvious criticism of this decomposition approach is that the measurement of the within-industry component is sensitive to the level of aggregation adopted. Each sector used in the decomposition contains a mixture of heterogeneous constituent industries. Some of these will be skill-intensive and expanding, others will be intensive in low-skills and contracting. By aggregating across these different types we may mask the true within-industry fall in skill intensity that occurs within the more disaggregated industries. Where it has been possible to move to a much more disaggregated level of decomposition, the predominance of the within-industry effects remains unchanged. This evidence remains inconclusive, as it will always be possible to argue that whatever level of 'industry' is used remains too aggregated. Rather than continue what could be an irresolvable discussion we take another route, focusing on the shifts in the skill structure in the non-traded sectors.

3.   Looking for Trade Effects in Disaggregated Non-Traded Sectors

Probably the most persuasive piece of evidence in Desjonqueres, Machin, and Van Reenen (1999) is a test of the impact of trade that effectively reverses the usual focus of the trade model. Instead of looking directly at trade, it asks what implications increased trade has for the structure of wages and employment in those industries that are not affected by the opening-up to trade—that is, sectors producing non-traded goods. The Heckscher–Ohlin model has very clear implications for non-traded sectors. The model predicts that the wages of the less skilled should fall as a consequence of rising international competition. This makes less-skilled workers relatively cheaper, and therefore one should see employers demanding more unskilled workers even in sectors that have not been exposed to international trade. Put more starkly, one should see increases in the employment shares of the unskilled in non-traded sectors. This is a very clear and easily testable implication of the Heckscher–Ohlin approach.

So, a strict interpretation of the trade model presented earlier would imply that, in the absence of offsetting factors, the non-traded sectors should show significant within-industry shifts in skill structure towards the less skilled, who, with the development of trade, become (relatively) cheaper to employ. Yet, looking at changes in within-industry shares of skilled employment in non-traded sectors, we observe a striking degree of skill upgrading. Table 9.1 reports changes in skill structure (with skill measured by education) for several countries in a number of non-manufacturing industries that one can plausibly characterize as non-traded. The pattern that emerges from Table 9.1 is of relative increases in the employment shares of skilled workers in *all* of the industries considered. This pattern of skill upgrading throughout the non-traded sectors is clearly at odds with the predictions of the pure trade-based model.

Could this seemingly perverse pattern be due to the fact that the general wage trends favourable to skilled workers are, for some reason, not present in these industries? It could be the case, for example, that skilled workers are unable to find employment in 'good jobs' and are therefore forced to take lower-paid jobs in these non-traded sectors. Table 9.1 shows that this cannot be the full story. Wage differentials have generally moved in favour of skilled workers in the non-traded industries at the same time as the employment shares of the skilled have been rising. These simultaneous changes in relative wages and in the skill structure in favour of skilled workers are clearly showing shifts in relative demand in favour of skilled workers in these disaggregated non-traded sectors. A process of skill upgrading is taking place that trade seemingly cannot adequately explain.

Table 9.1. Changes in relative employment shares and wage differentials in disaggregated non-traded sectors

Country	Industry	Time period	High-education employment share		High/low-education relative wage	
			Last period level	Change	Last period level	Change
Brazil	Personal and household services	1981–9	0.016	0.010	3.55	0.50
	Hotels and restaurants	1981–9	0.044	0.019	3.79	1.31
	Wholesale trade	1981–9	0.084	0.032	3.23	0.83
Germany	Personal and household services	1982–9	0.017	0.002	—	—
	Hotels and restaurants	1982–9	0.031	0.010	—	—
	Wholesale trade	1982–9	0.048	0.011	—	—
Japan	Hotels and restaurants	1981–90	0.074	0.055	1.52	0.12
	Wholesale trade	1981–90	0.114	0.043	1.26	0.01
UK	Personal and household services	1981–90	0.021	0.006	—	—
	Hotels and restaurants	1981–90	0.021	0.005	—	—
	Wholesale trade	1981–90	0.057	0.006	—	—
USA	Personal and household services	1980–90	0.055	0.013	1.54	0.13
	Beauty parlours and hairdressers	1983–90	0.029	0.003	1.65	0.07
	Hotels and restaurants	1983–90	0.085	0.024	2.22	−0.04
	Eating and drinking places	1983–90	0.066	0.005	2.08	0.16
	Wholesale trade	1983–90	0.22	0.08	1.87	0.11

Note: The high-education classification denotes workers with a degree or higher.

Source: calculated from country-specific sources—Brazil: National Survey of Households (Pesquisa Nacional Amostra de Domicilios); Germany: *Mikrozensus*; Japan: Japanese Wage Survey; UK: Labour Force Survey; USA: Current Population Survey. Reproduced from Desjonqueres, Machin, and Van Reenen (1999: table 4).

4.   An Input–Output Approach to Evaluating Trade against Technology

The results in the previous section, although apparently clear-cut, may be argued to identify the role of skill-bias in technological change only indirectly, by demonstrating that trade is an insufficient explanation for the major degree of skill upgrading observed within industries. The second methodology that we apply confronts the measurement of technological change directly. This then allows a quantitative comparison of the relative impacts of trade and technological change on the skill structure of employment.

The analytical framework, developed in Gregory, Zissimos, and Greenhalgh (2001), combines the 'factor content of trade' (FCT) methodology originated by Leontief (1951) with the input–output-based approach to the analysis of patterns of economic growth pioneered by Chenery and associates (Chenery, Shishido and Watanabe 1962; Chenery and Syrquin 1975). The approach evaluates the total use of skills, economy-wide, to produce final output, with input–output linkages capturing the use of skills back through each sector's supply chains. The approach is applied at a detailed sectoral level to the UK economy in the 1980s.

As with the between industry and within industry shifts above, the change in skill use between any two periods can be divided between the changes in sectoral outputs, notionally at given skill use, and the changes in skill use per unit of output, for given outputs:

$$\Delta N = \mathbf{n}\Delta X + \Delta \mathbf{n}X$$

where N is employment by skill group, X the vector of sectoral gross outputs, and $\mathbf{n}$ the matrix of skill-use coefficients (the number of workers of each skill type required to produce one unit of a sector's gross output).

Extending the open Leontief input–output framework in obvious ways, economy-wide output is:

$$X = (\mathbf{I} - k\mathbf{J} - h\mathbf{A})^{-1}(fF + E)$$

where $\mathbf{A}$ and $\mathbf{J}$ are the inter-industry matrices of intermediate and capital goods requirements, F is the vector of final consumption of domestic goods by households and government (i.e. final demand excluding gross investment), and E the vector of exports. f, h, and k are the home shares in final consumption, intermediates, and new capital goods respectively, with $(1 - f)$, $(1 - h)$ and $(1 - k)$ measuring import penetration in each area. fF, $h\mathbf{A}$, and $k\mathbf{J}$ are formed as element-by-element products. Differencing this expression allocates the economy-wide change in sectoral outputs among the channels identified in the Leontief expression: the growth of domestic final consumption (F), the change in exports (E), increasing import penetration in final consumption $(1 - f)$, in purchases of intermediate $(1 - h)$ and capital $(1 - k)$ goods, and changes in the use of intermediate and capital goods $(\mathbf{A}, \mathbf{J})$. Combining this with the expression for the change in employment given above allocates the change in the skill structure of employment across the economy among the effects of trade (exports and import penetration), effects defined as 'technological change', and the growth of domestic final consumption.

Within this framework technological change has a precise definition. First, and familiarly, it comprises the change in the use of skills within each sector, $\Delta \mathbf{n}$. This has many sources, involving the substitution of labour by capital, energy, or other inputs,

Table 9.2. Change in employment by skill level and source of employment change, UK, 1979–1990 (%)

Skill group	Employment change by source			
	Total employment change	Final demand	Net exports	Technological change
	(1)	(2)	(3)	(4)
High skill	28.8	28.2	−4.1	4.6
Intermediate skill	0.1	21.1	−4.8	−16.2
Low skill	−14.9	17.9	−5.7	−27.1
Total	3.5	22.0	−4.8	−13.7
Actual change (000)	784	5,006	−1,101	−3,121

Source: Gregory, Zissimos, and Greenhalgh (2001: table 2).

and subsuming technological innovation as commonly identified (for example, the use of microprocessors); it also encompasses qualitative changes in employment practices. The second element is the indirect use or 'buying-in' of skills, embodied in firms' purchases of components, services, and capital equipment as inputs to the production process. Where the skill intensity of a sector changes through the outsourcing of activities previously carried on in-house (including services such as recruitment, IT, and accountancy as well as the supply of components), the effect on the use of skills economy-wide is still captured. This means that the estimates measure the implications of industrial restructuring and reorganization for economy-wide skill use, and not simply their first-round, within-sector effects. By covering the whole economy rather than just manufacturing, the approach gives appropriate prominence to the service sectors, the largest and fastest-growing area of the economy, and an increasingly important constituent of trade, both directly, in traded services, and indirectly, through the service content (marketing and so on) of traded goods.

   This decomposition is applied to UK data for three broad skill groupings, high, intermediate, and low skilled. The skill classification is derived from the detailed occupations of the Standard Occupational Classification (SOC). This focuses on the job that the individual currently performs, allocating this to an occupation at the appropriate level on the basis of the education, skills, and experience required for competent performance of the job's tasks.

   The main findings for the UK economy over the 1980s are summarized in Table 9.2. This was a period of modest employment growth overall, with a net expansion of under 0.8 million full-time-equivalent jobs, 3.5 per cent over the eleven years (column (1)). However, the change in the skill structure was stark. High-skill employment expanded by 29 per cent; the number of intermediate skill jobs remained virtually unchanged; low-skilled jobs experienced a decline of 15 per cent. The overall growth

Table 9.3. Trade and technology: impact on the skill structure of employment (% change)

Skill group	Employment change due to			
	Trade		Technological change	
	Exports (1)	Imports (2)	Direct labour use (3)	Indirect labour use through intermediate and capital goods (4)
High skill	6.2	−10.3	−12.4	17.0
Intermediate skill	6.8	−11.6	−34.7	18.5
Low skill	6.2	−11.8	−34.9	7.8
Total	6.5	−11.4	−29.1	15.4
Actual change (000)	1,478	2,579	−6,614	3,493

Source: Gregory, Zissimos, and Greenhalgh (2001: table 2).

of 0.8 million jobs was the result of major, but mutually offsetting, developments. The growth of domestic final consumption was massively employment-creating, generating the equivalent of five million new full-time jobs, a 22 per cent expansion on 1979 levels. Trade and particularly technological change, on the other hand, were strongly employment-reducing. Trade destroyed the equivalent of 1.1 million jobs, while technological change, as we define it, eliminated 3.1 million jobs, 13.7 per cent of the number existing in 1979. The estimated impact of technological change on overall employment was therefore around three times as great as the impact of trade.

Skill bias is evident in each area, but is dramatic in the case of technological change. In spite of its overall thrust towards employment reduction, technological change had a *positive* impact on employment of the high skilled, increasing it by 4.6 per cent (column (4)). On the other hand, it imposed heavy job losses on the intermediate and, particularly, the low-skilled groups. Trade gave rise to job losses at all skill levels, least for the high skilled and greatest for the low skilled (column (3)), although both the levels and the differences are small. The growth of domestic consumption gave rise to a substantial increase in employment at all skill levels, with the higher skill groups gaining particularly strongly (28 per cent of 1979 levels); even though low-skill employment gained least, the number of jobs created was still substantial (18 per cent). The structure of this decomposition reminds us that, although demand growth and its skill bias are typically omitted from the trade versus technology debate, their role is none the less highly significant.

The effects of trade on employment reflect both job creation through exports and job loss owing to imports. As shown in Table 9.3, the rate of job creation through exports was only around one-half of the rate of job destruction from import penetration over this period (columns (1) and (2)). The growth of imports destroyed more low-skilled than high-skilled jobs, consistent with the Hecksher–Ohlin theory, but the difference was small. The pattern of jobs created by export growth, on the other hand, was effectively skill neutral. On this very different approach the Hecksher–Ohlin explanation again gains little support.

Columns (3) and (4) of Table 9.3 divide the employment-reducing effects of technological change between direct labour-saving in production, and the indirect effects embodied in firms' purchases of intermediate inputs and capital goods. Direct labour-saving occurred on a huge scale, with one-third of 1979 jobs eliminated by 1990 (column (3)). But over half of the jobs lost were replaced by jobs created with suppliers (column (4)). This is striking evidence of the way in which over this period technological change was working through specialization and outsourcing of component supplies and services. In both aspects the skill bias is clear. Direct labour-saving eliminated intermediate and low-skilled jobs at a huge rate, destroying these almost three times as fast as it eliminated high-skilled jobs. Similarly, contracting-out and increasingly complex and integrated supply chains generated new jobs at high and intermediate skill levels more than twice as rapidly as low-skilled jobs.

These results indicate that over the 1980s in the UK technological change had a major influence on the relative demands for skills, while the effects of trade were relatively small. This is broadly consistent with the findings of other studies, using different methodologies, for both the UK and the USA (Borjas, Freeman, and Katz 1992; Lawrence and Slaughter 1993; Sachs and Shatz 1994; Dewatripont, Sapir, and Sekkat 1998). Further, while the bias in favour of skills was evident in both categories, it was much more striking in the case of technological change. However, an even larger effect, typically overlooked in the trade versus technology debate, came from the growth of domestic demand. This generated a substantial volume of new employment at all skill levels, again tending to favour the higher skilled. The other significant channel for employment expansion to emerge from this analysis is the role of job creation through supply chains (column (4) of Table 9.3). Disaggregating to the sectoral level reveals the major contribution of the services sector in this, as both purchasers and providers of new jobs (Gregory, Zissimos, and Greenhalgh 2001). The service sector has been the major creator of high-skilled jobs, even more strongly than low-skilled jobs. Equally strikingly, much of this employment growth derives from the increasing role of services as an intermediate input, and to service producers even more than to manufacturers. This provides important pointers to key sectors and key linkages, which should be highly relevant to the formulation of policies on employment and skills.

5.   Industry Skill Upgrading

The final area of evidence we consider further reinforces these findings that technology matters more than trade. This draws on work that looks at the correlations between measures of skill upgrading and observable measures of both trade and technology.

Table 9.4. Industry changes in relative skill demand and technology

Technology measure	Census of Production 1982–9 change in non-production share of wage bill	Census of Production 1980–5 change in non-production share of wage bill	United Nations General Industrial Statistics Database 1973–89 change in non-production share of wage bill	General Household Survey 1974–94 change in graduate share of wage bill (men)	General Household Survey 1974–94 change in graduate share of wage bill (women)
	(1)	(2)	(3)	(4)	(5)
R & D/sales	0.065 (0.026)	—	—	—	—
1970s innovation count	—	0.092 (0.053)	—	—	—
Computer usage	—	—	0.010 (0.004)	0.014 (0.008)	0.010 (0.006)
Controls included	Change in log(capital stock), change in log(real sales), time period dummies	Change in log(capital stock), change in log(real sales), time period dummies	Change in log(capital stock), change in log(value added), time period dummies	Change in log(employment), time period dummies	Change in log(employment), time period dummies
Time periods covered	1982–9	1980–5	1973–89	1974–80, 1980–90, 1990–4	1974–80, 1980–90, 1990–4
Sample size	128	96	255	27	27

Notes: Each cell contains a coefficient estimate (standard error in parentheses) from a regression of the change in skilled wage bill shares on a technology variable, plus other controls, as detailed in the table.

Sources: technology measures—R & D/sales: Business Monitor Surveys, 1981, 1983, 1985–89; innovation count: Science Policy Research Unit database on commercially significant innovations introduced in the UK between 1945 and 1983; computer usage: British Social Attitudes Survey. Columns (1) and (2) are taken from Machin (1996*b*); column (3) is from Machin and Van Reenen (1998); columns (4) and (5) are from Harkness and Machin (1998).

5.1. *Skill Upgrading and Technology*

Table 9.4 (taken from Machin 1999, and derived from several earlier pieces of work) summarizes some recent findings, again for the UK, on the association between industry-level skill upgrading and indicators of technology. These are based on regressions of skill upgrading, measured by changes in the share of skilled workers in the industry wage bill, and measures of technological change. Again, two measures of skill are adopted, the wage bill share of non-production workers in columns (1)–(3) and the wage bill share of graduates in columns (4) and (5).

Columns (1) and (2) show that more R & D-intensive industries and more innovative industries, as measured by their innovation count, were those that experienced faster increases in non-production wage bill shares in the 1980s. Column (3) shows the same to be true of industries with higher computer usage. Columns (4) and (5) present regressions of changes in the graduate wage-bill share on computer usage, based on data from the General Household Survey, which extends into the 1990s. In both cases (column (4) for men and column (5) for women) the graduate wage bill share rose by more in industries with higher computer usage. The similarity of this industry-based evidence extending into the 1990s with the measures for the 1970s and 1980s is in line with the idea that technology is still shaping the more recent changes in skill structure that have occurred.

Cross-country evidence further confirms the importance of technology. Regressions of industry skill upgrading on R & D intensity for the same industries across different countries display a positive association. Table 9.4 reports coefficients on R & D intensity (R & D/Value added) for regressions in six countries (Denmark, Germany, Japan, Sweden, the UK, and the USA), and in all cases a positive and significant association is revealed.

The relationship between skill upgrading and R & D intensity derived from these econometric estimates is graphed in Fig. 9.5. In all six countries there is a clear upward-sloping relationship between skill upgrading and R & D. Such regularities are uncommon and not easy to find in international comparisons and suggest an important link between the extent of demand shifts in favour of the more skilled and observable measures of technology.

5.2   Skill Upgrading and International Competition

But is there any correlation between skill upgrading and rising import competition from developing countries? A clear answer emerges. There seems to be no systematic relation between industrial skill upgrading and those directly observed measures of increased international linkages with developing countries.

Fig. 9.6 plots the relationship for the six countries (derived from regressions using data in Machin and Van Reenen 1998). The slopes are more or less flat, display no consistent pattern and reveal much less of a relationship between directly observed measures of increased trade linkages with developing countries and skill upgrading compared to the technology correlations in Fig. 9.5.

It should be pointed out that, in terms of actually testing the trade-based explanation of shifts in relative demand, this approach may be much too crude, as it could be the threat of trade that actually matters. In this scenario one need not see any correlation between skill upgrading and import ratios. So far no one has produced

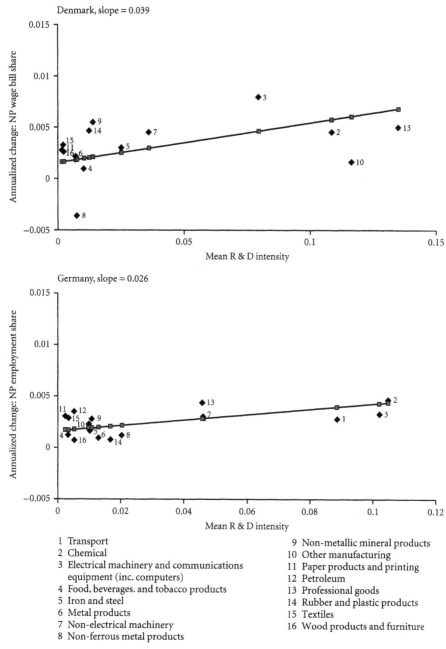

Fig. 9.5. The relationship between industrial skill upgrading and R & D intensity

Source: Machin (1999).

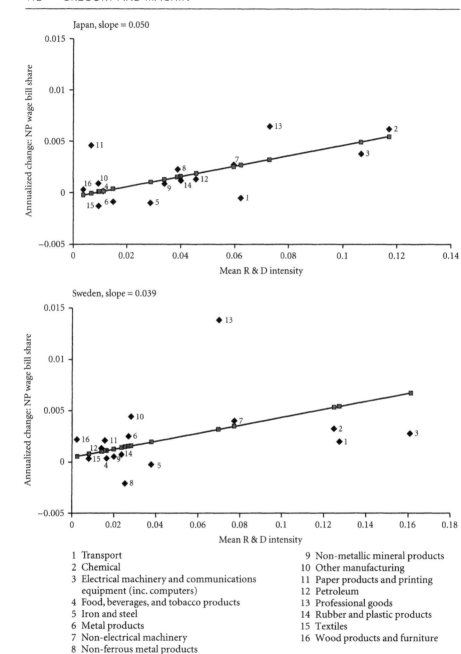

Fig. 9.5. (cont'd).

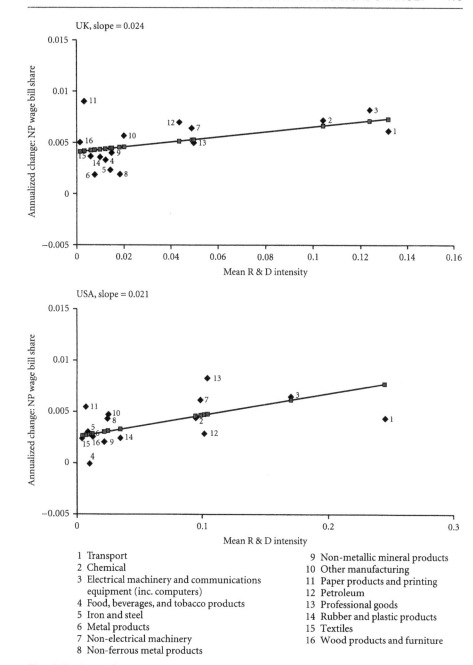

1 Transport
2 Chemical
3 Electrical machinery and communications
  equipment (inc. computers)
4 Food, beverages, and tobacco products
5 Iron and steel
6 Metal products
7 Non-electrical machinery
8 Non-ferrous metal products

9 Non-metallic mineral products
10 Other manufacturing
11 Paper products and printing
12 Petroleum
13 Professional goods
14 Rubber and plastic products
15 Textiles
16 Wood products and furniture

Fig. 9.5. (cont'd).

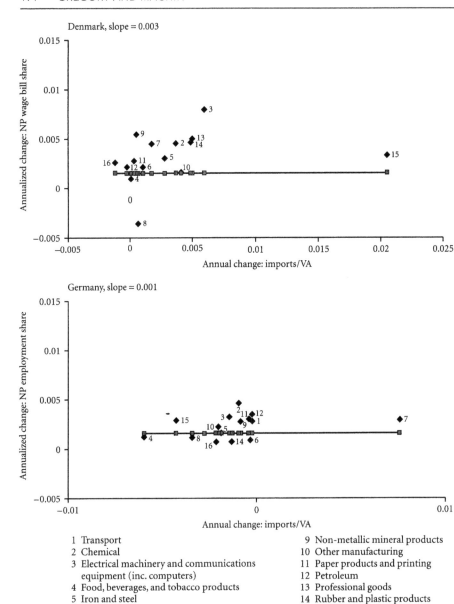

Fig. 9.6. The relationship between industrial skill upgrading and changes in import competition from developing countries

Note: The statistical models control for industry R & D intensity, changes in capital intensity, and output.

Source: Machin (1999).

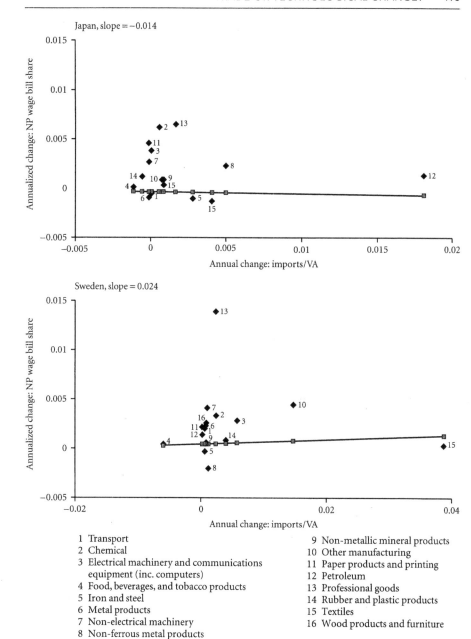

1 Transport
2 Chemical
3 Electrical machinery and communications
    equipment (inc. computers)
4 Food, beverages, and tobacco products
5 Iron and steel
6 Metal products
7 Non-electrical machinery
8 Non-ferrous metal products

9 Non-metallic mineral products
10 Other manufacturing
11 Paper products and printing
12 Petroleum
13 Professional goods
14 Rubber and plastic products
15 Textiles
16 Wood products and furniture

Fig. 9.6. (cont'd)

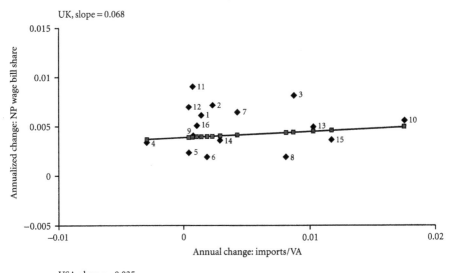

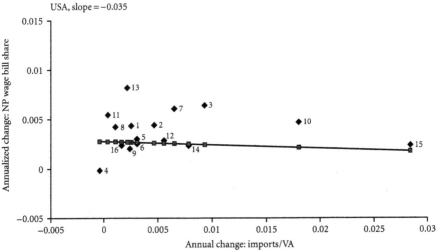

1 Transport
2 Chemical
3 Electrical machinery and communications
    equipment (inc. computers)
4 Food, beverages, and tobacco products
5 Iron and steel
6 Metal products
7 Non-electrical machinery
8 Non-ferrous metal products

9 Non-metallic mineral products
10 Other manufacturing
11 Paper products and printing
12 Petroleum
13 Professional goods
14 Rubber and plastic products
15 Textiles
16 Wood products and furniture

Fig. 9.6. (cont'd)

any persuasive evidence that points to important effects from the threat of trade. Furthermore, other observations cast doubt that trade has had a big impact to date. First, the trade flows from developing countries are still very small, as most trade in the developed world takes place with other developed countries. Secondly, as discussed above, one sees skill upgrading occurring in non-traded sectors. Both of these make it rather difficult to argue that trade is the key factor behind rising labour market inequalities in the developed world.

6.   Conclusions

The adverse demand shifts that worked against less-skilled workers in the last twenty or thirty years of the twentieth century, and what lies behind them, form an important question for government policy. The evidence that exists points to a strong connection between the declining demand for skilled workers and the new forms of technology that are rapidly diffusing into modern workplaces across the globe. But any association with increased exposure to international markets and higher trade flows seems much less marked. These findings are directly relevant to the formulation of policies. If trade is indeed not contributing importantly to these developments, policies should not be oriented towards intervening in these directions. The important orientations for policy lie towards the development of education and the fostering of skills that will link into, and take advantage of, technological progress.

10 Skills and Low Pay: Upgrading or Overeducation?

LEX BORGHANS AND ANDRIES DE GRIP

A significant development in labour markets has been the trend towards people with higher levels of education, notably college graduates, holding jobs previously held by people with lower levels of education, such as school-leavers. This chapter examines the principal explanations of the processes giving rise to this. The 'overeducation' view sees it as evidence of the underutilization of skills, which is socially wasteful. The 'upgrading' view, on the other hand, emphasizes the higher skills now required within occupations; although the job is formally the same, it now involves greater complexity. Both views, however, have pessimistic implications for the position of low-skill workers. On the overeducation view the increased supply of more educated workers pushes the low skilled into the least-favoured jobs, or even crowds them out altogether from the working population. The upgrading view sees low-skill workers as increasingly marginalized as their skill levels no longer meet the minimum requirements of the labour market. In the literature it is often assumed that this bumping-down process results from rigid markets in which so-called job competition regulates allocation. We will show, however, that even in a perfect market, with wage competition, bumping-down might result. Crucial for these processes are the elasticities of demand for each skill level and elasticities of substitution between skill levels. Interpretation of these developments is crucial for public policies towards education and training. In the case of bumping-down, additional investment in education is not effective. Upgrading, on the other hand, requires an increase in educational investment. However, training that increases educational levels below those where upgrading tendencies occur only further stimulates the process of bumping-down.

One of the first studies to put forward the pessimistic view was Freeman's *Overeducated American* (Freeman 1976), in which he suggested that students were overinvesting in education. Acting on out-of-date information about the labour market, they expected good job prospects after graduation. In reality, however, the increasing supply of more highly educated people could not be absorbed by the market, forcing many college graduates to accept a job requiring fewer skills than they had actually obtained. The trend towards graduates taking jobs previously held by people with lower qualifications is, therefore, often associated with (i) overinvestment

The authors wish to thank Peter Sloane, who provided an extensive overview of studies on underutilization, which has been used in Section 2.

in education, (ii) a waste of acquired knowledge, (iii) a decrease in pay for the skilled. Furthermore, (iv) these underutilized workers who occupy jobs below their educational level take away jobs appropriate for lower-skilled workers. This leads to (v) a 'bumping-down' process in the labour market, ultimately pushing low-skilled workers into low-paid jobs, or crowding them out of work altogether.

In contrast to this rather negative picture, the importance of knowledge in our society is increasingly emphasized in both academic and policy debates. This discussion perhaps begins with Leontief (1953), who suggested that it was not physical capital endowment, but rather its endowments in terms of skills, that explained the apparently paradoxical trade pattern of the USA. Recently the European Commission (1996) has claimed that education and training should be a priority for European competitiveness, and suggested that material investment and investment in training should be treated on an equal basis. Similarly the OECD (1996b) notes that 'OECD governments are strongly committed to improving the skills of their citizens as one of the principal means for dealing with current economic uncertainty'. As with technological progress, productivity growth may be obtained by the input of more skills into the production process—that is, an upgrading of the skill level of the labour force. According to Porter (1990), human capital will become the decisive factor in international competitiveness. Recent economic literature focuses on the causes of this upgrading in the technology versus trade debate in particular (e.g. Wood 1994; Machin, Ryan, and Van Reenen 1996).[1]

The overeducation versus upgrading debate is related to the debate on the development of the skilled-to-unskilled wage gap (e.g. Davis and Reeve 1997; Johnson 1997; Topel 1997). The upgrading of required skills is often cited as a major cause of the increased earnings differential between high- and low-skilled workers (e.g. Bound and Johnson 1992; Katz and Murphy 1992), whereas others explain the increase in wage inequality in countries such as Sweden and the Netherlands by an overeducation of the workforce (e.g. Muysken and ter Weel 2000). In a perfect market this link between the demand for educated labour and wages will hold, but, as will be shown in this chapter, where there is market failure an overeducated workforce does not necessarily lead to a narrowing of the earnings differential. Low wages for high-skilled workers who are overeducated for their job may occur alongside high wages for those with a level of education appropriate to it. Furthermore, formal qualifications may not represent a constant level and mix of skills over time. Screening theory (Lang 1994; Weiss 1995) suggests that increased enrolment may result in a reduction in the average ability of graduates, while Grogger and Eide (1995) explain part of the rise in the college premium by increased skills among graduates.

Although very different in character and policy implications, the overeducation and upgrading views share important empirical evidence about the role of skills in the

---

[1] This 'technology versus trade' debate also focuses on the explanation of the shift in demand towards the high skilled. This debate, however, deals particularly with the question of the extent to which this shift can be explained by changes in the industrial structure of the economy, while the 'upgrading versus overeducation' debate focuses on the explanation of the changed allocation of skills within occupations.

labour market. First, both views are consistent with the tendency for higher-educated people to obtain jobs previously held by lower-skilled workers. From the overeducation perspective, this illustrates the underutilization of skills, while from the upgrading view it illustrates the higher skills now required within occupations. Secondly, both views are pessimistic on prospects for low-skilled workers. From the overeducation perspective, low-skilled workers will be pushed into the least-favoured jobs, or even crowded out from the working population, irrespective of their real abilities or potential productivity, whereas the upgrading view predicts that low-skilled workers will become more and more marginalized, as their skill level no longer meets the minimum requirements of the labour market.

Knowledge about the allocation of skills across occupations will, therefore, not provide a direct answer to the questions on the role of skills in the labour market. To establish the significance of education and training for economic progress and for the position of low-skilled workers in the labour market, a better understanding is needed of the skills that people have and the way they utilize these skills in work. Unfortunately, much less is known about how workers' productivity is related to the way in which they use their skills than is known about the allocation of workers in the labour market. Because of the difficulty of measuring skills, the evidence available remains limited on the one hand to detailed case studies, and on the other hand to rough indicators of skills representative of the labour market as a whole.

The upgrading and overeducation views have opposite implications concerning the effectiveness of further investment in education and training, indicating that it is extremely important for policy purposes to gain a better understanding of the way in which an increase in the human capital investments of low-skilled workers is absorbed into the labour market. Whether additional investments in education and training are required because of upgrading within occupations or whether they lead only to overeducation of the workforce links naturally with debates about the way the labour market functions. Upgrading is associated with the neoclassical view in which additional skills are automatically rewarded by the market. Overeducation is associated with market failure, in which wages are insufficiently flexible and allocation is far from efficient.

We will show that the issue of the 'macro-efficiency' of further investment in education and training is not in the first instance related to the efficiency of the market. The effects of educational investments depend on specific characteristics of the segment of the labour market concerned, such as the elasticity of demand for each occupation and the substitutability between different skill levels within each occupation. We will show that even in a perfectly functioning market low elasticities of demand may lead to a bumping-down process, while, on the other hand, limited substitutability between skills might urge the need for an upgrading of the skill level of the labour force. Market failures bring a further level of complication, but only in addition to this.

Many advocates of the promotion of skills to combat the alleged increase in international competitiveness in a knowledge-intensive economy regard it as the role of government to stimulate the acquisition of skills. This illustrates that even proponents of the upgrading view acknowledge market failures. Moreover, although the differing explanations for the shift of higher-educated people towards low-level jobs are analytically in competition, in practice both processes may simultaneously be changing the labour market.

Effective policy formulation requires assessment of the macro-efficiency of investment in education and training. The aim of this chapter is to discuss the effects of changes in supply and demand on the utilization of skills, and the way in which shifts in the skill structure of employment influence the effectiveness of policies on education and training. We first examine what determines the optimum level of education for a job and the different ways underutilization is measured in economic literature. We develop a typology of economic theories on the possible causes and consequences of the observed changes in the allocation of skilled labour, and their policy implications in regard to the (macro)-efficiency of training for the low skilled.

The remainder of the chapter is organized as follows. Section 1 examines the meaning of the skill level of a job. By comparing the occupational productivity profile with the education–wage profile, it will be shown that the optimal skill level in an occupation can be viewed as an interaction between potential productivity in the occupation, on the one hand, and supply and demand developments in the labour market, on the other. The measurement of underutilization of skills is discussed in Section 2. Three different approaches to the measurement of underutilization can be distinguished in existing research. These are discussed in the light of the investigation of the optimal skill level, with empirical examples. Section 3 gives an overview of possible causes of shifts in the educational structure of occupations, presenting different theories that explain the movement within jobs towards the employment of higher educated, with their consequences for both higher- and lower-skilled workers. Finally, Section 4 concludes with a discussion of the implications of the various theoretical points of view for the macro-efficiency of training policies for low-skilled and low-paid workers.

1.   What is the Right Level of Education for a Job?

In everyday language it is common to state that an occupation requires a certain level of education. In this simple picture of the relationship between education and work it is implicitly assumed that jobs at a given level cannot be performed by a worker with lower qualifications: the productivity of the latter is zero. On the other hand, people with higher qualifications than are required are thought to waste their excess qualifications: their productivity in a job below their educational level equals the productivity of workers with only a sufficient educational background for the job.

Many empirical studies, however, question this rigid interpretation and suggest a looser relationship between productivity and educational background. Hartog and Jonker (1998) provide an overview of many empirical studies that show a gradual, non-linear relationship between the education level of workers and

Table 10.1. Hourly wages by job level relative to 'adequate match' by education in the Netherlands

Relative job level	Level of education				
	Lower	Extended lower	Intermediate	Higher vocational	University
Below	—	0.063	0.288	0.508	0.536
		(1.68)	(7.80)	(11.05)	(11.04)
Equal	—	0.170	0.440	0.607	0.860
		(6.04)	(10.49)	(15.77)	(14.19)
Above	0.115	0.330	0.478	0.829	—
	(2.65)	(8.30)	(10.35)	(10.52)	

Note: *t*-values in parentheses.
Source: Hartog (1985).

productivity.[2] This is illustrated in Table 10.1, which shows for the Netherlands the wage effects of (mis)match between the job level and the level of education of workers. The productivity (wage) of a worker with a given level of education increases with the level of the occupation. In most cases the productivity of higher-educated people in lower-level jobs exceeds the productivity of the lower educated at the same job level. (Academics are an exception to this.) In general the extra earnings for a job above the worker's educational level are less than the lost earnings in jobs below it. Hartog tests whether the influences of education and occupational level on the wage are additive, but rejects this hypothesis. This suggests the existence of comparative advantage, with educational levels keying into appropriate job levels.

1.1. *Occupational Productivity Profiles and the Education–wage Profile*

In assignment or matching theory as introduced by Roy (1950, 1951) and Tinbergen (1956, 1975), the productivity associated with a given level of education becomes specific to each occupation, and therefore the relationship between productivity and level of education, which we denote the 'occupational productivity profile', varies

---

[2] All empirical results that demonstrate this gradual non-linear relationship between education and productivity are based on the assumption that wages reflect productivity. The neoclassical law that productivity equals wages assumes, however, an optimal allocation of workers over the jobs. Since these analyses try to catch the consequences on productivity when allocation is changed, and therefore compare people with the same qualifications in jobs at different levels, this assumption is violated. Although illustrative of the idea that productivity depends on allocation, the estimates are in fact based on an inconsistency. Neoclassical theory would state that either workers with the same educational background are indifferent between jobs at different levels—e.g. because the wages are equal in each job—or that there must be differences in skills between these people with a formally equal qualification. More insight is therefore needed about the way in which skills differences influence allocation and productivity.

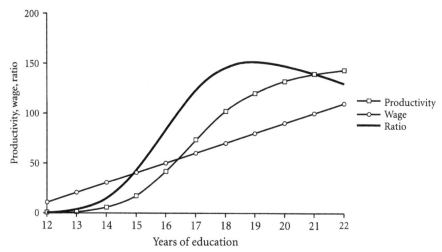

Fig. 10.1. An occupational productivity profile, and an education–wage profile, together determining the optimal skill level for a specific occupation

across jobs. In a perfect labour market, by contrast, the relationship between the wage and level of education, the 'education–wage profile', is equal for all occupations, and varies only with developments in the labour market as a whole.

Fig. 10.1 illustrates these relationships for an individual occupation, with occupational productivity profiles as introduced by Knight (1979). In this example the education–wage profile increases linearly with the level of education, while productivity rises sharply around fifteen–eighteen years of schooling. With low years of schooling, productivity is low and remains below the rising wage. At high levels of schooling again the additional productivity of one further year of schooling does not compensate for the increase in the wage. The ratio between productivity and the wage shows that workers with nineteen years of schooling provide the optimal combination of productivity and wages.

Fig. 10.1 also shows that, although the productivity/wage ratio reaches its maximum at nineteen years of schooling, it takes only modestly lower values at eighteen–twenty years of schooling. This might imply that employers are more or less indifferent between people with educational backgrounds within this interval. This is confirmed by the way the US Bureau of Labor Statistics indicates the educational requirements for an occupation, in terms of 'at least this level, but some/ many employers prefer . . .' (BLS 1985).

Fig. 10.2 gives an alternative representation, showing a job characterized by an occupational productivity profile that increases continuously with the level of education. The education–wage profile rises very similarly. As a consequence, employers will be almost indifferent to the exact amount of human capital which an employee brings, within the range of fifteen–twenty-two years of education. Empirical research

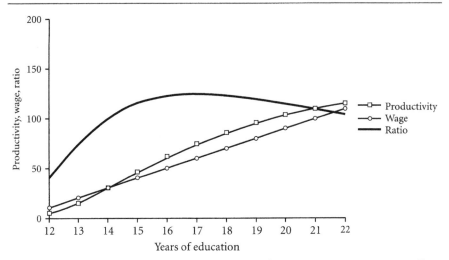

Fig. 10.2. An occupation in which productivity and wages increase proportionally with the skill level

shows that there are indeed occupations in which people of differing educational levels are employed. Borghans, De Grip, and Smits (1997) show that, while jobs such as the lower-level occupations in the printing and chemical industries are matched exclusively to one educational level (Intermediate Vocational Education), other occupations such as lower technical, industrial, and transport occupations seem to allow for a wide variety of educational levels. It is important to note that, although employers may be indifferent between workers with an educational background within this interval, productivity will not be equal for all workers in this group. Workers with more education are more productive, but also have higher wage costs. Within the indifference interval, however, productivity increases proportionally to the wage. Allocation theory suggests that the higher educated handle work differently, or perhaps carry out the more complicated tasks, and therefore are more productive than their colleagues with lower qualifications.

Although the education–wage profile has been introduced in Figs. 10.1 and 10.2 as exogenous, in neoclassical theory it has to be regarded as the outcome of an equilibrium process. Given the wage structure in the overall labour market, it is possible to determine the required educational level and the demand for workers in each occupation. Therefore the aggregate demand at each educational level can be determined. If supply is assumed to be given—that is, participation does not depend on the wage—this aggregate demand for workers at a particular educational level might differ from the supply. Educational levels with excess supply will face falling wages, while those for which demand exceeds supply will show wage increases. The adjustment of wages will ultimately lead to an equilibrium of supply and demand for each educational level. Teulings (1995) estimates such a model in which wages and allocation are investigated simultaneously.

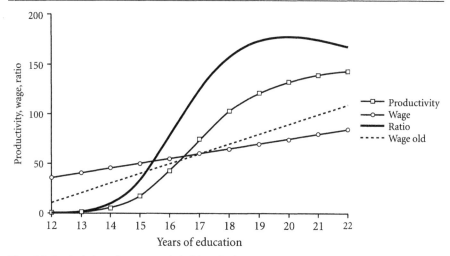

Fig. 10.3. A shift in the optimal skill level of an occupation owing to a shift in the education–wage profile, caused by changes in demand or supply

The education–wage profile in this equilibrium indicates the returns to education. For each additional year of schooling it provides the additional wage an employee can expect. If students anticipate these returns properly, their educational investment decisions will adjust to these returns to education. If some levels of schooling exhibit low returns, fewer students will invest in them, raising the returns again. Assuming a perfect market for education in which students perfectly foresee the returns on their human capital investments, the capital market is not restricted and the only benefits from education are the returns in the form of future wages, then the education–wage profile will become approximately linear with a slope that depends on the discount rate.[3]

1.2. *Shifts in the Education–wage and Occupational Productivity Profiles*

Allocation theory provides an explanation of a specific educational level being 'required' for an occupation. It refers to the match that is optimal given production possibilities and the supply of labour. This required level is not fixed but will be changed by shifts in the education–wage profile (owing to changes in occupational demand or in supply at that educational level) or to changes in the occupational production profile due to technological or organizational developments.

A change in the optimal skill level owing to a shift in the education–wage profile is illustrated in Fig. 10.3. Compared to Fig. 10.1 the optimal level of education increases

[3] Since more education will also shorten the period in which returns are obtained, the slope will rise slightly with years of schooling. Borghans (1993) discusses the effects on educational decisions of imperfect information about the returns; Kodde (1986) analyses the impact of constraints in the capital market, and Oosterbeek and Webbink (1995) discuss the impact on educational decisions from a consumption effect of education.

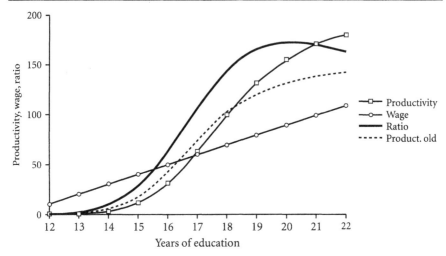

Fig. 10.4. A shift in the optimal skill level of an occupation owing to a change in the occupational productivity profile, caused by the introduction of new technology

from nineteen to twenty years of education. Fig. 10.4 shows the effect of a change in the occupational productivity profile on the optimal skill level. Compared to Fig. 10.1 the optimal level of education in this occupation again increases from nineteen towards twenty years of education.

Both the change in the supply of educated labour, which results in lower wages for the higher educated, as shown in Fig. 10.3, and the change in the occupational productivity profile, as shown in Fig. 10.4, result in a situation in which people employed in this occupation have a higher educational background than previously. Such a shift might easily be associated with overeducation or underutilization. However, in Fig. 10.3 the flattening of the education–wage profile (excess supply of higher skilled workers) has increased the optimal level of education in the occupation concerned. This figure therefore illustrates the overeducation view. However, the figure also shows that this does not mean that the more highly educated workers employed in this occupation do not utilize their extra skills; their productivity in this occupation is higher than the productivity of the workers with fewer years of education. Furthermore, given labour market conditions, it is not possible for them to reach a higher level of productivity.

Fig. 10.4 illustrates the upgrading view. Here a change in the production process owing to technological or organizational developments increases the demand for more highly educated workers. This means that more highly educated workers will be employed in this occupation, which used to be the domain of people with lower qualifications. The productivity of these higher-educated workers will, however, not be lower than the productivity they have, and used to have, in their traditional occupational domain. The new technologies have opened up opportunities to utilize the education of these people productively in these new jobs as well. Therefore there is no underutilization of their level of qualification.

Thus, allocation theory can explain the tendency for more highly educated people to occupy jobs that used to be held by the lower educated, from both a supply side and a demand-side perspective. Within this neoclassical framework, skills are always utilized optimally, given labour market conditions. In fact three grades of under-utilization of skills can be distinguished:

- First, a worker may be employed in a job where people of his educational background used to have lower productivity than in their original occupational domain, but where productivity is now at least equal to the productivity in this original domain. This is the case when upgrading occurs, and one can speak only of *alleged underutilization* of skills.
- Second, a worker may be employed in a job where he has lower productivity than people of his educational background used to have, but which equals their current productivity. This occurs in a situation of excess supply on a perfect labour market and might be called *inter-temporal underutilization* of skills.

Overeducation is, however, generally associated with underutilization of skills in a labour market that is far from perfect, and where part of the workforce with a given skill level is occupied in jobs where they are less productive than others; therefore

- Third, workers may be employed in a job where they have lower productivity than other people with the same educational background currently have. This is *genuine underutilization* of skills, and is not explained by allocation theory.

2.   How should Underutilization be Measured?

As both the overeducation ('bumping-down') and upgrading views are consistent with the stylized fact that people with higher education levels are being appointed to jobs previously held by lower-skilled workers, these views are difficult to distinguish empirically. This problem is increased by the fact that, despite the large number of empirical studies, the measurement of underutilization of skills is far from straight-forward. Moreover, various terms are used to describe essentially similar situations (Shockey 1989). Thus skill underutilization, overeducation, overqualification, under-employment, overtraining, and occupational mismatch are often used interchangeably.

Underutilization is most simply defined as a level of educational attainment greater than the requirement of the occupation in which the person is employed.[4] However the previous section has shown that it makes no sense to speak about a 'required level'

---

[4] Exceptions are the studies of Sloane, Battu, and Seaman (1996) and Borghans and Smits (1997), who distinguish different levels of underutilization.

of education for an occupation. Harvey, Moon, and Geall (1997) suggest that the distinction between graduate and non-graduate jobs is artificial, because graduates alter the nature of a job. Further, technological change and shifts in demand may also alter the relative demand for different levels of skills within an occupation. It has been argued that employers hire educated workers for jobs with lower educational requirements precisely because the more educated are more productive and reduce the cost of training (Sicherman 1991). This recognizes the fact that education is only one form of human capital and one that can be substituted for on-the-job training to the extent that more-educated workers take a shorter period of time to become fully proficient.

A study by Mason (1997) of engineering supervisors in the USA and Britain finds that only 20 per cent of production supervisors in British plants were graduates compared to 35 per cent in the USA. However, British managers recognized several advantages in employing graduate engineers alongside traditional supervisors trained on the shop floor. For example, graduates were better at utilizing computer systems and keeping up to date with technological developments. They played a key role in planning and implementing new work systems, and had the ability to combine the previously separate roles of manufacturing manager (usually office rather than shop-floor based) and production supervisor. This kind of evidence again suggests that more highly educated workers perform differently within an occupation, leaving open the question whether this can be viewed as underutilization.

Many empirical studies suggest, however, that a substantial proportion of workers do not fully utilize their skills, being employed in jobs for which lower skills would be sufficient. Their productivity is, therefore, lower than it would be in appropriate jobs. This is what we call underutilization of skills. Since it means that at least part of the potential productivity of the labour force is not utilized, it can be compared with unemployment. The International Labour Office (ILO 1996) therefore speaks about workers being 'underemployed' in a situation where similar people hold more productive jobs; underutilization is then treated on an equal basis with part-time unemployment.

To support the claim about the underutilization of skills, measurement is needed. However, direct measurement of the way in which people organize their work and thereby utilize their skills is rare. An interesting example of such research is provided by Stasz (1998). Using extensive observations of people at work, she draws conclusions about the role of competences such as problem solving, communications, and teamwork at the workplace. Mason, van Ark, and Wagner (1994) and Lam (1996) also provide interesting detailed studies of the utilization of skills. Studies such as these require large resources, however, and therefore can never provide a complete picture of developments across the labour market. To obtain a more general view on the developments in skill utilization indirect methods are needed.

There are three main alternative measures of underutilization. The *objective measure* involves systematic evaluation by professional job analysts, who attempt to specify the level and type of education required in particular occupations. The best-known source of data of this sort is the Dictionary of Occupational Titles

(DOT) established by the US Employment Service and used in a number of studies of overeducation. On this approach a job is analysed in two different establishments in one state and then in two different establishments in another state. Worker charac- teristics are assessed in terms of six components: training time, aptitude, interest, temperament, physical demands, and working conditions (see Rumberger 1981). The US Department of Labor's (1972) *Handbook for Analysing Jobs* shows that the training time requirements are derived from two questions. The first asks the level of general education necessary to give the worker the background knowledge required to per- form the work. The second asks the duration of the vocational training required for a worker with a specified level of educational attainment to become fully qualified on the job. European equivalents to DOT are few and far between. One is the *ARBI*-code developed by the Dutch Department of Social Affairs (*Arbeidsvoorziening beroepsin- deling* (employment services occupational classification)); this involves a classifica- tion into seven levels of job complexity ranging from very simple work with a training time of a few days (level one) to work on a scientific basis at level seven (Hartog and Oosterbeek 1988). The classification takes into account both the job content and the employee's ability and knowledge in attaining the required level of proficiency.

The second approach is based on worker self-assessment and can therefore be referred to as *subjective assessment*. Examples include the question in the Michigan Panel Study of Income Dynamics that asks 'How much formal education is required to get a job like yours?', or the question in the British Social Change and Economic Life Initiative (SCELI) data set that asks 'If they were applying today, what qualifications if any would someone need to get the type of job you have now?' In similar vein, Green and his colleagues (2000) distinguish 'credentialism' from underutilization of skills. Credentialism occurs where an employer requires a certain level of skills although these are not utilized. Workers with an appropriate level of qualifications are simply not recruited. A slightly different variant is the Spanish Living and Working Con- ditions Survey of 1985 (*Encuesta de Condiciones de Vida Trabajo (ECVT)*), which has been analysed by Alba Ramirez (1993). This includes two separate questions. The first asks 'Considering the job you do, how long would it take someone with the required education, who begins the job, to do it correctly?' Such periods of time may be inter- preted as on-the-job training requirements, but may be influenced not only by the complexity of the job, but also by the ability of the individual. The second question in the *ECVT* survey, asks 'What kind of education does a person need in order to perform the job?' This recognizes the possibility that there may be a distinction between the actual requirements of the job and the customary hiring requirement. This is con- sistent with the screening hypothesis that suggests that the labour market is char- acterized by imperfect information and education is used as a signal to identify to employers the more able, ambitious, or productive workers. Finally, some data sets may allow for the fact that there is no unique educational requirement—for example, asking for minimum entry requirements. As Hartog (1997) notes, the above defini- tions are clearly different from one another, but they may not necessarily be perceived as such by the respondents.

The third approach focuses on the distribution of educational qualifications within an occupation. Most commonly underutilization is defined as a level of education more than one standard deviation above the mean, and undereducation as a level of education more than one standard deviation below the mean (see e.g. Verdugo and Verdugo 1989). This so-called *empirical method* clearly differs from the measures above in defining underutilization as being substantially underutilized. Borghans, de Grip, Smits, and Zuurbier (1997) formulate criteria that allow the identification on an empirical basis of a range of skill levels as appropriate.

It is clear that the above approaches to the measurement of underutilization of skills can lead to divergent estimates. All three have been criticized on various grounds. As Hartog (1997) notes, conceptually the job analysis approach has the advantages of being objective, and having clear definitions and a detailed measurement methodology. Yet there are a number of sources of potential bias. First, estimates of mean years of required schooling in an occupation are constructed by aggregating various jobs within that occupation, ignoring the fact that there is likely to be a distribution of required education across those jobs. Some workers may, therefore, be misclassified as overeducated as a result of variation within the occupation in job-specific schooling requirements (Halaby 1994). Second, required schooling levels may vary for each occupation according to the abilities of incumbents. As Rumberger (1987) and others have pointed out, workers with higher levels of ability may require fewer educational qualifications to perform tasks effectively. Education and ability are substitutes. Third, converting job scores, as in the DOT approach in the USA, into years of schooling is far from uncontentious, though in European studies that use educational dummies this sort of problem may be avoided. Fourth, levels of education ignore the type of education received and some workers who are mismatched may be misclassified. As Halaby (1994) puts it, 'if plumbing requires a high school diploma then plumbers who work in any occupation requiring a high school diploma would be classified as matched even if plumbing skills are not used in the work'.

Most important, however, is that, fifth, such studies make the assumption that the educational requirements of occupations are fixed, whilst in practice both tasks and the required level of knowledge alter over time (Smith 1986). Since the objective method is very expensive and time-consuming, occupational classifications become available long after they have been measured, and are typically used for a very long time period, assuming no changes in the required level. However, as explained in Section 1, the optimal level of skills for an occupation depends on market forces, and is changed by technological and organizational developments. Measurement of changes in underutilization based on the objective method therefore includes shifts in the optimal level. In practice, the objective method picks up all three forms of skills underutilization distinguished in Section 1 and is not able to separate real from alleged underutilization of skills. It is, therefore, not surprising that it tends to produce high levels of underutilization of skills and also strong increases in these levels. Indeed, a study by Van der Velden and van Smoorenburg (1997), comparing the results of the objective and the subjective methods on a Dutch data set, finds that the job analysis method systematically overestimates the actual level of underutilization.

Worker self-assessment has been criticized as subjective, and it is claimed that workers may not have a clear insight into the actual level of education required. For example, they may be inclined to overstate the requirements of their job in order to enhance their perceived status. Stasz (1998), however, found that employees report the actual skill requirements much more accurately than employers. By contrast with the job analysis method, workers will be able to identify their own job rather than the occupation in general. Furthermore, workers may report changes in job requirements as soon as they show up. The method therefore might have clear advantages for measuring pure developments in underutilization, without incorporating biases due to changes in the optimal levels of skills within an occupation. Given a suitably worded question, correctly understood and accurately reported by the worker, the subjective measure reflects genuine underutilization of skills. There is, however, a severe risk that workers relate their situation to productivity standards from the past. In that case the subjective measure would adjust only gradually to new allocation equilibria and tend towards a measure of inter-temporal underutilization of skills. Employees might furthermore simply state current hiring standards. Any tendency to credentialism may be underestimated by the subjective method.

The empirical approach has the advantage that it takes the theoretical foundation of allocation theory as its point of departure. When the labour market functions reasonably well, it might be expected that the majority of workers within an occupation will have an appropriate educational background. Moreover, this approach will be very sensitive to labour market conditions and technological developments, picking up changes in skill requirements quickly. Ideally, the method therefore reflects genuine underutilization of skills. Measurement based on the labour force as a whole might be hampered by stickiness of existing work contracts, leading to some elements of inter-temporal underutilization being included. However, based on information about school-leavers or other new matches on the labour market, the information might be very responsive to new allocation equilibria. Another advantage of this method is that it incorporates the possibility that a range of educational levels is appropriate for a given occupation, as in Fig. 10.2. The empirical method will therefore do a good job in identifying the appropriate level of education for a particular occupation and changes in it. The demarcation line between adequate levels and levels at which underutilization occurs will, however, be largely arbitrary, since the method is based on criteria of frequency. If underutilization occurs more than only incidentally the method might therefore fail, while furthermore it will not provide very precise measures of the degree of underutilization.

It can be concluded that, although it seems to be clear that occupations that used to be occupied by lower skilled workers tend now to be occupied by people with higher levels of education, it is not evident to what degree this really indicates underutilization of the acquired skill level. Therefore, empirical information about such trends has to be treated with care.

3.   The Shifting Allocation of Skilled Labour: Causes and Consequences

To assess the likely consequences of a policy of education for the low skilled, we need to know the reasons for the shift in employment towards the higher skilled. This section will therefore discuss theories explaining this observed tendency and their implications for the labour market position of both higher- and lower-skilled workers.

In Section 1 the concept of the optimum level of education for a job was analysed in order to provide a benchmark for the measurement of skill utilization. It was shown that even in a perfect labour market, where workers with different skill levels are allocated optimally, changes in the matching of workers with jobs might occur. Theories that explain the shift of higher-educated workers towards jobs that used to be held by less-educated workers can therefore be distinguished in two groups: theories within the framework of allocation theory and theories that claim that the actual allocation deviates from the optimum of allocation theory. In the first group three explanations for shifts in the employment structure are possible. First, they may be caused by changes in supply and demand for different levels of education or, second, by technological progress, expressed in a changing occupational productivity profile. Section 3.1 will focus on changes in supply and demand, while in Section 3.2 the process of upgrading will be discussed. A third explanation that does not violate the essence of allocation theory can be found in the heterogeneity of workers with the same formal educational level. This will be discussed in Section 3.3.

Although the allocation model seems able to explain both processes of bumping-down and upgrading, there is empirical evidence of deviations from the optimal allocation of labour. These deviations have serious implications for the interpretation of developments in the educational structure in the labour market. In Section 3.4 the consequences of screening in the labour market are discussed. Section 3.5 continues with efficiency wage theories. In Section 3.6 inflexible wages will be discussed. The theoretical positions elaborated in these sections will be illustrated by some stylized facts from the UK and the Netherlands. Finally, in Section 3.7 a typology of the various theories on the causes and consequences of the shift of the occupational domain of high-skilled workers will be given.

3.1.   Increasing Supply or Decreasing Demand for the Higher Educated

In allocation theory, described in Section 1, the allocation of people with different levels of education is regulated by the balance between the higher wages and the increased productivity of the higher educated. The relative wages of the various levels of education reflect their scarcity. Changes in the supply of skills or demand for occupations will therefore influence wages and the allocation of workers over the occupations. If supply of the highest educational level goes up, or demand for the jobs they are initially matched to goes down, the optimal match of these people will shift towards the lower level occupations. As they become relatively cheaper, employers with jobs that 'require' lower levels of education will consider the higher educated as a serious alternative, as soon as their wages are low enough to be compensated by the higher productivity that their education will bring. Also employment opportunities within their traditional occupational domain will increase as costs fall. The extent of the increase in employment in their own occupational domain depends on the elasticity of demand in the relevant product market. Assuming that this elasticity is low, the wage of the higher educated will decrease until there is sufficient demand from the lower-qualified jobs for which they become attractive. Workers with higher education levels will therefore occupy part of the market in jobs at one level below their own skill level. As a consequence, demand for workers with this lower skill level will fall. This effect is likely to be amplified owing to the higher productivity of the more educated workers. The decrease in demand at the lower educational level will also push down wages there. This will lead to a chain of shifts in the occupational domains, that can be typified as a process of bumping-down.

If the wage elasticity of demand is low in all markets for educated labour, this wave will be transmitted to the lowest part of the labour market. The lower the wage elasticities of demand for the various levels of educated labour, the more severely this tidal wave will ravage the lowest part of the market, resulting in either very low wages or high unemployment for low-skilled workers. If the demand for unskilled labour is elastic, an increase in this unskilled work, with very low wages, will result. If demand is inelastic or if a minimum wage hampers wage adjustment, unemployment will result. Note that productivity does not go down because these workers have lower skills, but because the market value of their skills has gone down owing to competition with more educated workers. The above shows that even within allocation theory it is possible to explain a process of bumping-down, leading to increased low-paid jobs or unemployment for the least skilled.

In the case of an inelastic labour demand any exogenous decrease in demand, for high- or low-skilled jobs, will be transmitted to the lower part of the labour market. Empirical research has indeed shown that the unemployment rate among lower-skilled workers is very sensitive to the business cycle. Teulings (1990) provides unemployment figures by skill level for the Netherlands in 1979 and 1985, shown in Table 10.2.[5] In 1979 total unemployment was relatively low, while in 1985 the economy was in a deep recession. The table shows that the low skilled are indeed hurt much more by this recession than those with higher levels of education. Teulings (1990: 200) states that these results show that actual labour market dynamics deviate from those of neoclassical theory: 'in a standard neo-classical model of the labour market there is no room for unemployment. Wage flexibility guarantees supply to be equal to demand in every market segment.' The main difference between Teulings's 'standard neoclassical model' and the matching theory presented here is the endogeneity

---

[5] A more recent overview of unemployment rates by level of education indicates that in various OECD countries the unemployment rate for low-skilled workers is still much higher than the unemployment rate for high-skilled workers (see Glyn and Salverda, this volume).

Table 10.2. Unemployment by level of education in the Netherlands, 1979 and 1985 (%)

Education level	Unemployment	
	1979	1985
Lower	6	24
Extended lower	3.2	14
Intermediate	⎧	7.6
Higher vocational	⎨ 2.2	6.3
University	⎩	6.2
Total	3.2	12.7
In persons × 1,000	167	751

Source: Teulings (1990).

of the optimal match between the different levels of education and occupations. Teulings assumes that every level of education has its own occupational domain and thus supply and demand always have to equilibriate within this domain.

3.2. Upgrading

The alternative explanation that allocation theory offers for the movement of people with a given level of education towards lower-level jobs in the employment structure is the upgrading of the skills required in these jobs. Suppose that the occupational productivity profile changes in one specific occupation: productivity goes up, owing to the introduction of new technologies. Spenner (1985: 126) describes this as 'the logic of industrialisation [that] involves a division of labour that evolves along the lines of greater differentiation and efficiency. Technological change raises productivity, requiring a broader variety of skills and higher average skills from the work force.' As a consequence, within an occupation that faces an increase in complexity, the optimal level of education will go up, even if wages for this group rise owing to their increased scarcity. Murnane, Willett, and Levy (1995) indeed find that the market value of cognitive skills has been rising. Empirically this will lead to an increase of employment of these higher-educated people in jobs that were formerly occupied by lower educated. Since the new technologies imply increased productivity, employment may, furthermore, be reduced within the occupation if product demand is inelastic.

Wages will increase for the level of education concerned. For workers in the educational level that has lost this occupational domain, demand will fall, *ceteris paribus*. Again assuming a low elasticity of demand, their wages will go down. These lower

Table 10.3. Qualifications required in Britain, 1986 and 1997 (%)

Educational level	1986	1997
High level	20.2	23.8
Level 3	15.3	13.3
Level 2	18.5	21.4
Level 1	7.7	8.9
None	38.3	31.4

Source: Green *et al.* (2000).

wages might make them competitive again with the higher educated who took over their jobs, or might lead to a changed match of these skill levels with jobs at a further lower level of qualifications. Therefore these groups will also be observed occupying jobs previously occupied by lower-qualified workers. While upgrading means an improvement in labour market position for the skill levels directly affected by the changed occupational productivity profiles, for lower-educated workers the effects are equivalent to the situation of decreasing demand described in the previous subsection. So upgrading will again induce a chain of shifts in the occupational domain accompanied by wage decreases for the lower educational levels. Which might again finally push low-skilled workers into low-wage jobs or unemployment. For the lower parts of the labour market, the consequences of upgrading are not completely opposite to those of excess supply of higher-educated people, as is often suggested. Only if the trend to upgrading occurs at all job levels does increasing the education of the low skilled seem a fruitful response.

Table 10.3 provides information about the changes in required qualifications in Britain between 1986 and 1997 from Green and his colleagues (2000). Except for level 3, all educational levels experienced an increase in demand. If these figures are interpreted as a measure of inter-temporal skills utilization, this would clearly indicate a trend to upgrading in Britain for this period. Robinson (1997) estimates, however, that the shift of higher-educated workers to lower occupations exceeds this increase in demand for higher skills, suggesting that the upgrading process is only a part of the explanation. According to Table 10.3, workers with no qualifications experienced a severe decline in demand between 1986 and 1997. The labour market position of approximately 25 per cent of this group could have been improved by additional education, up to level 1. This might have improved the labour market position both of those who received this additional education, and also of those who did not, since the decreasing number of low-skilled jobs would be available for a smaller group of workers. Assuming low elasticities of demand, this would lead to an oversupply at level 1, possibly inducing a bumping-down process that again would hurt the people without qualifications. In addition to the training for the non-qualified, additional

Table 10.4. Underutilization of education in the Netherlands, based on workers' self-assessment (%)

Utilization level	1974	1982	1995
Underutilized	17	16	24
Adequately matched	53	62	63
Overutilized	30	22	12

Source: Hartog and Jonker (1998).

education would also be necessary to increase the skills of some of the workers with levels 1, 2, and 3.

3.3. *Heterogeneity of Labour within an Educational Category*

Although allocation theory is able to explain the shifts in the occupational domain of skill groups adequately from both a bumping-down and an upgrading perspective, there is empirical evidence that its main assumptions do not hold. This derives from the observation that some of those at a given educational level are always found to be 'under-utilized', whatever measure is used. Table 10.4 provides an example from Hartog and Jonker (1998), showing a subjective measure of underutilization in the Netherlands rising from 17 to 24 per cent between 1974 and 1995. In addition to the increase, the figures show that only a fraction of the workers with a given skill level work below their educational level. Since allocation theory predicts that people with the same skills will end up in the same position in the labour market, this finding contradicts the theory. In allocation theory this outcome can occur only when people are equally well off in both types of job. But the data show that workers working below their educational level systematically earn less than those suitably matched.

A straightforward explanation for this is worker heterogeneity within the given level of education. If qualifications do not adequately reflect skills (OECD 1998*b*; Steedman 1999), then a given qualification in fact represents a distribution of skills. Different levels of skills within this distribution may be allocated differently (Borghans and Smits 1997). Underutilization based on formal qualifications rather than actual measurement of skills does not therefore indicate at a non-optimal allocation. Heterogeneity might, however, go together with other explanations for the under-utilization of skills. Pryor and Schaffer (1999) show that in the USA the growth of low-skilled jobs has been greater than the growth of high-skilled jobs. As a consequence, higher-educated workers have been forced to accept lower-level jobs. Pryor and Schaffer also show that cognitive abilities vary among the higher educated. Their analysis, based on the US National Adult Literacy Survey, shows that those among the higher educated who have lower cognitive abilities are employed in lower-level jobs. This sheds another light on the interpretation of 'overeducation' of these workers.

3.4. Screening

An important issue in the economics of education is whether the education process delivers a constant output when the throughflow increases. By contrast with human capital theory (Becker 1962), which treats education as a production process producing skills, screening theory (Spence 1973) stresses the selectivity role of education. People differ in initial abilities, but employers lack information about these abilities. If it is assumed that children with greater ability can go through education more easily, education can become a screening device, enabling pupils to signal their abilities to employers. In a so-called separating equilibrium, youngsters who stay longer in school are associated with higher abilities and therefore earn higher wages. For the youngsters with lower ability, a longer spell in education is not worthwhile. Although they would be able to indicate high ability, the costs to them in completing the course would be too high.

There is extensive evidence that screening at least partially explains the income effects of education (Blaug 1976; Weiss 1995). Furthermore, the importance of screening may have increased[6] (Lang 1994; Borghans 1998). As a consequence, people with the same abilities will now stay longer in education. This implies that, as a scale to measure skills, years of schooling not only contain measurement error, as in the case of heterogeneity, but also shift over time. This process of increased screening might therefore explain the changing occupational domains of certain skill groups. A given qualification will after some time lead to lower-level jobs and a lower wage. In reality, however, people with the same level of skills, correctly measured by their initial abilities, remain allocated to the same jobs at the same wage. Only the time they spend in education increases. From a social point of view, this implies overinvestment in education. However, this does not mean that the initial abilities of workers are underutilized.

3.5. Efficiency Wages and Search Equilibria

As mentioned above, it is an important stylized fact that workers with the same educational background are not equally well off. An alternative explanation to heterogeneity is that the labour market position achieved is to some degree random. People might have the same probability of achieving a job appropriate to their level of education, but the *ex post* outcome might differ. The reason for this lottery might be that only a limited number of adequate jobs are available. Because of wage rigidity, supply might structurally exceed demand. Excess supply then leads to unemployment or to employment at lower job levels.

---

[6] There is, however, also evidence that the return to 'educational signals' declines as additional work experience allows more direct estimates of production to be made by employers (Belman and Heywood 1997; Battu, Belfield, and Sloane 1999). This has the implication that the proportion of workers who are 'properly matched' according to their formal qualifications may decline with age, which is referred to by Belman and Heywood (1997) as a 'sheepskin effect'.

It is generally regarded as a weakness of fixed wage theories that no explanation is offered for employers not adjusting wages when supply and demand are not in equilibrium. Efficiency wage theory has been developed as a foundation for wage inflexibility (Weiss 1990 provides an overview). Also the equilibrium unemployment theories (Mortensen and Neumann 1988; Mortensen 1990) typically depend on the assumption of an efficiency wage. An efficiency wage model introduces a relationship between productivity and the costs of losing one's job. Assuming that employers will not be able to monitor effort perfectly, higher costs of job loss will motivate employees to be productive in order to avoid the firing that would follow the employer's discovery of their low level of effort. Employers will therefore pay more than the competitive wage in order to increase productivity. Since this argument holds for all employers, all will pay the same wage. With full employment there would be no costs of being fired. Efficiency wages therefore lead to unemployment—that is, an equilibrium in which the average duration of unemployment times the reduction in income in that situation equals a level that optimally increases the worker's productivity. However, without loss of argument, this equilibrium might refer to underutilization of labour instead of unemployment (Gautier 2000).

Although efficiency wage models explain wages that deviate from competitive equilibrium, wages are not fixed. Although a substantial number of the workers at a given skill level are employed below their educational level, there is no reason to expect that an increase in supply will lead only to an increase of the number employed below their skill level. The underutilization of a fraction of the workers with this skill level indicates only the existence of a natural rate of underutilization. Additional supply will also face this natural rate, but the fraction of workers whose skills are underutilized will remain unchanged.

3.6. Fixed Wages: The Job Competition Model

So far it has been assumed that wages reflect the marginal productivity of the people at each educational level. In the explanations of shifts in the occupational domain and bumping-down, workers' skills are utilized optimally in some sense. It is often claimed, however, that the labour market does not clear in the way assumed by neoclassical theory. The absence of wage adjustments—that is, fixed wages for each occupation—leads to job competition rather than wage competition. In this subsection we will discuss the consequences of such fixed occupational wages.

In the bumping-down model above, a decrease in demand for higher-educated workers ultimately pushes low-skilled workers into badly paid work or unemployment, and additional education will not improve their situation on the labour market. An important characteristic of this model is, however, that higher-educated labour will receive lower wages. Since in a neoclassical framework wages will be equal for all labour with the same personal characteristics, the wage will fall not only for those who have to accept a lower job, but also for the workers employed in their 'traditional' occupational domain. Although productivity might be higher within the higher-level jobs, wage competition among workers with equal characteristics for these scarce jobs 'at their own level' will push wages down until they are equal to productivity in the lower-skill jobs that have to be accepted by part of this group.

Although wage competition might therefore lead to a bumping-down process, it will also diminish the returns to education. If students adequately anticipate these returns and base their educational investments on its expected benefits, educational investments will diminish. This leads to an adjustment of labour supply to the demand shock. However, although many countries faced the shifts of higher-educated workers to lower-level jobs, a reduction of average investment in education has never been observed.

These observations might suggest that the labour market is regulated not by wage competition but by job competition. In the job competition model of Thurow (1975)[7] it is assumed that wages do not directly reflect marginal productivity. Rather, it is assumed that every type of job is characterized by a constant wage. In more recent literature, these non-clearing wages are often explained by mark-ups owing to monopolistic competition (Snower 1983; Nishimura 1989; Matsuyama 1995; Zwick 2000). Knight (1979) shows that, if the productivity of workers increases with their educational level, then all employers will prefer to recruit the most highly qualified, even if the additional productivity is very slight. This creates a queue of workers. The workers with the highest skill levels are in the front of the queue, with plenty of choice between different jobs, and will therefore choose the best-paid occupations. For people with lower qualifications, the best-paid jobs will not be available. Therefore, a job queue will arise similar to the queue of workers. The outcome of this allocation process will be that the worker at the top of the queue will be matched with job number one, and so on. If demand decreases in the best-paid jobs, everyone will shift some places downwards in the queue. Reduced demand or excess supply for the high-level jobs will therefore again result in a bumping-down process, bringing unemployment or low-paid jobs for the people at the end of the queue.

Although the wage competition and job competition models are often considered as opposing theories, both seem able to explain the process of bumping-down. However, there are three important differences between them. In the first place a bumping-down process is not an inevitable consequence of the neoclassical matching model. Only in combination with the assumption of low elasticities of demand is a decrease in demand for higher-level jobs transmitted to the lower part of the labour market. In the job competition model the bumping-down process will always take place. The reason is that with constant wages *de facto* no demand elasticity exists. Wage competition therefore seems to be able to predict a wider range of market mechanisms among which the extreme bumping-down case is one.

The assumption of job-dependent constant wages,[8] however, creates two further differences between wage and job competition, which obstruct efficiency in the job

---

[7] Reder (1955) introduced the idea of occupational wage differentials two decades before Thurow.

[8] In contrast with occupation-specific fixed wages, wages might also be fixed by level of education. Except for the influence of minimum wages on unemployment, not much attention is paid in literature to this situation, although many other institutional arrangements like wage bargaining agreements could explain

Table 10.5. The average wage of school-leavers from higher vocational education in the Netherlands relative to the fraction of school-leavers with a job below their educational level

Required education level for job	Constant	% below educational level
Lower plus extended lower	14.76 (9.75)	6.44 (1.09)
Intermediate	18.84 (26.91)	−2.70 (0.98)
Higher vocational	21.45 (26.34)	−5.25 (1.63)
University	21.45 (24.16)	−2.34 (0.67)
Total group	21.31 (30.66)	−6.13 (2.24)

Note: *t*-values in parentheses.
Source: Borghans and Smits (1997).

competition model. The marginal benefits of educational investments in the job competition model do not equal the wage in the marginal job. If one more worker is schooled for the highest educational level, this will push one of the workers with the highest education into a less-favourable job. In contrast to the wage competition model, the marginal benefits are larger than the wage in this marginal job. Decreasing demand will therefore not provide a signal to reduce educational investments.

Second, the allocation between workers and jobs might be obscured in the job competition model. Since wages are constant for each occupation, workers will not be allocated to the jobs where their productivity is optimal; instead, everyone will try to obtain the best-paid jobs. If the jobs with the highest wages do not provide the highest comparative advantage for the most skilled people, talent will be wasted in less productive jobs. Murphy, Schleifer, and Vishny (1991) provide the example of highly rewarded lawyer jobs reducing national growth rates by preventing people becoming engineers.

The wage competition model is less pessimistic than the job competition model regarding the effectiveness of additional training for low-skilled workers. Crucial in the job competition model is the difference in wage between those who are lucky enough to find a job that matches their educational level, and those who have to accept a job below their skill level. The burden of excess supply is borne by the losers in the competition for the favourable jobs (Borghans and Smits 1997; Borghans, Bruinshoofd, and de Grip 2000). Table 10.5 shows that school-leavers from Dutch higher vocational education receive higher wages if they are employed in jobs for

the absence of wage flexibility within an educational level. Teulings (1990) provides a short description of the consequences. Changes in demand and supply will have no effect on the match between level of education and jobs. Assuming an education–wage profile that is less steep than in equilibrium would lead to high levels of unemployment in the lower part of the labour market. Underutilization would not, however, occur, while shocks in supply and demand will not be transmitted to the market segments for other levels of education.

which higher educational levels are required. This confirms the findings of Hartog (1985) shown in Table 10.1. This wage is, however, found to be responsive to labour market conditions. The larger the percentage of school-leavers finding a job below the educational level within a labour market segment, the lower the average wage they receive. However, a deterioration of the labour market affects the wages of those with a job matching their educational level substantially more than the wages of the underutilized workers. This suggests that increased competition in the labour market leads to wage competition within the traditional occupational domain. The smaller wage effects for those in a job below or above the higher vocational education level can be explained by heterogeneity. These arguments also predict a positive relationship between the average wage and the percentage of workers below the educational level at the lowest level (lower vocational education).

Van Ours and Ridder (1995) reject the job competition model. They estimate that, where the higher educated face a low number of vacancies within their own occupational domain in the job-matching process, they do not substantially reduce the matching probabilities of lower-qualified people within other segments of the labour market. Higher unemployment rates among low-skilled people are, according to Van Ours and Ridder (1995), explained by higher quit rates. Although their findings provide interesting insights into the functioning of the labour market, it is not clear why the job competition model requires the reallocation induced by shifts in demand and supply to be realized through changing matching behaviour rather than changes in the quit ratio.

3.7. A Typology of the Theories on the Shifts in the Allocation of Labour

Table 10.6 recaps with a typology of the theories that could explain a shift in the occupational domain of higher-skilled workers towards lower job levels.

4.   Policy Conclusions

The aim of this chapter was to discuss the effects of changes in supply and demand on the utilization of skills, and the way in which shifts in the skill structure of the workers within occupational groups affect the effectiveness of education and training policies for the low skilled. For this purpose we developed a typology of the theories that explain the possible causes and consequences of the observed changes. The overeducation and upgrading views provide the two extreme positions. Analyses of the relationship between the acquisition of skills and labour market dynamics show that aspects of both may be involved.

For the policy issue of whether labour market developments make additional investments in schooling worthwhile, the opposing positions of the wage competition and job competition models are not crucial. The crucial point is whether increased employment of the higher educated in jobs at lower levels indicates a bumping-down

Table 10.6. Typology of theories that explain a shift in the occupational domain and their consequences

Consequences	Within allocation theory			Outside allocation theory		
	Upgrading	Increase in supply	Heterogeneity	Screening	Efficiency wages	Job competition
Overinvestment	No	No	No	Yes	No	Yes
Wastage of skills	No	No	No	No	No	Yes
Lower wages	No, higher wages	Yes	No	Yes, people end up with the same wage regardless of their qualifications	No	Yes, people end up with the same wage regardless of their qualifications
Take away jobs of lower educated	No, create job opportunities for lower educated	Yes, especially when elasticity of demand is low	Yes	No, but forces people to increase their educational investments to keep the same job	Yes	Yes
Bumping-down process	Upgrading in high-level jobs might result in bumping-down on the lower end of the labour market	Yes, especially when elasticity of demand is low	No	No	No	Yes

process initiated by excess supply of the more educated, or whether it points to a process of upgrading. Bumping-down can result in both the job competition model and the neoclassical matching model, suggesting that additional investment in education is not very effective. Upgrading, on the other hand, requires an increase in educational investment. Upgrading versus bumping-down therefore seems to be the most fundamental conflict for the macro-efficiency of training policies for the low skilled.

Two differences between the job competition and the wage competition models remain important, however. First, from the point of view of the wage competition model, bumping-down is only an extreme case. The model does not exclude additional demand absorbing part of the extra supply of skills that results from training policies. The effects of training therefore need not to be totally cancelled out by a bumping-down process, but might lead to new employment opportunities at higher wages, depending on the elasticity of demand at the higher job levels. In the job competition model, however, the elasticity of demand equals zero, since wages do not react to changes in supply and demand. Second, although in a world of job competition and in a world of wage competition upgrading might occur, in the sense that jobs become more complex, in the job competition case the labour market will provide no signals for this. In the case of wage competition it might be very difficult to distinguish upgrading from bumping-down, since both processes will lead to a shift in the employment structure, with higher-educated people taking jobs that used to be occupied by the lower educated. Upgrading does, however, manifest itself in a changing employment structure. In the case of job competition, neither the allocation of workers nor their wages will be changed owing to upgrading. The increased productivity of the higher educated, which might make more educational investments fruitful, will therefore remain unobserved.

Finally, it is interesting to note that not every form of training will be a useful instrument to cope with upgrading. It has been shown that upgrading in a specific group of occupations might induce bumping at lower levels of education. Training is fruitful only if it increases the supply at a level of education for which the upgrading process creates new demand. Training that increases educational levels below those where the upgrading tendencies occur only further stimulates the process of bumping-down.

References

Abowd, J. M., and Kramarz, F. (1998), 'The Cost of Hiring and Separations', NBER Working Paper 6110, revised, Cambridge, Mass.

—— Corbel, P., and Kramarz, F. (1999), 'The Entry and Exit of Workers and the Growth of Employment', *Review of Economics and Statistics*, 81 (2), 170–87.

Ahrne, G., and Persson, I. (1997) (eds.), *Familj, makt och jämställdhet (Family, Power and Equality between Women and Men)*, Stockholm: SOU 1997: 138.

Alba Ramirez, A. (1993), 'Mismatch in the Spanish Labor Market: Over-education?', *Journal of Human Resources*, 28 (2), 259–78.

Albæk, K., Arai, M., Asplund, R., Barth, E., and Strøjer Madsen, E. (1998), 'Measuring Wage Effects of Plant Size', *Labour Economics*, 5 (4), 425–48.

Alpin, C., Shackleton, J. R., and Walsh, S. (1997), 'Over and Under-Education in the UK Graduate Labour Market', mimeo.

Arai, M., Asplund, R., and Barth, E. (1998), 'Low Pay, A Matter of Occupation', in R. Asplund, P. J. Sloane, and I. Theodossiou (eds.), *Low Pay and Earnings Mobility in Europe*, Aldershot: Edward Elgar.

Armstrong, P., Glyn, A., and Harrison, J. (1991), *Capitalism since 1945*, Oxford: Basil Blackwell.

Asplund, R. (1998a), 'Private vs. Public Sector Returns to Human Capital in Finland', *Journal of Human Resource Costing and Accounting*, 3 (1), 11–44.

—— (1998b), 'The Gender Wage Gap in Finnish Industry 1980–94', in I. Persson and C. Jonung (eds.), *Women's Work and Wages*, London: Routledge. (Revised version of a more comprehensive working paper with the same title published as Discussion Paper 541 by the Research Institute of the Finnish Economy, ETLA, Helsinki.)

—— and Bingley, P. (1996), *Wage Mobility in Finnish Industry in 1980–1994*, Helsinki: The Research Institute of the Finnish Economy, ETLA, Series B, 123.

—— —— and Westergård-Nielsen, N. (1997), 'Wage Mobility in the Danish and Finnish Private Sectors', paper presented at the EALE Conference, Aarhus.

—— —— —— (1998), 'Wage Mobility for Low-Wage Earners in Denmark and Finland', in R. Asplund, P. J. Sloane, and I. Theodossiou (eds.), *Low Pay and Earnings Mobility in Europe*, Aldershot: Edward Elgar.

—— Sloane, P. J., and Theodossiou, I. (1998) (eds.), *Low Pay and Earnings Mobility in Europe*, Aldershot: Edward Elgar.

Atkinson, A. B. (1973), 'Low Pay and the Cycle of Poverty', in F. Field (ed.), *Low Pay*, London: Arrow.

—— (1985), 'How Should We Measure Poverty?', ESRC Programme on Taxation, Incentives and the Distribution of Income, Discussion Paper 82, London: London School of Economics.

—— (1987), 'On the Measurement of Poverty', *Econometrica*, 55 (4), 749–64.

—— (1995), *Incomes and the Welfare State*, Cambridge: Cambridge University Press.

—— Bourguignon, F., and Morrisson, C. (1992), *Empirical Studies of Earnings Mobility*, London: Harwood.

—— Rainwater, L., and Smeeding, T. (1995), *Income Distribution in OECD Countries*, Paris: OECD.

Bardone, L., Gittleman, M., and Keese, M. (1998), 'Causes and Consequences of Earnings Inequality in OECD Countries', *Lavoro e relazioni industriali: Rivista di economia applicata*, 4 (2), 1–25.

Battu, H., Belfield, C. R., and Sloane, P. J. (1999), 'Over-Education among Graduates: A Cohort View', *Education Economics*, 7 (1), 21–38.

Bazen, S. (1988), 'On the Overlap between Low Pay and Poverty', ESRC Programme on Taxation, Incentives and the Distribution of Income, Discussion Paper 120, London School of Economics.

—— and Benhayoun, G. (1995), 'Les Effets du salaire minimum sur l'emploi: Une analyse sectoriel', in S. Bazen and G. Benhayoun (eds.), *Salaire minimum et bas salaires*, Paris: L'Harmattan.

—— —— (1996), *Les Bas Salaires en Europe*, Paris: Presses Universitaires de France.

—— and Marimoutou, V. (1997), 'Looking for a Needle in a Haystack? A Re-Examination of the Time Series Relationship between Teenage Employment and Minimum Wages in the United States', LARE-CNRS Document de Travail 97/12.

—— and Martin, J. (1991), 'The Impact of Minimum Wages on the Earnings and Employment of Young People and Adults', *OECD Economic Studies*, 16, 199–221.

—— and Skourias, N. (1997), 'Is there a Negative Effect of the Minimum Wage on Youth Employment in France?', *European Economic Review*, 41 (3–5), 723–32.

—— Benhayoun, G., and Skourias, N. (1995), 'The Impact of Minimum Wages on Employment in France: A Regional Approach', paper presented at the EALE Conference, Lyons.

—— Gregory, M., and Salverda, W. (1998a), 'Low-Paid Employment in France, Great Britain and the Netherlands', in S. Bazen, M. Gregory, and W. Salverda (eds.), *Low-Wage Employment in Europe*, Aldershot: Edward Elgar.

—— —— —— (1998b) (eds.), *Low-Wage Employment in Europe*, Aldershot: Edward Elgar.

Becker, G. S. (1962), 'Investment in Human Capital: A Theoretical Analysis', *Journal of Political Economy*, 70 (S), 9–49.

Bell, B. D., and Pitt, M. K. (1998), 'Trade Union Decline and the Distribution of Wages in the UK: Evidence from Kernel Density Estimation', *Oxford Bulletin of Economics and Statistics*, 60 (4), 509–28.

Bell, L., and Freeman, R. (1996), 'Why do Americans and Germans Work Different Hours?', in F. Buttler, W. Franz, R. Schettkat, and D. Soskice (eds.), *Institutional Frameworks and Labor Market Performance*, London: Routledge.

Belman, D., and Heywood, J. S. (1997), 'Sheepskin Effects by Cohort: Implications of Job Matching in a Signalling Model', *Oxford Economic Papers*, 49 (4), 623–37.

Benhayoun, G. (1990), 'Le Salaire minimum et l'emploi des jeunes', Centre d'Économie Regionale, Université d'Aix Marseille III.

—— (1994), 'The Impact of Minimum Wages on Youth Employment in France Revisited: A Note on the Robustness of the Relationship', *International Journal of Manpower*, 15 (2–3), 82–5.

Berman, E., Bound, J., and Griliches, Z. (1994), 'Changes in the Demand for Skilled Labor within US Manufacturing Industries: Evidence from the Annual Survey of Manufacturing', *Quarterly Journal of Economics*, 109 (2), 367–98.

—— —— and Machin, S. (1998), 'Implications of Skill Biased Technological Change: International Evidence', *Quarterly Journal of Economics*, 113 (4), 1245–79.

Bigard, A., Guillotin, Y., and Lucifora, C. (1998), 'Earnings Mobility: An International Comparison of Italy and France', *Review of Income and Wealth*, 44 (4), 535–54.

Bingley, P., Bjørn, N. H., and Westergård-Nielsen, N. (1995), 'Wage Mobility in Denmark 1980–90', CLS Working Paper 95–10, Aarhus.

Bjorklund, A., and Freeman, R. (1996), 'Generating Earnings Equality and Eliminating Poverty: The Swedish Way', in R. Freeman, B. Swedenborg, and R. Topel (eds.), *Reforming the Welfare State*, Chicago: Chicago University Press.

Blanchflower, D., and Freeman, R. (1992), 'Unionism in the US and Other OECD Countries', *Industrial Relations*, 31 (1), 56–79.

Blank, R., Card, D., and Robins, P. (1999), 'Financial Incentives for Increasing Work and Income among Low-Income Families', NBER Working Paper 6998, Cambridge, Mass.

Blau, F. D. (1998), 'Trends in the Well-Being of American Women, 1970–1995', *Journal of Economic Literature*, 36 (1), 112–65.

—— and Kahn, L. M. (1996), 'International Differences in Male Wage Inequality: Institutions versus Market Forces', *Journal of Political Economy*, 104 (4), 791–836.

—— Simpson, P., and Anderson, D. (1998), 'Continuing Progress? Trends in Occupational Segregation in the United States over the 1970s and 1980s', *Feminist Economics*, 4 (3), 29–71.

Blaug, M. (1976), 'The Empirical Status of Human Capital Theory: A Slightly Jaundiced Survey', *Journal of Economic Literature*, 14 (3), 827–55.

Blondal, S., and Pearson, M. (1995), 'Unemployment and Other Non-employment Benefits', *Oxford Review of Economic Policy*, 11 (1), 136–69.

BLS (1984): Bureau of Labour Statistics, *Occupational Outlook Handbook*, 1984–5 edition, Washington: US Department of Labor.

Bonnal, L., Fougère, D., and Sérandon, A. (1997), 'Evaluating the Impact of French Employment Policies on Individual Labor Market Histories', *Review of Economic Studies*, 64 (4), 683–713.

Borghans, L. (1993), 'Educational Choice and Labour Market Information', ROA Dissertation Series, no. 1, Maastricht: ROA.

—— (1998), 'Human Capital and Screening with Heterogeneous Learning Activities', paper presented at the EALE Conference, Blankenberge.

—— and Smits, W. (1997), 'Under-Utilization and Wages of HVE graduates', paper presented at Applied Econometrics Association, Maastricht.

—— Bruinshoofd, A., and de Grip, A. (2000), 'Low Wages, Skills, and the Utilization of Skills', in L. Borghans and A. de Grip (eds.), *The Over-Educated Worker? The Economics of Skill Utilization*, Aldershot: Edward Elgar.

—— —— and Smits, W. (1997), 'Future Developments in the Job Level and Domain of Low-Skilled Workers', paper presented at the LoWER Conference, Bordeaux.

—— —— —— and Zuurbier, H. (1997), *Het beroependomein van opleidingen* (The Occupational Domain of Type of Education), ROA-R-1997/2, Maastricht.

Borjas, G. J., Freeman, R. B., and Katz, L. F. (1992), 'On the Labor Market Effects of Immigration and Trade', in G. J. Borjas and R. B. Freeman (eds.), *Immigration and the Work Force: Economic Consequences for the United States and Source Areas*, NBER Project Report, Chicago and London: University of Chicago Press.

Bound, J., and Johnson, G. (1992), 'Changes in the Structure of Wages in the 1980s: An Evaluation of Alternative Explanations', *American Economic Review*, 82 (3), 371–92.

Brown, C., Gilroy, C., and Kohen, R. (1982), 'The Effect of the Minimum Wage on Employment and Unemployment', *Journal of Economic Literature*, 20 (2), 487–528.

Brunetta, R., and Dell'Aringa, C. (1990), *Labour Relations and Economic Performance*, Macmillan: London.

Buchinsky, M., and Hunt, J. (1996), 'Wage Mobility in the United States', NBER Working Paper 5455, Cambridge, Mass.

Buhman, B., Rainwater, L., Schmaus, G., and Smeeding, T. (1988), 'Equivalence Scales, Well-Being, Inequality and Poverty: Sensitivity Estimates across Ten Countries Using the Luxembourg Income Study Database', *Review of Income and Wealth*, 33 (2), 115–42.

Bulletin on Women and Employment in the EU (1994), 4, Brussels: European Commission, DGV.

Burkhauser, R., and Finegan, T. (1989), 'The Minimum Wage and the Poor: The End of the Relationship', *Journal of Policy Analysis and Management*, 8, 53–71.

—— Holtz-Eakin, D., and Rhody, S. (1995), 'Mobility and Inequality in the 1980s: A Cross-National Comparison of the United States and Germany', mimeo.

Callan, T., and Nolan, B. (1991), 'Concepts of Poverty and the Poverty Line', *Journal of Economic Surveys*, 5 (3), 243–61.

Calmfors, L., and Driffill, J. (1988), 'Bargaining Structure, Corporatism and Macroeconomic Performance', *Economic Policy*, 6, 14–61.

Cantillon, S., and Nolan, B. (1998), 'Are Married Women More Deprived than their Husbands?', *Journal of Social Policy*, 27 (2), 151–71.

—— Marx, I., and Van den Bosch, K. (1997), 'The Challenge of Poverty and Social Exclusion, in OECD, *Family, Market and Community: Equity and Efficiency in Social Policy*, Paris: OECD.

Cappellari, L. (1998), 'Wage Inequality Dynamics in the Italian Labour Market: Permanent Changes or Transitory Fluctuations?', Istituto di Economia dell'Impresa e del Lavoro Working Paper 23, Università Cattolica, Milan.

Card, D. (1998), 'The Impact of Declining Unionization on Wage Inequality', NBER Working Paper 5520, Cambridge, Mass.

—— and Krueger, A. (1995), *Myth and Measurement: The New Economics of the Minimum Wage*, Princeton: Princeton University Press.

—— —— (1998), 'A Re-Analysis of the Effect of the New Jersey Minimum Wage Increase on Employment Using Representative Payroll Data', NBER Working Paper 6386, Cambridge, Mass.

—— Kramarz, F., and Lemieux, T. (1999), 'Changes in the Relative Structure of Wages and Employment: A Comparison of the United States, Canada and France', *Canadian Journal of Economics*, 32 (4), 843–77.

Caroli, E., and Aghion, P. (1998), 'Inequality and Growth', mimeo, University College London.

CEA (1998): Council of Economic Advisers, *Good News for Low Income Families: Expansions in the Earned Income Tax Credit and the Minimum Wage*, Washington: CEA.

CERC (1991): Centre d'Études des Revenus et des Coûtes, *Les Bas Salaires dans les pays de la Communauté Économique Européenne*, Paris: CERC.

Chenery, H., and Syrquin, M. (1975), *Patterns of Development: 1950–1970*, Oxford: Oxford University Press.

—— Shishido, S., and Watanabe, T. (1962), 'The Pattern of Japanese Growth 1914–54', *Econometrica*, 30 (1), 98–131.

Contini, B., Filippi, M., and Villosio, C. (1998), 'Earnings Mobility in the Italian Economy', in R. Asplund, P. J. Sloane, and I. Theodossiou (eds.), *Low Pay and Earnings Mobility in Europe*, Aldershot: Edward Elgar.

Coulter, F., Cowell, F., and Jenkins, S. P. (1992), 'Equivalence Scale Relativities and the Extent of Inequality and Poverty', *Economic Journal*, 102 (Sept.), 1067–82.

Davis, D. R., and Reeve, T. A. (1997), 'Human Capital, Unemployment, and Relative Wages in a Global Economy', NBER Working Paper 6133, Cambridge, Mass.

Deaton, A. (1997), 'Letter from America', *Royal Economic Society Newsletter*, 99: 6–7.

De Grip, A., and Borghans, L. (2000) (eds.), *Skill Utilization and Bumping Down*, Aldershot: Edward Elgar.

Delame, E., and Kramarz, F. (1997), 'Entreprises et formation continue' (firms and In-Service Training), *Économie et prévision*, 127, 63–82.

Dell'Aringa, C., and Lucifora, C. (1994), 'Wage Dispersion and Unionism: Do Unions Protect Low Pay?', *International Journal of Manpower*, 15 (2–3), 221–32.

Desjonqueres, T., Machin, S., and Van Reenen, J. (1999), 'Another Nail in the Coffin? Or Can the Trade Based Explanation of Changing Skill Structures be Resurrected?', *Scandinavian Journal of Economics*, 101 (4), 533–54.

Dewatripont, M., Sapir, A., and Sekkat, K. (1998), *Trade and Jobs in Europe: Much Ado About Nothing?*, Oxford: Oxford University Press.

Dickens, R. (1997a), 'Caught in a Trap? Wage Mobility in Great Britain: 1975–94', Centre for Economic Performance Discussion Paper 365, London School of Economics.

—— (1997b), 'Male Wage Inequality in Great Britain: Permanent Divergence or Temporary Differences?', in P. Gregg (ed.), *Jobs, Wages and Poverty*, Centre for Economic Performance, London School of Economics.

—— Machin, S., and Manning, A. (1994), 'Minimum Wages and Employment: A Theoretical Framework with an Application to the UK Wages Councils', *International Journal of Manpower*, 15 (2–3), 26–48.

DiNardo, J., Fortin, N., and Lemieux, T. (1996), 'Labor Market Institutions and the Distribution of Wages, 1973–1992: A Semi-Parametric Approach', *Econometrica*, 64 (5), 1001–44.

Dolado, J. J., Felgueroso, F., and Jimeno, J. F. (1998), 'The Effects of Minimum Wages: Evidence from Spain', in S. Bazen, M. Gregory, and W. Salverda (1998) (eds.), *Low-Wage Employment in Europe*, Aldershot: Edward Elgar.

—— Kramarz, F., Machin, S., Manning, A., Margolis, D., and Teulings, C. (1996), 'The Economic Impact of Minimum Wages in Europe', *Economic Policy*, 23, 317–72.

Ducos, G., and Plassard, J. M. (1991), 'Salaire minimum et demande de travail des jeunes', paper presented at Premières Journées du SESAME, Clermont Ferrand.

Duncan, G., Gustafsson, B., Hauser, R., Schmaus, G., Jenkins, S., Messinger, H., Muffels, R., Nolan, B., Ray, J. C., and Voges, W. (1995), 'Poverty and Social Assistance in the United States, Canada, and Europe', in K. McFate, R. Lawson, and W. J. Wilson (eds.), *Poverty, Inequality and the Future of Social Protection*, New York: Russell Sage Foundation.

Eissa, N., and Liebman, J. (1996), 'Labor Supply Response to the Earned Income Tax Credit', *Quarterly Journal of Economics*, 112 (2), 605–37.

Eriksson, T. (1998), 'Long-Term Earnings Mobility of Low-Paid Workers in Finland', in R. Asplund, P. J. Sloane, and I. Theodossiou (eds.), *Low Pay and Earnings Mobility in Europe*, Aldershot: Edward Elgar.

European Commission (1996), *Teaching and Learning: Towards the Learning Society*, Brussels: Commission of the European Communities.

Eurostat (1998a), *Labour Force Survey: Results 1997*, Luxembourg: Office for Official Publications of the European Communities.

—— (1998b), *Low Income and Low Pay in a Household Context (EU-12)*, in series 'Statistics in Focus: Population and Social Conditions, 1998/6', Luxembourg: Office for Official Publications of the European Communities.

Fagan, C., and Rubery, J. (1996), 'Transitions between Family Formation and Paid Employment', in G. Schmid, J. O'Reilly, and K. Schomann (eds.), *International Handbook of Labour Market Policy and Evaluation*, Aldershot: Edward Elgar.

—— O'Reilly, J., and Rubery, J. (1998), 'Le temps partiel aux Pay-Bas, en Allemagne et au Royaume-Uni: Un nouveau contrat social entre les sexes?', in M. Maruani (ed.), *Les Nouvelles Frontières de L'inégalité: Hommes et Femmes sur le Marché du Travail*, Paris: La Découverte/Mage.

Ferber, M. A. (1998) (ed.), *Women in the Labor Market*, 2 vols., International Library of Critical Writings in Economics, Aldershot: Edward Elgar.

Fortin, N., and Lemieux, T. (1997), 'Institutional Change and Rising Wage Inequality', *Journal of Economic Perspectives*, 11 (2), 75–96.

Förster, M. (1994), 'Family Poverty and the Labour Market', LIS Working Paper 114, Luxembourg Income Study/CEPS, Luxembourg.

Foster, J. E., and Shorrocks, A. F. (1988), 'Poverty Orderings', *Econometrica*, 56 (1), 173–77.

Freeman, R. B. (1976), *The Over-Educated American*, New York: Academic Press.

—— (1980a), 'The Exit-Voice Trade-off in the Labour Market: Unionism, Job Tenure, Quits, and Separations', *Quarterly Journal of Economics*, 94 (June), 643–73.

—— (1980b), 'Unionism and the Dispersion of Wages', *Industrial and Labor Relations Review*, 34 (1), 3–24.

—— (1993), 'How Much Has De-Unionization Contributed to the Rise in Male Earnings Inequality?', in S. Danziger and P. Gottschalk (eds.), *Uneven Tides: Rising Inequality in America*, New York: Russell Sage Foundation.

—— (1994), 'How Labor Fares in Advanced Economies', in R. B. Freeman (ed.), *Working under Different Rules*, New York: Russell Sage Foundation.

—— (1995), 'Are Your Wages Set in Beijing?', *Journal of Economic Perspectives*, 9 (3), 15–32.

—— (1996a), 'The Minimum Wage as a Redistributive Tool', *Economic Journal*, 106 (May), 639–49.

—— (1996b), 'Labour Market Institutions and Earnings Inequality', *New England Economic Review*, May–June, 157–72.

—— (forthcoming), *Labour Market Institutions and Economic Success*, Clarendon Lectures in Economics, Oxford: Oxford University Press.

—— and Gottschalk, P. (1998), *Generating Jobs: How to Increase Demand for Less-Skilled Workers*, New York: Russell Sage Foundation.

—— and Medoff, J. L. (1984), *What Do Unions Do?*, New York: Basic Books.

—— and Schettkat, R. (1999), 'Skill Compression, Wage Differentials and Employment: Germany vs. the US', Leverhulme Programme on The Labour Market Consequences of Technical and Structural Change, Discussion Paper 39.

Friedman, M., and Kuznets, S. (1954), *Income from Independent Professional Practice*, New York: NBER.

Gautier, P. A. (2000), 'Do More High Skilled Workers Occupy Simple Jobs during Bad Times?', in L. Borghans and A. de Grip (eds.), *The Over-Educated Worker? The Economics of Skills Utilization*, Aldershot: Edward Elgar.

Gittleman, M., and Joyce, M. (1995), 'Earnings Mobility in the United States, 1967–91', *Monthly Labour Review*, 118 (9), 3–13.

—— —— (1996), 'Earnings Mobility and Long-Run Inequality: An Analysis Using Matched CPS Data', *Industrial Relations*, 35 (2), 180–96.

Glyn, A., and Miliband, D. (1994) (eds.), *Paying for Inequality: The Economic Cost of Social Injustice*, London: Institute for Public Policy Research and Rivers Oram Press.

Gosling, A. (1996), 'Minimum Wages: Possible Effects on the Income Distribution', *Fiscal Studies*, 17 (4), 31–48.

—— et al. (1997), *The Dynamics of Low Pay and Unemployment in Early 1990s Britain*, London: Institute for Fiscal Studies.

Gottschalk, P. (1982), 'Earnings Mobility: Permanent Change or Transitory Fluctuations?', *Review of Economics and Statistics*, 64 (3), 430–56.

—— (1997), 'Inequality, Income Growth and Mobility: The Basic Facts', *Journal of Economic Perspectives*, 11 (2), 21–40.

—— and Moffitt, R. (1994), 'The Growth of Earnings Instability in the US Labor Market', *Brookings Papers on Economic Activity*, 2, 217–72.

—— and Smeeding, T. M. (1997), 'Cross-National Comparisons of Earnings and Income Inequality', *Journal of Economic Literature*, 35 (2), 633–87.

—— Johnson, G. E., Topel, R. H., Fortin, N. M., and Lemieux, T. (1997), Symposium 'Wage Inequality', *Journal of Economic Perspectives*, 11 (2), 21–96.

Granqvist, L., and Persson, H. (1997), 'Karriärer inom varuhandeln—spelar kön någon roll?' ('Careers within Retailing—Does Gender Matter?'), in I. Persson and E. Wadensjö (eds.), *Glastak och glasväggar? Den könssegregerade svenska arbetsmarknaden* (*Glass Ceilings and Glass Walls? The Sex Segregated Swedish Labour Market*), Stockholm: SOU 1997: 137.

Green, A., and Steedman, H. (1997), *Into the Twenty-First Century: An Assesment of British Skill Profiles and Prospects*, Special Report, Centre for Economic Performance, London School of Economics.

Green, F., Ashton, D., Burchell, B., Davies, B., and Felstead, A. (2000), 'Are British Workers Becoming More Skilled?', in L. Borghans and A. de Grip (eds.), *The Over-Educated Worker? The Economics of Skill Utilization*, Aldershot: Edward Elgar.

Gregg, P. (1997) (ed.), *Jobs, Wages and Poverty*, Centre for Economic Performance, London School of Economics.

—— and Wadsworth, J. (1995), 'Making Work Pay', *New Economy*, 214: 120–13.

—— —— (1996), 'More Work in Fewer Households?', in J. Hills (ed.), *New Inequalities: The Changing Distribution of Income and Wealth in the UK*, Cambridge: Cambridge University Press.

—— —— (1999) (eds.), *The State of Working Britain*, Manchester: Manchester Univesity Press.

Gregory, M., and Elias, P. (1994), 'Earnings Transitions of the Low-Paid in Britain, 1976–91: A Longitudinal Study', *International Journal of Manpower*, 15 (2–3), 170–88.

—— and Jukes, R. (1998), 'The Effects of Unemployment on Future Earnings: Low Paid Men in Britain, 1984–1994', in R. Asplund, P. J. Sloane, and I. Theodossiou (eds.), *Low Pay and Earnings Mobility in Europe*, Aldershot: Edward Elgar.

—— and Thomson, A. W. J. (1990) (eds.), *A Portrait of Pay, 1970–82: An Analysis of the New Earnings Survey*, Oxford: Oxford University Press.

—— Zissimos, B., and Greenhalgh, C. (2001), 'Jobs for the Skilled: How Technology, Trade and Domestic Demand Changed The Structure of UK Employment, 1979–90', *Oxford Economic Papers*, 53(1); previously 'The Impact of Trade, Technological Change and Final Demand on the Skills Structure of UK Employment', Leverhulme Programme on 'The Labour Market Consequences of Technical and Structural Change' Discussion Paper 29.

Grogger, E., and Eide, E. (1995), 'Changes in College Skills and the Rise in the College Wage Premium', *Journal of Human Resources*, 30 (2), 280–310.

Gustafsson, B. (1994), 'The Degree and Pattern of Income Immobility in Sweden', *Review of Income and Wealth*, 40 (1), 67–86.

Hagenaars, A., de Vos, K., and Zaidi, M. A. (1994), *Poverty Statistics in the Late 1980s: Research Based on Micro-Data*, Luxembourg: Office for Official Publications of the European Communities.

Halaby, C. (1994), 'Over-Education and Skill Mismatch', *Sociology of Education*, 67, 47–59.

Hakim, C. (1996), *Key Issues in Women's Work: Female Heterogeneity and the Polarisation of Women's Employment*, London: Athlone Press.

Harkness, S., and Machin, S. (1998), 'Changes in the Wage Returns to Education in Britain: Supply Changes and the Evolution of Wage Differentials by Sex and Subject of Study', mimeo.

—— —— and Waldfogel, J. (1997), 'Evaluating the Pin Money Hypothesis: The Relationship between Women's Labour Market Activity, Family Income and Poverty in Britain', *Journal of Population Economics*, 10 (2), 37–158.

Hartog, J. (1985), 'Earnings Functions: Testing for the Demand Side', *Economics Letters*, 19, 281–5.

—— (1997), 'On Returns to Education: Wandering Along the Hills of Our Land', paper presented at Applied Econometrics Association, Maastricht.

—— and Jonker, N. (1998), 'A Job to Match your Education: Does it Matter?', in H. Heijke and L. Borghans (eds.), *Towards a Transparent Labour Market for Educational Decisions*, Aldershot: Ashgate.

—— and Oosterbeek, H. (1988), 'Education, Allocation and Earnings in the Netherlands: Overschooling?', *Economics of Education Review*, 7 (2), 185–94.

Harvey, L., Moon, S., and Geall, V. (1997), 'Graduates Work: Organisational Change and Students' Attributes', University of Central England.

Hirsch, B. T., and Addison, J. T. (1986), *The Economic Analysis of Unions*, Boston: Allen & Unwin.

Horrigan, M., and Mincey, R. (1993), 'The Minimum Wage and Earnings and Income Inequality', in S. Danziger and P. Gottschalk (eds.), *Uneven Tides: Rising Inequality in America*, New York: Russell Sage Foundation.

Horvath, F. (1982), 'Forgotten Employment: Recall Bias in Retrospective Data', *Monthly Labor Review*, 104 (3), 40–3.

Hughes, G., and Nolan, B. (1998), 'Competitive and Segmented Labour Markets and Exclusion from Retirement Income', paper presented at the LoWER Conference, Groningen.

Hultin, M., and Szulkin, R. (1997), 'De lågavlönade på arbetsmarknaden—en analys av kvinnor och män under två decennier' ('The Low-Paid in the Labour Market—An Analysis of Women and Men over Two Decades'), in I. Persson and E. Wadensjö (eds.), *Kvinnors och mäns löner—varför så olika? (Wages of Women and Wages of Men—Why So Different?)*, Stockholm: SOU 1997: 136.

ILO (1996): International Labour Office, *Underemployment*, Geneva: ILO.

ISSAS (1990): Institute of Social Studies Advisory Service, *Poverty in Figures: Europe in the Early 1980s*, Luxembourg: Eurostat.

Jenkins, S. (1991), 'Poverty Measurement and the Within-Household Distribution: Agenda for Action', *Journal of Social Policy*, 20 (4), 457–83.

Jensen, P., and Verner, M. (1997), 'Do Low-Wage Individuals Experience More Unemployment?', paper presented at the LoWER Conference, London.

Jepsen, M., Meulders, D., and Terraz, I. (1998), *Working-Time, Women and Low Wages*, paper presented at the EALE Conference, Blankenberge.

—— —— Plasman, O., and Vanhuynegem, P. (1997), *Individualisation of the Social and Fiscal Rights and the Equal Opportunities between Women and Men*, Département d'Économie Appliquée de l'Université Libre de Bruxelles, Brussels.

Johnson, G. E. (1997), 'Changes in Earnings Inequality: The Role of Demand Shifts', *Journal of Economic Perspectives*, 11 (2), 41–54.

—— and Stafford, F. P. (1998), 'Alternative Approaches to Occupational Exclusion', in I. Persson and C. Jonung (eds.), *Women's Work and Wages*, London: Routledge.

Jonung, C. (1998a), 'Occupational Segregation by Sex and Change over Time', in I. Persson and C. Jonung (eds.), *Women's Work and Wages*, London: Routledge.

—— (1998b), 'Yrkessegregeringen mellan kvinnor och män' ('Occupational Segregation between Women and Men'), in I. Persson and E. Wadensjö (eds.), *Glastak och glasväggar? Den könssegregerade svenska arbetsmarknaden* (*Glass Ceilings and Glass Walls? The Sex Segregated Swedish Labour Market*), Stockholm: SOU 1997: 137.

Joshi, H. (1998), 'Gender Equity and Low Pay: A Note Based on Britain', in C. Lucifora and W. Salverda (eds.), *Policies for Low Wage Employment and Social Exclusion*, Milan: Franco Angeli.

—— and Paci, P. (1998), *Unequal Pay for Women and Men*, Cambridge, Mass.: MIT Press.

Katz, L., and Murphy, K. (1992), 'Changes in Relative Wages 1963–1987: Supply and Demand Factors', *Quarterly Journal of Economics*, 107 (1), 35–78.

Kaufman, R. (1989), 'The Effects of Statutory Minimum Rates of Pay on Employment in Great Britain', *Economic Journal*, 99 (Dec.), 1040–53.

Keane, M. R., Moffitt, R., and Runkle, D. (1988), 'Real Wages over the Business Cycle: Estimating the Impact of Heterogeneity with Micro Data', *Journal of Political Economy*, 96 (6), 1232–65.

Keese, M. (1998), 'Are Statutory Minimum Wages an Endangered Species?', in C. Lucifora and W. Salverda (eds.), *Policies for Low Wage Employment and Social Exclusion*, Milan: Franco Angeli.

—— and Swaim, P. (1997), 'The Incidence and Dynamics of Low-Wage Employment in OECD Countries', paper presented at the LoWER Conference, Bordeaux.

—— Puymoyen, A., and Swaim, P. (1998), 'The Incidence and Dynamics of Low-Paid Employment in OECD Countries', in R. Asplund, P. Sloane, and I. Theodossiou (eds.), *Low Pay and Earnings Mobility in Europe*, Aldershot: Edward Elgar.

Knight, J. B. (1979), 'Job Competition, Occupational Production Functions, and Filtering Down', *Oxford Economic Papers*, 31 (2), 187–204.

Kodde, P. A. (1986), 'Uncertainty and the Demand for Education', Ph.D. thesis, Rotterdam.

Koutsogeorgopoulou, V. (1994), 'The Impact of Minimum Wages in Greece', *International Journal of Manpower*, 15 (2–3), 86–99.

Kramarz, F., and Philippon, T. (1998), 'The Impact of Differential Payroll Tax Subsidies on Minimum Wage Employment Effects', CREST-INSEE Working Paper, Paris.

Krueger, A. (1993), 'How Computers have Changed the Wage Structure', *Quarterly Journal of Economics*, 108 (1), 33–60.

—— and Pischke, J.-S. (1997), 'Observations and Conjectures on the US Employment Miracle', NBER Working Paper 6146, Cambridge, Mass.

Lam, A. (1996), 'Work Organisation, Skills Development and Utilisation of Engineers: A British–Japanese Comparison', in R. Crompton, D. Gallie, and K. Purcell (eds.), *Changing Forms of Employment*, London: Routledge.

Lang, K. (1994), 'Does the Human-Capital/Educational-Sorting Debate Matter for Development Policy?', *American Economic Review*, 84 (1), 353–8.

Laroque, G., and Salanié, B. (1999), 'Breaking Down Female Non-Employment in France', CREST Working Paper 9931, Paris.

Lawrence, R. Z., and Slaugher, M. J. (1993), 'Trade and US Wages: Great Sucking Sound or Small Hiccup?', *Brookings Papers on Economic Activity; Microeconomics*, 161–210.

Layard, R., Piachaud, D., and Stewart, M. (1978), *The Causes of Poverty*, Background Paper 5, Royal Commission on the Distribution of Income and Wealth, London: HMSO.

Le Grand, C. (1997), 'Kön, lön och yrke—yrkessegregering och lönediskriminering mot kvinnor i Sverige' ('Gender, Wage and Occupation—Occupational Segregation and Wage Discrimination against Women in Sweden'), in I. Persson and E. Wadensjö (eds.), *Kvinnors och mäns löner—varför så olika? (Wages of Women and Wages of Men—Why So Different?)*, Stockholm: SOU 1997: 136.

Leontief, W. W. (1951), *The Structure of the American Economy 1919–39: An Empirical Application of Equilibrium Analysis*, New York: Oxford University Press.

—— (1953), 'Domestic Production and Foreign Trade: The American Position Re-Examined', *Proceedings of the American Philosophical Society*, 38: 386–407.

Leuven, E., and Oosterbeek, H. (1997), 'Explaining International Differences in Male Wage Inequality by Differences in Demand and Supply of Skills', mimeo, University of Amsterdam.

Lewis, H. G. (1986), *Union Relative Wage Effects: A Survey*, Chicago: University of Chicago Press.

Lillard, L., and Willis, R. J. (1978), 'Dynamic Aspects of Earnings Mobility', *Econometrica*, 41 (5), 985–1012.

Low Pay Commission (1998), *The National Minimum Wage*, First Report of the Low Pay Commission, London: Stationery Office.

Lucifora, C. (1997), 'Winners and Losers: An Analysis of Earnings Mobility in Italy and France', in P. Gregg (ed.), *Jobs, Wages and Poverty*, London: Centre for Economic Performance, London School of Economics.

—— (1998), 'Working Poor? An Analysis of Low-Wage Employment in Italy', in R. Asplund, P. J. Sloane, and I. Theodossiou (eds.), *Low Pay and Earnings Mobility in Europe*, Aldershot: Edward Elgar.

—— (1999), 'Wage Inequalities and Low Pay: The Role of Labour Market Institutions', Fondazione Eni Enrico Mattei, Note di lavoro, no. 13/99.

—— and Salverda, W. (1998) (eds.), *Policies for Low Wage Employment and Social Exclusion*, Milan: Franco Angeli.

—— —— and Nolan, B. (2000) (eds.), *Policy Measures for Low Wage Employment in Europe*, Aldershot: Edward Elgar.

Lundberg, S., and Pollak, R. A. (1996), 'Bargaining and Distribution in Marriage', *Journal of Economic Perspectives*, 10 (4), 139–58.

—— —— and Wales, T. J. (1997), 'Do Husbands and Wives Pool their Resources? Evidence from the United Kingdom Child Benefit', *Journal of Human Resources*, 32 (3), 463–80.

Machin, S. (1996a), 'Wage Inequality in the UK', *Oxford Review of Economic Policy*, 12 (1), 49–62.

—— (1996b), 'Changes in the Relative Demand for Skills in the UK Labour Market', in A. Booth and D. Snower (ed.), *The Skills Gap and Economic Activity*, Cambridge: Cambridge University Press.

—— (1997), 'The Decline of Labour Market Institutions and the Rise in Wage Inequality in Britain', *European Economic Review*, 41 (3–5), 647–57.

—— (1998), 'Recent Changes in Wage Inequality and the Wage Returns to Education in Britain', *National Institute Economic Review*, 166, 87–96.

—— (1999), 'Wage Inequality in the 1970s, 1980s, and 1990s', in P. Gregg and J. Wadsworth (eds.), *The State of Working Britain*, Manchester: Manchester University Press.

—— and Manning, A. (1994), 'The Effects of Minimum Wages on Wage Dispersion and Employment: Evidence from the UK Wages Councils', *Industrial and Labor Relations Review*, 47 (2), 319–29.

—— —— (1997), 'Minimum Wages and Economic Outcomes in Europe', *European Economic Review*, 41 (3–5), 733–42.

—— and Van Reenen, J. (1998), 'Technology and Changes in Skill Structure: Evidence from Seven OECD Countries', *Quarterly Journal of Economics*, 113 (4), 1215–44.

—— Ryan, A., and Van Reenen, J. (1996), 'Technology and Changes in Skill Structure: Evidence from an International Panel of Industries', Leverhulme Programme on 'The Labour Market Consequences of Technical and Structural Change' Discussion Paper 4, Institute of Economics and Statistics, Oxford.

McKnight, A. (1998), 'Low Wage Mobility in a Working Life Perspective', in R. Asplund, P. J. Sloane, and I. Theodossiou (eds.), *Low Pay and Earnings Mobility in Europe*, Aldershot: Edward Elgar.

Mage Network (1995, 1996, 1997a, 1998), *Les Cahiers du Mage*, Paris: CNRS.

—— (1997b), Seminar on 'Protection Sociale et Genre', *Les Cahiers du Mage*, 3–4, 67–139.

Magnac, T. (1997), 'State Dependence and Heterogeneity in Youth Employment Histories', CREST Working Paper 9747, Paris.

Maier, F. (1994), 'Institutional Regimes of Part-Time Working', in G. Schmid (ed.), *Labour Market Institutions in Europe: A Socioeconomic Evaluation of Performance*, London: M. E. Sharpe.

Martin, J. P. (1983), 'The Effects of the Minimum Wage on the Youth Labour Market in North America and France', *OECD Economic Outlook Occasional Studies*, June.

Marx, I., and Verbist, G. (1997), 'Low-Wage Employment and Poverty: Curse or Cure?', paper presented at the LoWER Conference, Bordeaux.

—— —— (1998), 'Low-Paid Work and Poverty: A Cross-Country Perspective', in S. Bazen, M. Gregory, and W. Salverda (eds.), *Low-Wage Employment in Europe*, Aldershot: Edward Elgar.

Mason, G. (1997), 'Back from the Dead Again? Production Supervisors in the United States, Britain and Germany', National Institute of Social and Economic Research Discussion Paper 120, London.

—— van Ark, B., and Wagner, K. (1994), 'Productivity, Product Quality and Workforce Skills: Food Processing in Four European Countries', *National Institute Economic Review*, Feb., 62–83.

Matsuyama, K. (1995), 'Complementarities and Cumulative Processes in Models of Monopolistic Competition', *Journal of Economic Literature*, 33 (2), 701–29.

Meulders, D., Plasman, R., and Vander Stricht, V. (1993), *Position of Women on the Labour Market in the European Community*, Aldershot: Dartmouth Publishing Company.

Meyerson, E., and Petersen, T. (1997a), 'Lika lön för lika arbete' (Equal Pay for Equal Work), in I. Persson and E. Wadensjö (eds.), *Kvinnors och mäns löner—varför så olika?* (*Wages of Women and Wages of Men—Why So Different?*), Stockholm: SOU 1997: 136.

—— —— (1997b), 'Finns det ett glastak för kvinnor?' ('Is there a Glass Ceiling for Women?'), in I. Persson and E. Wadensjö (eds.), *Glastak och glasväggar? Den könssegregerade svenska arbetsmarknaden* (*Glass Ceilings and Glass Walls? The Sex Segregated Swedish Labour Market*), Stockholm: SOU 1997: 137.

Mishel, L., Bernstein, J., and Rassell, E. (1995), 'Who Wins with a Higher Minimum Wage?', Briefing Paper, Economic Policy Institute, Washington.

Mortensen, D. T. (1990), 'Equilibrium Wage Distributions: A Synthesis', in J. Hartog, G. Ridder, and J. Theeuwes (eds.), *Panel Data and Labor Market Studies*, North-Holland: New York, 279–96.

—— and Neumann, G. R. (1988), 'Estimating Structural Model of Unemployment and Job Duration in Dynamic Econometric Modeling', *Proceedings of the Third International Symposium in Economic Theory and Econometrics*, Cambridge: Cambridge University Press.

Murnane, R., Willett, J., and Levy, F. (1995), 'The Growing Importance of Cognitive Skills in Wage Determination', NBER Working Paper 5076, Cambridge, Mass.

Murphy, K. M., Schleifer, A., and Vishny, R. (1991), 'The Allocation of Talent; Implications for Growth', *Quarterly Journal of Economics*, 106 (2), 503–30.

Muysken, J., and ter Weel, B. (2000), 'Overeducation and Crowding Out of Low-Skilled Workers', in L. Borghans and A. de Grip (eds.), *The Over-Educated Worker? The Economics of the Underutilization of Skills*, Aldershot: Edward Elgar.

Neumark, D., and Wascher, W. (1997), 'Do Minimum Wages Fight Poverty?', NBER Working Paper 6127, Cambridge, Mass.

Nickell, S. (1996), 'The Low-Skill Low-Pay Problem: Lessons from Germany for Britain and the US', *Policy Studies*, 17 (1), 7–21.

—— (1997), 'Unemployment and Labor Market Rigidities: Europe versus North America', *Journal of Economic Perspectives*, 11 (3), 55–74.

—— and Bell, B. (1995), 'The Collapse in the Demand for the Unskilled and Unemployment across the OECD', *Oxford Review of Economic Policy*, 11 (1), 40–62.

—— and Layard, R. (1997), 'Labour Market Institutions and Economic Performance', Leverhulme Programme 'The Labour Market Consequences of Technical and Structural Change' Discussion Paper 23, Institute of Economics and Statistics, Oxford.

—— —— (1999), 'Labor Market Institutions and Economic Performance', in O. Ashenfelter and D. Card (eds.), *Handbook of Labor Economics*, vol. 3C, Amsterdam: North Holland Elsevier.

Nishimura, K. (1989), 'Indexation and Monopolistic Competition in Labor Markets', *European Economic Review*, 33 (8), 1606–23.

Nolan, B. (1998a), *Low Pay in Ireland*, Volume II of the Report of the National Minimum Wage Commission, Dublin: Stationery Office.

—— (1998b), 'Low Pay, the Earnings Distribution and Poverty in Ireland, 1987–1994', in S. Bazen, M. Gregory, and W. Salverda (eds.), *Low-Wage Employment in Europe*, Aldershot: Edward Elgar.

—— and Watson, D. (1998), *Women and Poverty in Ireland*, Dublin: Oak Tree Press.

—— and Whelan, C. T. (1996), *Resources, Deprivation and Poverty*, Oxford: Oxford University Press.

OECD (1989, 1993, 1996a, 1997a, 1998a), *Employment Outlook*, Paris: OECD.
——— (1992), *Technology and the Economy* (Paris: OECD).
——— (1994), *The OECD Jobs Study: Evidence and Explanations*, Paris: OECD.
——— (1996b), *Measuring What People Know*, Paris: OECD.
——— (1996c), *Education at a Glance* (Paris: OECD).
——— (1996d), *Historical Statistics* (Paris: OECD).
——— (1997b), *Literacy Skills for the Knowledge Society*, Paris: OECD.
——— (1998b), *Human Capital Investment: An International Comparison*, Paris: OECD.
——— (1998c), *Key Employment Policy Challenges Faced by OECD Countries*, Labour Market and Social Policy Occasional Paper 31, Paris: OECD.
O'Higgins, M., and Jenkins, S. P. (1990), 'Poverty in the EC: Estimates for 1975, 1980 and 1985', in R. Teekens and B. Van Praag (eds.), *Analysing Poverty in the European Community*, Luxembourg: Eurostat.
Ohlsson, J., and Öhman, J. (1997), 'Kvinnliga och manliga chefer—finns det ett glastak?' ('Male and Female Bosses—is there a Glass Ceiling?'), in I. Persson and E. Wadensjö (eds.), *Glastak och glasväggar? Den könssegregerade svenska arbetsmarknaden* (*Glass Ceilings and Glass Walls? The Sex Segregated Swedish Labour Market*), Stockholm: SOU 1997: 137.
Oosterbeek, H., and Webbink, D. (1995), 'Enrolment in Higher Education in the Netherlands', *De Economist*, 143 (3), 367–80.
Oswald, A. (1996), 'A Conjecture on the Explanation for High Unemployment in the Industrial Nations', Warwick Economic Research Papers 475, University of Warwick.
Pekkarinen, J., Pohjola, M., and Rowthorn, B. (1992), *Social Corporatism: A Superior Economic System?* Oxford: Oxford University Press.
Persson, I. (1990) (ed.), *Generating Equality in the Welfare State: The Swedish Experience*, Oslo: Norwegian University Press.
——— (1993), *Svenska kvinnor möter Europa: Ekonomisk integration och social harmonisering ur ett kvinnoperspektiv* (*Swedish Women Encounter Europe: Economic Integration and Social Harmonization from Women's Perspective*), Stockholm: Supplement 16 to SOU 1992: 19.
——— and Jonung, C. (1997) (eds.), *Economics of the Family and Family Policies*, London: Routledge.
——— ——— (1998) (eds.), *Women's Work and Wages*, London: Routledge.
——— and Wadensjö, E. (1997a) (eds.), *Kvinnors och mäns löner—varför så olika?* (*Wages of Women and Wages of Men—Why So Different?*), Stockholm: SOU 1997: 136.
——— ——— (1997b) (eds.), *Glastak och glasväggar? Den könssegregerade svenska arbetsmarknaden* (*Glass Ceilings and Glass Walls? The Sex Segregated Swedish Labour Market*), Stockholm: SOU 1997: 137.
——— ——— (1998) (eds.), *Välfärdens genusansikte* (*The Gendered Face of Welfare Systems*), Stockholm: SOU 1998: 3.
Porter, M. (1990), *The Competitive Advantage of Nations*, London: Macmillan.
Pryor, F., and Schaffer, D. (1999), *Who's Not Working and Why: Employment, Cognitive Skills, Wages, and the Changing U.S. Labor Market*, Cambridge: Cambridge University Press.
Reder, M. (1955), 'The Theory of Occupational Wage Differentials', *American Economic Review*, 65 (5), 833–50.
Ribeiro, M. (1995), 'L'Impact du salaire minimum au Portugal', in S. Bazen and G. Benhayoun (eds.), *Salaire minimum et bas salaires*, Paris: L'Harmattan.
Robinson, P. (1997), 'Underskilled or Overqualified? Qualifications, Occupations and Earnings in the British Labour Market', paper presented at the LoWER Conference, London.

Roy, A. D. (1950), 'The Distribution of Earnings and of Individual Output', *Economic Journal*, 60 (Sept.), 489–501.

—— (1951), 'Some Thoughts on the Distribution of Earnings', *Oxford Economic Papers*, 3 (2), 135–46.

Rubery, J., Fagan, C., and Maier, F. (1996), 'Occupational Segregation, Discrimination and Equal Opportunity', in G. Schmid, J. O'Reilly, and K. Schomann (eds.), *International Handbook of Labour Market Policy and Evaluation*, Aldershot: Edward Elgar.

Rumberger, R. W. (1981), *Over-Education in the US Labor Market*, New York: Praeger.

—— (1987), 'The Impact of Surplus Schooling on Productivity and Earnings', *Journal of Human Resources*, 22 (1), 24–50.

Russo, G., and Schettkat, R. (1998), 'The Institutional-Division and the Product-Division of Industry', paper presented at the Tilburg and Utrecht Universities Workshop, Amsterdam.

Sachs, J. D., and Shatz, H. J. (1994), 'Trade and Jobs in US Manufacturing', *Brookings Papers on Economic Activity*, 1, 1–84.

Saeger, S. (1995), 'Industrial Structure and Employment: Evidence from the OECD', mimeo, Harvard.

Sainsbury, D. (1996), *Gender, Equality and Welfare States*, Cambridge: Cambridge University Press.

Salverda, W. (1992), *Youth Unemployment: Dynamics of the Dutch Labour Market 1955–1988*, Groningen: Wolters-Noordhoff.

Santos, M., Mendes Oliveria, M., and Kiker, B. F. (1996), 'Over-Education and Under-Education: Evidence for Portugal', paper presented at the EALE Conference, Crete.

Schmid, G., O'Reilly, J., and Schomann, K. (1996) (eds.), *International Handbook of Labour Market Policy and Evaluation*, Aldershot: Edward Elgar.

Schmitt, J., and Bernstein, J. (1998), *Making Work Pay: The Impact of the 1996–97 Minimum Wage Increase*, Washington: Employment Policy Institute.

Scholz, J. K. (1996), 'In-Work Benefits in the United States: The Earned Income Tax Credit', *Economic Journal*, 106 (1), 156–69.

Shockey, J. W. (1989), 'Over-Education and Earnings: A Structural Approach to Differential Attainment in the US Labor Force 1970–82', *American Sociological Review*, 54, 856–64.

Shorrocks, A. F. (1978a), 'The Measurement of Mobility', *Econometrica*, 46 (5), 1013–24.

—— (1978b), 'Income Inequality and Income Mobility', *Journal of Economic Theory*, 19 (2), 376–93.

Sicherman, N. (1991), 'Over-Education in the Labor Market', *Journal of Labor Economics*, 9 (2), 101–22.

Siebert, H. (1997), 'Labor Market Rigidities: At the Root of Unemployment in Europe', *Journal of Economic Perspectives*, 11 (3), 37–54.

Sloane, P. J., and Theodossiou, I. (1996), 'Earnings Mobility, Family Income and Low Pay', *Economic Journal*, 106 (May), 657–66.

—— —— (1998), 'An Econometric Analysis of Low Pay and Earnings Mobility in Britain', in R. Asplund, P. J. Sloane, and I. Theodossiou (eds.), *Low Pay and Earnings Mobility in Europe*, Aldershot: Edward Elgar.

Sloane, P., Battu, H., and Seaman, P. (1996), 'Over-Education and the Formal Education/ Experience and Training Trade-Off', *Applied Economics Letters*, 3 (8), 511–15.

Smith, A. (1776), *The Wealth of Nations*, repr. London: Penguin, 1986.

Smith, H. (1986), 'Over-Education and Underemployment: An Agnostic Review', *Sociology of Education*, 59, 85–99.

Snower, D. (1983), 'Imperfect Competition, Underemployment and Crowding Out', *Oxford Economic Papers*, 35 (suppl.), 245–70.

Spence, M. (1973), 'Job Market Signalling', *Quarterly Journal of Economics*, 87 (3), 355–74.

Spenner, K. L. (1985), 'The Upgrading and Downgrading of Occupations: Issues, Evidence and Implications for Education', *Review of Educational Research*, 55, 125–54.

Stasz, C. (1998), 'Generic Skills at Work: Implications for Occupationally-Oriented Education', in W. J. Nijhof and J. N. Streumer (eds.), *Key Qualifications in Work and Education*, Dordrecht: Kluwer.

Steedman, H. (1999), 'Measuring the Quality of Educational Outputs: Some Unresolved Problems', in R. Alexander, P. Broadfoot, and D. Philips (eds.), *Learning from Comparing: New Directions in Comparative Education Research*, Wallingford: Symposium Books.

Stewart, M. B. (1998), 'Low Pay, No Pay Dynamics', paper prepared for HM Treasury Workshop, London.

—— (1999), 'Low Pay in Britain', in P. Gregg and J. Wadsworth (eds.), *The State of Working Britain*, Manchester: Manchester University Press.

—— and Swaffield, J. K. (1998), 'The Earnings Mobility of Low-Paid Workers in Britain', in R. Asplund, P. J. Sloane, and I. Theodossiou (eds.), *Low Pay and Earnings Mobility in Europe*, Aldershot: Edward Elgar.

—— —— (1999), 'Low Pay Dynamics and Transition Probabilities', *Economica*, 66 (1), 23–42.

Sundin, E. (1998), *Män passar alltid (Men are Always Right)*, Stockholm: SOU 1998: 4.

Sutherland, H. (1997), *A National Minimum Wage and In-Work Benefits*, Economic Report, Employment Policy Institute, London.

Teulings, C. (1990), 'Conjunctuur en Kwalificatie', (The Business Cycle and Qualifications) SEO Report, University of Amsterdam.

—— (1995), 'The Wage Distribution in a Model of the Assignment of Skills to Jobs', *Journal of Political Economy*, 103 (2), 280–315.

—— (1998), 'The Contribution of Minimum Wages to Increasing Wage Inequality', in C. Lucifora and W. Salverda (eds.), *Policies for Low Wage Employment and Social Exclusion*, Milan: Franco Angeli.

Thurow, L. (1975), *Generating Inequality*, London: Macmillan.

Tinbergen, J. (1956), 'On the Theory of Income Distribution', *Weftwirtschaftliches Archiv*, 77, 156–73.

—— (1975), *Income Distribution: Analysis and Policies*, Amsterdam: North-Holland.

Topel, R. (1997), 'Factor Proportions and Relative Wages: The Supply-Side Determinants of Wage Inequality', *Journal of Economic Perspectives*, 11 (2), 55–74.

US Department of Labor (1972), *Handbook for Analysing Jobs*, Washington: Department of Labor.

Van den Bosch, K., Callan, T., Estivill, J., Hausman, P., Jeandidier, B., Muffels, R., and Yfantopoulos, J. (1993), 'A Comparison of Poverty in Seven European Countries and Regions using Subjective and Relative Measures', *Journal of Population Economics*, 6 (3), 235–59.

Van Opstal, R., Waaijers, R., and Wiggers, G. (1998), 'Wage Growth of Low- and High-Skilled Workers in the Netherlands', in R. Asplund, P. J. Sloane, and I. Theodossiou (eds.), *Low Pay and Earnings Mobility in Europe*, Aldershot: Edward Elgar.

Van Ours, J. C., and Ridder, G. (1995), 'Job Matching and Job Competition: Are Lower Educated Workers at the Back of Job Queues?', *European Economic Review*, 39 (9), 1717–31.

Van der Velden, R. K. W., and van Smoorenburg, M. S. M. (1997), 'The Measurement of Over-Education and Under-Education: Self Report vs Job Analyst Method', paper presented at the EALE Conference, Aarhus.

Van Soest, A. (1989), 'Minimum Wage Rates and Unemployment in the Netherlands', *De Economist*, 137 (3), 279–309.

—— (1994), 'Youth Minimum Wage Rates: The Dutch Experience', *International Journal of Manpower*, 15 (2/3), 100–17.

Verdugo, R. R., and Verdugo, N. T. (1989), 'The Impact of Surplus Schooling on Earnings: Some Additional Findings', *Journal of Human Resources*, 24 (4), 629–43.

Walby, S. (1998), 'Les figures emblématiques de l'emploi flexible', in M. Maruani (ed.), *Les Nouvelles Frontières de L'inégalité: Hommes et Femmes sur le Marché du Travail*, Paris: La Découverte/Mage.

Weiss, A. (1990), *Efficiency Wages: Models of Unemployment, Layoffs, and Wage Dispersion*, Princeton: Princeton University Press.

—— (1995), 'Human Capital vs. Signalling Explanations of Wages', *Journal of Economic Perspectives*, 9 (4), 133–54.

Whitehouse, E. (1996), 'Designing and Implementing In-Work Benefits', *Economic Journal*, 106 (1), 130–41.

Wood, A. (1994), *North–South Trade, Employment and Inequality: Changing Fortunes in a Skill Driven World*, Oxford: Oxford University Press.

—— (1995), 'How Trade Hurt Unskilled Workers', *Journal of Economic Perspectives*, 9 (3), 57–80.

—— (1998), 'Globalization and the Rise in Labour Market Inequalities', *Economic Journal*, 108 (Sept.), 1463–82.

Zwick, T. (2000), 'Overqualification Makes Low-Wage Employment Attractive: The Economics of Upgrading and Bumping Down', in L. Borghans and A. de Grip (eds.), *The Over-Educated Worker? The Economics of the Underutilization of Skills*, Aldershot: Edward Elgar.

Name Index

Subject Index

Lightning Source UK Ltd.
Milton Keynes UK
UKHW021857070223
416594UK00003B/448